GORDON RAMSAY

MAKES IT
easy

GORDON RAMSAY

with Mark Sargeant and Helen Tillott
photographs by Jill Mead

MAKES IT
easy

Quadrille

contents

Publishing consultant Anne Furniss
Art director Helen Lewis
Project editor Janet Illsley
Photographer Jill Mead
Food stylist Mark Sargeant
Home economist Helen Tillott
Production Vincent Smith

This edition first published in 2009 by
Quadrille Publishing Limited, Alhambra House
27–31 Charing Cross Road, London WC2H 0LS

Text © 2005 Gordon Ramsay
Photography © 2005 Jill Mead
Design and layout © 2005 Quadrille Publishing Limited

The rights of the author have been asserted.
All rights reserved. No part of this book may be reproduced,
stored in a retrieval system or transmitted in any form or by
any means, electronic, electrostatic, magnetic tape,
mechanical, photocopying, recording
or otherwise, without the prior permission in writing
of the publisher.

Cataloguing in Publication Data: a catalogue record for this
book is available from the British Library.

ISBN 978 184400 767 7

Printed in China

notes

All spoon measures are level unless otherwise stated:
1 tsp = 5ml spoon; 1 tbsp = 15 ml spoon.

All herbs are fresh and all pepper is freshly ground black pepper.

Egg sizes are specified where they are critical, otherwise use large eggs.
I recommend free-range eggs. If you are pregnant or in a vulnerable health group,
avoid those recipes that contain raw egg whites or lightly cooked eggs.

My oven timings are for fan-assisted ovens. If you are using a conventional
oven increase the temperature by 10°C (½ Gas Mark). Individual ovens can deviate
by as much as 10°C from the setting, either way. Get to know your oven and use
an oven thermometer to check its accuracy. My timings are provided as guidelines,
with a description of colour or texture where appropriate.

introduction

Cooking still excites and entices me, just as it did when I opened the doors of my first restaurant in 1993. Food is constantly evolving and I love the challenge of creating new dishes for my customers. However, I am not a fan of trendy, contrived food – it doesn't satisfy me. I would far rather eat a tasty homemade fish pie than a tower of fish smothered with an unidentifiable sauce. The quality of ingredients is paramount to the success of a dish and I always source foods from top quality producers. With every dish, I strive to achieve a balance of flavours, enhancing the individual tastes and textures of ingredients without masking or overpowering any of them.

Cooking with Tana and the family has opened up a whole new area for me. Above all, food is to be enjoyed, with family, friends and loved ones – but in our busy lives time for cooking is often limited. The solution is to choose dishes that taste great, are made from the best ingredients, but are simple in their execution. In this book, I hope to inspire you by using my experience to make things easy. Cooking and eating fabulous food together – whether it's a family meal, a barbecue with friends or a romantic dinner for two – is fun and rewarding. Enjoy...

breakfast
and brunch

There's nothing quite like a proper breakfast to start the day. I love a traditional English breakfast, and not necessarily first thing. A mid-morning brunch is essential fuel in the restaurants to get the brigade through lunch service. Easy nutritious food is what's needed and it's much the same at home. I encourage the family to vary their breakfasts, and make the most of seasonal fruit – a fresh cherry compote is popular in summer. My spiced breakfast bread is worth a try too – as an alternative to croissants or toast.

country garden breakfast

Serves 4

200g new potatoes

sea salt and pepper

4 large flat field
mushrooms, trimmed

4 large English tomatoes,
halved

1 tbsp butter, plus extra to
grease

4 free-range eggs

4 tbsp double cream

1 tbsp olive oil

Heat the oven to 200°C/Gas 6. Boil the new potatoes in salted water until just tender, then drain well and crush slightly.

Put the mushrooms and tomatoes in a large non-stick sauté pan, dot with the butter and season with pepper. Cover and leave to cook gently until softened.

Butter 4 ramekins, break an egg into each one and pour on the cream. Season with pepper and bake for 5–7 minutes.

Meanwhile, heat the olive oil in a small frying pan until hot but not smoking, add the potatoes and fry until golden brown and crispy.

Serve the baked egg ramekins on warm plates with the mushrooms, tomatoes and crispy potatoes.

salmon kedgeree

Serves 4

375g filleted salmon, skinned

1 tsp turmeric

225g basmati rice, rinsed

pinch of saffron threads

4 tbsp olive oil

100g cherry tomatoes, halved

4 free-range eggs

400ml fish stock (approximately)

2 spring onions or shallots, chopped

75g unsalted butter, in pieces

3 tbsp chopped flat-leaf parsley

sea salt and pepper

Cut the salmon into chunks, sprinkle with the turmeric and set aside to marinate.

Put the rice in a pan with 500ml cold water, bring to the boil and simmer for 7–8 minutes until the liquid is absorbed. Tip into a shallow bowl, sprinkle with the saffron and leave to stand.

Heat 2 tbsp olive oil in a frying pan and cook the salmon chunks for about 1 minute on each side. Remove and drain on kitchen paper.

Add the tomatoes to the pan with another 1 tbsp olive oil and cook, stirring, for 1 minute. Remove and set aside.

Boil the eggs for 6–8 minutes, then peel, halve and set aside. Bring the fish stock to the boil in a pan and keep at a low simmer.

Heat the remaining oil in a medium pan and cook the onions for 2–3 minutes to soften. Add a third of the butter, then the blanched rice and cook, stirring, to coat in the butter.

Add a ladleful of hot stock and stir until the liquid is absorbed. Continue to add the stock, a ladleful at a time, stirring over the heat, until the rice is cooked. Add the remaining butter and stir until melted.

Fork the salmon through the rice. Add the tomatoes, parsley and salt to taste, and heat through gently. Pile on to warm plates, add the halved boiled eggs and grind over some pepper. Serve immediately.

salmon kedgeree

"I like to eat my scrambled eggs topped with pan-fried mushrooms and cherry tomatoes on the vine"

sublime scrambled eggs
ON TOAST

Serves 2–3

6 large free-range eggs

25g ice-cold butter, cut into small dice

1 tbsp crème fraîche

sea salt and pepper

few chives, snipped

To serve:

2–3 chunky slices of rustic bread, such as pain Polaîne

Break the eggs into a cold, heavy-based pan, place on the lowest heat possible and add half the butter. Using a spatula, stir the eggs frequently to combine the yolks with the whites.

As the mixture begins to set, add the remaining butter. The eggs will take about 4–5 minutes to scramble – they should still be soft and quite lumpy. Don't let them get too hot – keep moving the pan off and back on the heat.

Toast the bread slices on both sides in the meantime.

Add the crème fraîche and season the eggs at the last minute, then add the snipped chives. Put the toast on warm plates, pile the softly scrambled eggs on top and serve immediately.

bubble and squeak
WITH SMOKED HADDOCK

Serves 4

550g Desirée potatoes, peeled

sea salt and pepper

500ml milk

300g smoked haddock fillet

180g Savoy cabbage, cored and finely chopped

1 onion, finely chopped

3 tbsp vegetable oil

25g butter

Boil the potatoes in salted water until soft, then drain and press through a potato ricer into a large bowl (or mash well). Put to one side.

Bring the milk to the boil in a small frying pan and poach the smoked haddock for 3–4 minutes. Take off the heat and allow to cool in the liquid.

Blanch the cabbage in boiling salted water for 2–3 minutes, then drain and refresh in cold water.

Sauté the onion in 1 tbsp oil until soft. Add to the potato with the butter and cabbage, mix well and season generously. Drain the haddock, flake and fold into the potato mixture.

Heat the remaining oil in a non-stick medium frying pan. Add the potato mixture and press down with the back of a spoon to form a 'cake'. Cook for 10 minutes until the base is golden brown.

Turn on to a plate, then slide the potato cake back into the pan and cook for a further 5–7 minutes. Serve immediately.

English breakfast

Serves 4

3 tbsp vegetable oil, plus
  extra to fry eggs

4 or 8 good-quality butcher's
  pork sausages

4 slices black pudding

8 smoked back bacon
  rashers

4 slices good, thick sliced
  bread

4 large flat or field
  mushrooms, trimmed

1 bunch vine-ripened cherry
  tomatoes, stalks removed

sea salt and pepper

4 free-range eggs (ideally
  duck's eggs)

Heat the oven to 120°C/Gas ½ and put 4 dinner plates and a large platter inside to warm.

Heat 3 tbsp oil in a large, heavy-based frying pan. Add the sausages and black pudding, and cook slowly for 6–8 minutes to release the fat. Turn up the heat, add the bacon and cook until it begins to crisp and the sausages are brown. Transfer to the warmed platter in the oven.

Heat the fat left in the pan until you can see a haze (adding a little more oil if needed). Add the bread and fry quickly on one side until golden brown. Remove and drain on kitchen paper, then add to the platter in the oven.

Lower the heat and add the mushrooms and tomatoes to the frying pan. Season with pepper, cover and cook for 5 minutes.

Meanwhile, heat a little oil in a small frying pan. Break an egg into a breakfast cup and carefully tip into the hot pan. Repeat with the other eggs (if fresh they will 'sit up' and not spread all over the pan). Cook until the white is completely set and firm.

Immediately transfer a fried egg to each warm plate and season with salt and pepper. Add the sausages, black pudding, bacon, fried bread, tomatoes and mushrooms. Serve at once.

English
breakfast

toasted bagel

" I love New York and the fresh hot bagel stalls on every other corner – perfect for a breakfast on the move. Smoked salmon and cream cheese may be the traditional filling but there's really no limit. I also like smoked chicken with rocket, and egg mayonnaise with grilled maple bacon"

Serves 4
4 bagels
4 large vine-ripened beef tomatoes
pepper
a little olive oil to brush
8 slices Serrano ham

Heat the grill to high. Split the bagels in half.

Cut the tomatoes into 5mm slices, place on a baking tray and season with pepper. Brush with olive oil and cook under the grill for a few minutes to soften. Remove the tray from the grill.

Toast the split bagels under the grill until crisp and golden brown on both sides.

Put the bagel bases on warm plates, pile the grilled tomato slices on top and cover with the Serrano ham slices. Sandwich together with the bagel tops and serve.

spiced breakfast bread

Makes 10–12 slices

butter to grease

3 free-range eggs

50g light brown sugar

250g thin honey

125ml milk

125g plain flour

125g buckwheat flour

1 tsp five-spice powder

1 tbsp ground mixed spice

2 tbsp baking powder

finely grated zest of
   2 oranges

Heat the oven to 160°C/Gas 3. Lightly butter a 25x10cm loaf tin.

Whisk the eggs and sugar together in a large bowl over a pan of hot water, using an electric whisk, until the mixture is pale and thickened (enough to leave a ribbon when the beaters are lifted). Remove the pan from the heat, but leave the bowl set over it.

Warm the honey and milk together in a small pan and gradually beat into the egg mixture until evenly mixed.

Sift the flours, spices and baking powder together into a large mixing bowl and carefully fold in the egg mixture, followed by the orange zest.

Spoon the mixture into the loaf tin and bake for 35–40 minutes until well risen, firm to the touch and golden brown on top. Leave in the tin for 5 minutes, then turn out and cool on a wire rack.

Serve warm, cut into slices. Best eaten on the day it is made (any leftover can be frozen). Delicious with a compote of cherries (see overleaf).

"We are so lucky to have such fabulous fruit in this country, why we ship vast quantities in from abroad rather than make the most of seasonal produce is beyond me. Sampling the different cherry varieties in a beautiful Kent orchard last autumn inspired me to create this simple recipe"

compote of cherries

Serves 6

1kg mixed fresh cherries
250ml fresh orange juice
100g sugar
pared zest of 1 lemon
few mint leaves

Pit the cherries and put into a stainless steel or non-reactive saucepan with the orange juice, sugar, lemon zest and mint leaves. Slowly bring to the boil and then simmer for 5 minutes, shaking the pan occasionally to prevent the cherries sticking.

Tip into a bowl and allow to cool, then remove the mint leaves and lemon zest. Cover and keep in the fridge until needed (up to 3 days), but bring back to room temperature to serve.

Serve the compote with Greek-style yogurt.

banana and passion fruit smoothie

Serves 4

4 bananas (in skins)
4 passion fruit, halved
400ml chilled natural yogurt
100ml chilled milk
2 tsp thin honey

Put the bananas in the freezer for an hour or two. (The skins will blacken, but that's fine.)

Scoop out the passion fruit pulp and press through a sieve into a blender. Peel the bananas and add to the blender with the yogurt, milk and honey. Whiz until smooth, pour into glasses and serve.

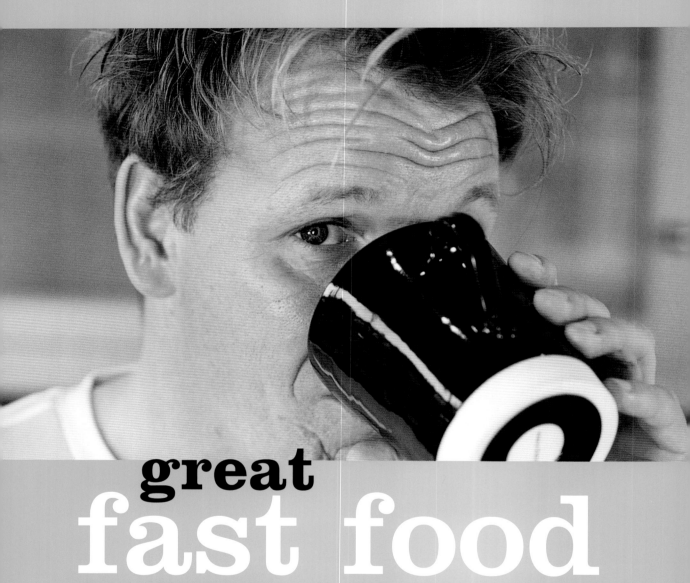

great

fast food

Fast food is now synonymous with ready-meals and take-aways, which is a sad state of affairs. So many fresh foods are incredibly quick to prepare and easily assembled into tempting fast meals – such as soups, omelettes, warm salads and pasta dishes. Keeping a well-stocked storecupboard is the key to great fast food. You will be amazed just how quick these recipes are to prepare. In the time it takes to reheat a ready-meal, you can put a homemade soup, smart pasta dish, or a creamy risotto on the table.

broccoli soup

Serves 4

1kg broccoli

sea salt and pepper

4 slices soft goat's cheese,
 or 4 baby chèvres

50g flaked almonds or
 walnuts, lightly toasted

extra virgin olive oil to drizzle

Cut the broccoli into florets. Bring 800ml salted water to the boil in a pan, add the broccoli and simmer for about 4 minutes until tender but still bright green. Drain, reserving the liquid.

Whiz the broccoli in a blender, with enough of the liquid to half-fill the goblet, to give a velvety texture.

Reheat the soup in the pan; adjust the seasoning. Put the goat's cheese slices into warm soup bowls and pour in the soup, to one side. Top with the nuts, grind over some pepper and drizzle with olive oil to serve.

seared scallops and lettuce
ON RUSTIC BREAD

Serves 4

olive oil to brush

16 medium to large scallops,
   shelled and cleaned

4 large slices rustic bread

butter to spread

2 Little Gem lettuces,
   separated into leaves

squeeze of lemon juice

extra virgin olive oil to drizzle

sea salt and pepper

lemon wedges to serve

Heat a griddle pan and brush with a little olive oil. When very hot, place the scallops on the griddle and cook for 2 minutes, then turn and cook for a further $1-1\frac{1}{2}$ minutes – no longer or they will toughen.

Meanwhile, toast the bread on both sides until golden. Butter very lightly, while still warm. Put a slice on each plate.

Pile the lettuce on to the toasted bread and tuck the griddled scallops between the leaves. Squeeze a little lemon juice over the scallops and drizzle with a little extra virgin olive oil. Season well with salt and pepper and serve, with lemon wedges.

"I admire the traditional baker. Having done two stints as a night baker, I appreciate the care that goes into each and every loaf. There are plenty of good bakeries producing excellent rustic bread, so find your nearest one and avoid synthetic white bread at all costs"

"This is a great way to use up leftover roast pork belly (see page 80); you can also buy crispy roast pork from Chinatown and some good deli counters"

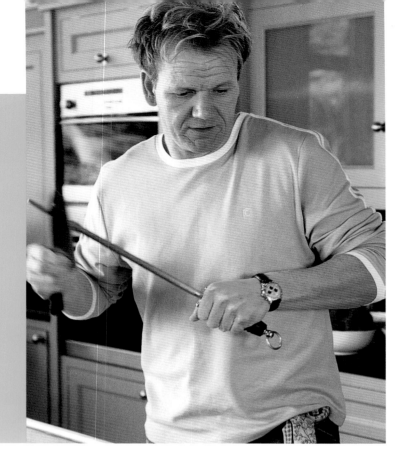

sandwich of crispy pork
WITH SOURDOUGH BREAD

Serves 4

1 tbsp olive oil, plus extra to brush
1 large red onion, finely sliced
1 garlic clove, finely chopped
8 thick slices sourdough bread
1 Little Gem lettuce, separated into leaves
4 slices roast pork belly
sea salt and pepper

Heat the olive oil in a heavy-based pan and sauté the onion and garlic over a low heat for 5–7 minutes to soften, without browning.

Lightly toast the bread on both sides. Put a slice on each of 4 plates. Brush lightly with olive oil and arrange the lettuce leaves on top.

Lay the pork slices on the lettuce and top with the sautéed onion. Season with salt and pepper. Sandwich together with the other toasted bread slices, cut in half and serve.

tortilla wrap
WITH CHICKEN AND AVOCADO

Serves 4

3–4 free-range boneless chicken breasts

3 tbsp olive oil

juice of 1 lime

1 tsp ground cumin

1 tsp ground coriander

1 onion, roughly chopped

1 red pepper, deseeded and roughly chopped

6 vine-ripened tomatoes, cut into quarters

8 tortilla wraps

1 tbsp chopped coriander leaves

2 avocados

125ml Greek-style yogurt

"Wraps are a convenient fast food option. As an alternative to chicken, use monkfish or salmon fillet, cut into medallions"

Cut the chicken into thin strips. Combine the olive oil, lime juice and spices in a bowl. Add the chicken, toss to mix and leave to marinate for 2 hours. Heat the oven to 200°C/Gas 6.

Heat a heavy-based frying pan or griddle until very hot. Add the chicken in its marinade, with the onion, red pepper and half the tomatoes. Cook for 4–5 minutes.

Wrap the tortillas in foil and warm in the oven for 5 minutes. Add the rest of the tomatoes to the frying pan and cook for a further 2 minutes. Scatter over the chopped coriander.

Halve, peel and thinly slice the avocados, discarding the stones. Divide the chicken mixture between the warm tortillas, add a few avocado slices and a dollop of yogurt to each one, then roll up. Serve two per person.

grilled fresh sardines
WITH A NEW POTATO AND CRÈME FRAÎCHE SALAD

Serves 4

12 new potatoes, such as Charlotte

sea salt and pepper

4 tbsp crème fraîche

1 tbsp lemon juice

2 tsp snipped chives, plus extra to garnish

8 small fresh sardines, cleaned, boned and butterflied

olive oil, to oil

1 Little Gem lettuce, separated into leaves

a little classic vinaigrette

lemon wedges to serve

Boil the new potatoes in their skins in salted water until tender. Drain, tip into a bowl and lightly crush with the back of a fork, then allow to cool. Add the crème fraîche, lemon juice and snipped chives, and season well with salt and pepper.

Heat the grill to maximum. Lay the sardines, skin-side up, in an oiled baking tray and grill for 3–4 minutes. Turn them over and cook for a further 2–3 minutes. Remove from the grill and season well.

Place a few lettuce leaves on each plate and pile the potato salad on top. Arrange the hot sardines, skin-side up, on the salad. Drizzle with a little vinaigrette and serve immediately, topped with a few chives and accompanied by lemon wedges.

open omelette
OF SMOKED SALMON AND CRÈME FRAÎCHE

Serves 4

6 free-range eggs

sea salt and pepper

1 tbsp olive oil

25g butter

200g smoked salmon, cut
   into strips

100ml crème fraîche

small bunch of chives,
   snipped

Heat the grill to high. Break the eggs into a bowl, whisk with a fork and season with pepper.

Heat the olive oil in a cast-iron frying pan, add the butter and allow to melt. Increase the heat to medium-high and, when the pan is hot, pour in the egg mixture. Leave until the eggs start to set, then with a metal spatula, draw the edge of the mixture towards the centre of the pan.

Cook for 30 seconds or so until the base of the omelette is set (the top will appear quite wet), then put the pan under the grill for 30 seconds or until the omelette is lightly set on top but not dry. Remove from the heat.

Scatter the smoked salmon on top of the omelette and dot with the crème fraîche. Sprinkle with the snipped chives and season with salt and pepper to taste. Loosen the edges, then slide the omelette out of the pan. Cut into wedges and serve immediately.

"If girolles are out of season and other wild mushrooms are hard to find, use a mixture of chestnut and oyster mushrooms"

risotto of wild mushrooms

Serves 4

750ml vegetable stock

3 tbsp olive oil

2 large shallots, finely diced

2 celery sticks, finely sliced

200g risotto rice

1 small glass dry white wine

1 tsp ground coriander
  seeds

sea salt and pepper

100g oyster mushrooms,
  cleaned and sliced

100g girolles, ceps or other
  wild mushrooms, cleaned
  and sliced

2 tbsp mascarpone or
  crème fraîche

1 tbsp chopped chervil or
  chives

2 tbsp freshly grated
  Parmesan

Bring the stock to the boil in a pan and keep it at a low simmer.

Heat 1 tbsp olive oil in a deep sauté pan, add the shallots and sauté for 2–3 minutes until softened but not coloured. Add the celery and cook for a further 2 minutes.

Stir in the rice and cook for 2 minutes. Pour in the wine and cook until it has been absorbed, then add a ladleful of the hot stock with the ground coriander and cook, stirring, until the liquid has been absorbed.

Continue to add the stock a ladleful at a time, allowing each addition to be absorbed before adding any more, until the rice is al dente (cooked but firm to the bite). The risotto should be very moist and creamy. Season with salt and pepper to taste.

Heat the remaining olive oil in a sauté pan, add the sliced mushrooms and cook, stirring frequently, until softened, then stir through the risotto.

Add the mascarpone or crème fraîche, stir and divide the risotto between warm plates. Scatter the herbs and Parmesan over and serve.

risotto of wild mushrooms

butternut squash puff 'pizza'
WITH SAGE AND SMOKED CHEDDAR

Serves 4

2 tbsp olive oil

450g chopped butternut
squash

330g ready-made puff
pastry

1 egg yolk beaten with 1 tsp
water (eggwash)

200g smoked Cheddar
cheese, grated

4 sage leaves, finely
chopped, plus extra to
garnish

sea salt and pepper

Heat the oven to 220°C/Gas 7. Heat the olive oil in a
pan, add the squash and sweat gently for 5 minutes.

Roll out the pastry to a large rectangle, about
15x25cm. Using a sharp knife, mark a 1cm border
around the edge of the pastry, without cutting right
through. Brush the border with eggwash.

Sprinkle half the cheese on the pastry within the
border and top with the squash. Scatter the chopped
sage over and season with salt and pepper.

Bake for 20 minutes, then scatter over the
remaining cheese and cook for a further 5 minutes.
Garnish with fresh sage leaves and serve.

salad of smoked eel
WITH BACON AND SAUTÉ POTATOES

Serves 4

12 new potatoes, such as La Ratte, cleaned

sea salt and pepper

2–3 tbsp olive oil

50g bacon lardons

300g smoked eel fillets

3 tbsp classic vinaigrette

2 Little Gem lettuce, separated into leaves

herby mascarpone (optional, see right)

"I sometimes serve this salad topped with a spoonful of herby mascarpone. Simply stir some chopped herbs (such as chervil, parsley and dill) salt, pepper and a squeeze of lemon juice into some mascarpone"

Par-boil the potatoes in salted water for 7–8 minutes until barely tender, then drain. Allow to cool, then halve lengthways.

Heat the olive oil in a frying pan. Add the potatoes, cut-side down, and cook quickly over a high heat until golden brown, adding a little more oil if needed. Drain on kitchen paper.

Remove excess oil from the pan with kitchen paper, then add the bacon lardons and cook over a high heat until crisp. Drain on kitchen paper.

Cut the eel fillets into strips and warm through gently in a small pan with 2 tbsp of the vinaigrette. Toss the lettuce leaves with the remaining vinaigrette.

Divide the lettuce between plates, scatter over the lardons and place the warm potatoes on top. Spoon the warm flaked eel in the centre and top with a dollop of herby mascarpone if you like.

spaghetti with lobster
IN A CREAMY TOMATO SAUCE

Serves 4

1 freshly cooked lobster,
  about 1kg

600g cherry tomatoes, diced

2–3 spring onions, finely
  sliced or shredded

1 chilli, deseeded and
  chopped

1 garlic clove, chopped

50g unsalted butter

sea salt and pepper

1 glass dry white wine

500g fresh spaghetti

1 tbsp olive oil

100ml double cream

handful of basil leaves,
  chopped

freshly shaved Parmesan
  to serve

olive oil to drizzle

To extract the lobster meat, cut through the body shell and take out the meat in one piece, pulling out the dirt sac from the third disc. Extract the meat from the claws by cracking the shells open with the back of a knife or a nutcracker. Chop the body and claw meat into bite-sized pieces; set aside.

Put the cherry tomatoes, spring onions, chilli, garlic and butter in a heavy-based pan and cook over a medium heat until soft but not coloured. Season with pepper, add the wine and cook until it has evaporated.

Add the spaghetti to a large pan of boiling salted water with the olive oil and cook until al dente (tender but firm to the bite), about 3 minutes.

Meanwhile, add the lobster to the sauce and stir in the cream and chopped basil. Warm through gently for a couple of minutes.

Drain the pasta and toss with the lobster sauce. Divide between warm plates, scatter the Parmesan over and drizzle with a little olive oil. Serve immediately.

"I love this incongruous combination of lobster – the king of shellfish – with simple spaghetti and fresh tomato. It's a great fast pasta dish for a special occasion"

macaroni cheese

WITH BEENLEIGH BLUE AND MUSHROOMS

Serves 4

250g dried macaroni

sea salt and pepper

1 tbsp olive oil

50g butter

100g ceps or chestnut mushrooms, sliced

200ml double cream

100g Beenleigh blue cheese

Add the macaroni to a large pan of boiling salted water with the olive oil and cook for 7–10 minutes until just tender. Drain and rinse under cold water to remove excess starch. Return to the pan and set aside.

Melt the butter in a small frying pan. Add the mushrooms and fry until softened and golden brown, then season with pepper. Heat the grill.

Add the cream to the macaroni and crumble in two-thirds of the blue cheese. Heat gently for a few minutes to melt the cheese. Season with pepper.

Transfer the macaroni cheese to a gratin dish and scatter on the mushrooms and remaining cheese. Place under the hot grill for 2–3 minutes to brown lightly, then serve.

"I recommend you always buy free-range organic chicken – the flavour is far superior to that of intensively reared birds fed on a limited diet with minimal exercise"

warm chicken salad

WITH JERUSALEM ARTICHOKES, SPINACH AND BACON

Serves 4

2 rosemary sprigs

3 thyme sprigs

1 bay leaf

2 garlic cloves, peeled

500ml chicken stock

2–3 free-range chicken
    breasts (part-boned)

4 tbsp olive oil

50g butter

150g Jerusalem artichokes,
    scrubbed or peeled

2 tbsp lemon juice

125g bacon rashers

50ml classic vinaigrette

1 tsp sherry vinegar

1 shallot, finely chopped

150g baby spinach

deep-fried onion rings to
    serve (optional)

Put the herbs, garlic and stock in a pan and bring to a simmer. Add the chicken breasts and poach gently for 3 minutes or until firm to touch. Cool in the liquor, then lift out and remove from the bone, keeping the skin intact.

Fry the chicken breasts, skin-side down, in half the olive oil for 4–5 minutes until the skin is golden brown and crisp. Add half the butter and cook for another 2 minutes.

Simmer the artichokes in water to cover, with the lemon juice added, for 5–6 minutes. Drain, cool and thickly slice. Fry the artichoke slices in the remaining oil and butter for 2–3 minutes each side until golden brown. Drain on kitchen paper. Pan-fry the bacon until crisp, drain and cut into pieces.

Whisk the vinaigrette with the sherry vinegar and shallot. Cut each chicken breast lengthways into 6 slices. Arrange the spinach, chicken, bacon and artichokes on plates and dress with the vinaigrette. Garnish with fried onion rings if you like and serve.

family and friends

Eating together as a family is important to me. My mother always made us sit down together to eat and I have fond memories of the food, as well as the laughter. Sunday is our family day and we often have a roast, but I also like to cook meals that are easy to prepare and serve. We never quite know how many of us there will be, so meals need to be flexible. My fish pie is a favourite, but the children also enjoy braised beef or a chicken casserole. Desserts are a must and we never tire of steamed pudding or trifle.

roasted cod and tomatoes
WITH OVEN CHIPS

Serves 4

700g Maris Piper potatoes

2 tbsp olive oil

25g butter

675g cod loin fillet, skinned
  and cut into 4 thick pieces

12 cherry tomatoes on the
  vine, cut into 4 clusters

juice of $\frac{1}{2}$ lemon

sea salt and pepper

2 tbsp chopped parsley

Heat the oven to 200°C/Gas 6. Peel the potatoes and cut into chunky chips. Add to a pan of boiling water and blanch for 4 minutes; drain well. Return to the dry pan, add the olive oil and shake the pan to coat the chips in the oil. Spread the chips out on a baking tray and bake for 10 minutes. Shake the tray to turn the chips and bake for a further 10–15 minutes.

Meanwhile, melt the butter in a cast-iron frying pan, add the fish and cook for 2–3 minutes. Turn and cook the other side for 2 minutes, then add the tomatoes to the pan and place in the oven. (If your pan isn't ovenproof, simply transfer to an oiled roasting pan.) Bake for 5 minutes.

Drizzle the lemon juice over the fish as you take it from the oven. Season with salt and pepper and then allow to rest in the pan for 5 minutes. Put the cooked chips into a warm bowl and season with salt.

Place the roasted cod and tomatoes on warm plates, scatter the parsley over and drizzle with the pan juices. Serve at once, with the oven chips.

fillets of red mullet
WITH A RUSTIC RATATOUILLE

Serves 4

4 small red mullet about 250g each, or
   2 larger ones about 500g each, filleted

2 tbsp olive oil

sea salt and pepper

Rustic ratatouille:

2 beef tomatoes

$\frac{1}{2}$ red pepper, deseeded

$\frac{1}{2}$ yellow pepper, deseeded

1 tbsp olive oil

2 garlic cloves, finely chopped

1 red onion, finely chopped

2 courgettes, chopped

1 aubergine, chopped

handful of basil leaves, roughly chopped

dash of balsamic vinegar

For the ratatouille, halve and deseed the tomatoes, then finely chop the flesh. Cut the peppers into 1cm dice. Heat the olive oil in a saucepan and cook the garlic and onion gently for 2 minutes to soften. Add the courgettes, aubergine, tomatoes and peppers, stir and cook for about 5 minutes to soften. Add the basil, balsamic vinegar and seasoning to taste. Take off the heat and keep warm.

To cook the red mullet, heat the olive oil in a heavy-based frying pan, then add the red mullet fillets, skin-side down, and cook for about 3 minutes until the skin is really crispy. Turn and cook for a further 30 seconds–1 minute, depending on the thickness of the fish. Remove from the heat, season with salt and pepper and leave to rest for a few minutes.

Spoon the ratatouille on to warm plates or a large platter. Top with the red mullet fillets and serve.

fillets of red mullet

gordon's fish pie

Serves 4

25g butter

4 shallots, finely chopped

250ml dry white wine

250ml Noilly Prat or dry
   vermouth

500ml fish stock

500ml double cream

sea salt and pepper

800g mixed white filleted
   fish (cod, haddock,
   monkfish etc)

juice of $\frac{1}{2}$ lemon

handful of tarragon, flat-leaf
   parsley or chervil, chopped

300g ready-made puff
   pastry

1 egg yolk, beaten with
   1 tsp water (eggwash)

Heat the butter in a pan and sweat the shallots until soft. Add the wine and vermouth and let bubble until reduced by half. Add the stock and reduce again by half.

Add the cream and boil until reduced to a sauce-like consistency. Season with salt and pepper to taste and allow to cool. Meanwhile, heat the oven to 180°C/Gas 4.

Check the fish for any small bones, removing any with tweezers, then cut into 3cm chunks. Add to the sauce with the lemon juice and herbs, toss to mix, then pour into an earthenware baking dish. Bake for about 15 minutes.

Meanwhile, roll out the pastry and cut out 4 oval shapes, using an individual pie dish as a guide. Place on a baking sheet and brush with eggwash to glaze.

Remove the fish from the oven and keep warm. Raise the oven temperature to 200°C/Gas 6, then bake the pastry ovals for 7–10 minutes until golden brown.

Spoon the fish and creamy sauce on to warm plates, top with the oval pastry 'lids' and serve.

"As a lad growing up in Scotland, I loved fishing and learnt to respect the industry. I still get a thrill from catching my own fish and cooking it. Very fresh fish doesn't smell or feel slimy. It has bright eyes and firm flesh. Ask your fishmonger for his best catch of the day. If he fillets the fish for you, then ask for the trimmings to make your own fish stock"

"Look for traditionally cured bacon produced from a suitable pig, such as an English saddleback or Sussex Black. Mass-produced bacon contains chemicals and water, shrinks to nothing and is quite tasteless"

roast pheasant
WITH CREAMED CABBAGE AND BACON

Serves 4–6

1 brace of pheasants

olive oil to brush

4 thyme sprigs, leaves
   stripped

2 bay leaves

10 dry-cured smoked
   streaky bacon rashers

200ml double cream

½ head of Savoy cabbage,
   cored

½ head of white cabbage,
   cored

sea salt and pepper

Heat the oven to 190°C/Gas 5. Brush the pheasants with olive oil, sprinkle with the thyme leaves and lay a bay leaf on top of each pheasant. Wrap 3 bacon rashers over each pheasant to keep the breast moist (and hold the bay leaf in place) and place in a roasting pan. De-rind the other rashers, cut into lardons and set aside.

Roast the pheasant in the middle of the oven for 45 minutes, then remove the bacon and roast for a further 15 minutes until the skin is golden. Allow to rest in a warm place for 15 minutes.

Cook the bacon lardons in a dry pan for a couple of minutes, then add the cream and simmer gently for 5 minutes.

Meanwhile, finely shred both cabbages and blanch in boiling salted water for a few minutes until just tender. Drain thoroughly and add to the bacon and cream mixture. Season with salt and pepper.

Carve the pheasant at the table and serve with the creamed cabbage.

chicken casserole
WITH CORIANDER DUMPLINGS

Put the chicken in a large oval casserole, add the stock and bring to the boil. Add the vegetables and bring back to a simmer. Add the herbs, ginger and plenty of seasoning. Cover and simmer very gently for about 40 minutes until the chicken is tender. Remove from the heat and allow to cool. (This can be done a day in advance.)

Skim off any fat from the surface of the casserole. Lift out the chicken pieces, remove the meat from the bone, discard the skin, then return to the pan. Check the seasoning.

To make the coriander dumplings, mix the flour, suet and coriander together in a bowl, adding enough cold water to form a soft pliable dough. Shape into small dumplings.

Reheat the casserole. When the liquid comes to a boil, drop in the dumplings. Lower heat, re-cover and simmer for 10–15 minutes or until the dumplings are doubled in size and fluffy. Discard ginger and herbs.

Serve in warm pasta bowls, with crusty bread for mopping up the juices.

Serves 4–6

8–12 chicken portions (legs, thighs etc)
1 litre chicken stock
4 celery sticks, halved
2 leeks (white part only), finely chopped
2 red onions, cut into wedges
4 carrots, chopped
2 parsnips, chopped
1 celeriac, finely diced
1 bay leaf
few thyme sprigs
1 lemongrass stalk
knob of fresh root ginger, bruised
sea salt and pepper

Coriander dumplings:

250g plain flour
100g shredded suet
3 tbsp chopped coriander

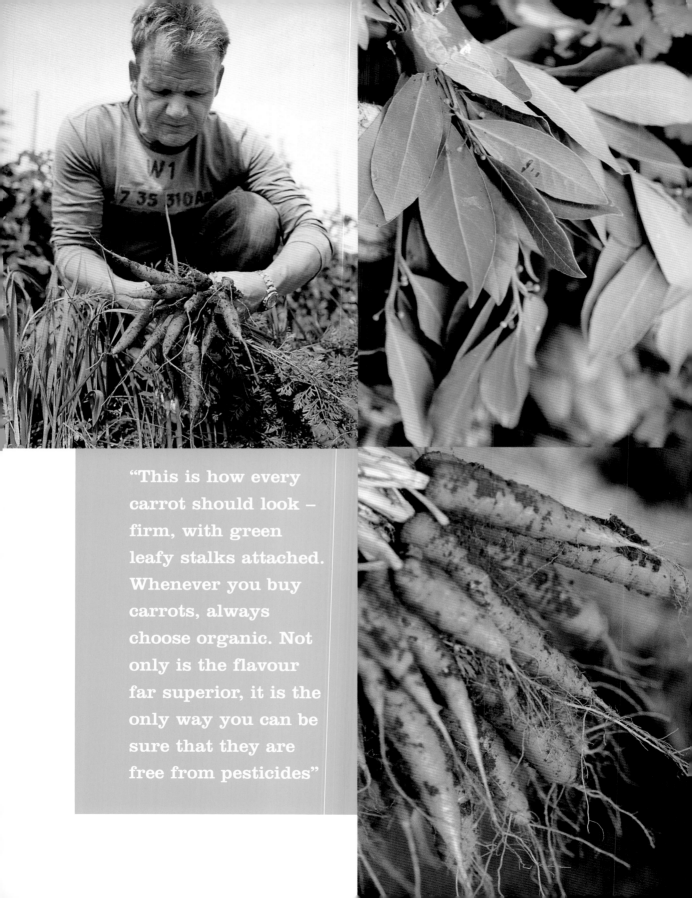

"This is how every carrot should look – firm, with green leafy stalks attached. Whenever you buy carrots, always choose organic. Not only is the flavour far superior, it is the only way you can be sure that they are free from pesticides"

chicken casserole

braised shin of beef
WITH BABY TURNIPS AND MANGETOUT

Serves 4–6

2 tbsp olive oil

2kg shin of beef (on the bone)

3–4 garlic cloves, peeled

1 onion, roughly chopped

1 carrot, sliced

2 celery sticks, halved

1 turnip, chopped

1 beef tomato, deseeded and
  roughly chopped

600ml red wine

600ml beef stock

1 bay leaf

2 thyme sprigs

1 star anise

1 tsp coriander seeds

sea salt and pepper

200g baby turnips, trimmed

200g mangetout

Heat the olive oil in a large casserole, add the beef and sear on all sides; remove and set aside. Add the garlic, onion, carrot, celery, chopped turnip and tomato, and sweat for 3–5 minutes to soften.

Return the meat to the casserole, pour in the red wine and bring to the boil, then add the stock. Bring back to the boil, then add the bay leaf, thyme, star anise and coriander seeds. Reduce the heat to a low simmer, cover and cook gently for 2–3 hours until the meat is tender.

Carefully lift out the meat and allow to cool. Strain the cooking liquid through a chinois into a clean pan, discarding the vegetables. Skim off the fat, then boil until the stock is reduced to a sauce-like consistency. Season with salt and pepper to taste. Meanwhile, take the cooled meat off the bone, discarding all fat and sinew.

Cook the baby turnips in boiling salted water for 5–7 minutes until tender. Blanch the mangetout for 2 minutes. Drain.

Add the meat to the reduced liquor and warm through gently. Serve on warm plates with the turnips and mangetout, and plenty of mash.

"The flavour of Aberdeen Angus beef organically raised on good grazing pastures is amazing. How an animal lives, eats and is slaughtered is as important as the breed of the animal to the taste of the meat. Fergal, the handsome bull pictured above, lives on a farm in Devon "

saddle of lamb
STUFFED WITH SPINACH

Heat the oven to 200°C/Gas 6. Open out the saddle of lamb; set aside the eye fillets. Halve the garlic, season and leave for a few minutes to draw out the juices.

For the stuffing, heat a splash of olive oil in a non-stick pan and sauté the mushrooms until softened and browned; drain in a colander. Heat a little more oil and a knob of butter in the pan, add the spinach, season lightly and cook until just wilted. Tip the mushrooms into a bowl, mix in the spinach, mascarpone and egg yolk, and season with nutmeg, salt and pepper.

Oil several sage leaves and place down the middle of the lamb. Rub the meat with the garlic bulb. Spoon the stuffing on top of the sage leaves. Cut the eye fillets horizontally (but not right through), open out and place over the stuffing. Fold one flap of the saddle over, then the other, wrapping firmly to make a neat roll. Secure with string at intervals and tuck the remaining sage leaves in at the ends.

Heat a splash of oil in a roasting pan, add the garlic bulb and sage sprigs and sauté briefly, then add the butter and allow to foam. Put the meat on top.

Roast for 30 minutes, then lower setting to 180°C/Gas 4 and roast for a further 30 minutes. Lift meat on to a warm platter and rest in a warm place for 20 minutes. Deglaze pan juices with sherry vinegar, add the wine and stock, and reduce by half. Strain and adjust seasoning. Serve the lamb thickly sliced, with the jus.

Serves 6–8

1 saddle of lamb, about
  2.4kg, boned out

1 garlic bulb

sea salt and pepper

splash of olive oil

few sage sprigs

knob of butter

Stuffing:

3–4 tbsp olive oil

250g mixed mushrooms,
  (shiitake, oyster, button),
  cleaned

knob of butter

250g young spinach, stalks
  removed

2–3 tbsp mascarpone

1 egg yolk

freshly grated nutmeg

6–8 sage leaves

Pan jus:

1 tbsp sherry vinegar

2 glasses red wine

125ml light stock

"Secure the meat with string at intervals but don't tie it too tightly – just enough to hold it together during roasting"

saddle of lamb

"I am delighted to see the revival of rare breed pigs raised in natural surroundings ... there is no doubt that you can taste the difference"

roast pork belly
WITH SAGE AND THYME

Serves 4–6

1kg boned piece of pork
   belly, skinned
sea salt and pepper
few thyme leaves
handful of sage leaves,
   roughly chopped
2–3 tbsp olive oil

Heat the oven to 220°C/Gas 7. Lay the pork, skinned-side up, on a board and season well with salt. Turn the meat, season with pepper and scatter the herbs over. Roll up from a long side and tie with string.

Heat the olive oil in a roasting pan on the hob, add the pork and sear on all sides. Transfer to the oven and roast for 10 minutes, then lower the setting to 150°C/Gas 2 and cook for a further 2 hours. Rest in a warm place for 10 minutes, then carve into slices. Serve with flavoured mash, baby carrots and cabbage.

creamy spinach tart

Roll out the pastry and line a 23cm flan tin, leaving some pastry overhanging the edge. Prick the base with a fork, line with greaseproof paper and fill with dried beans or rice. Chill for 20 minutes. Meanwhile, heat the oven to 200°C/Gas 6.

Steam the spinach (or cook in a pan with the minimum of water) until just wilted. Drain and set aside to cool.

Bake the pastry case for 15 minutes, then remove the paper and beans, and brush the base with the eggwash. Bake for a further 5 minutes. Allow to cool slightly, then trim the edge of the pastry level with the tin, using a very sharp knife. Lower the oven temperature to 180°C/Gas 4.

Lightly whisk the eggs and extra yolk together. Beat in the milk, crème fraîche, sea salt, cayenne and nutmeg. Mix in the spinach and pour into the pastry case. Bake for 25–35 minutes or until golden brown and set. Allow to cool slightly.

Serve the tart warm, cut into wedges, garnished with tomato slices.

Serves 4–6

300g ready-made shortcrust
    pastry
150g baby spinach, stalks
    removed
1 egg yolk, beaten with
    1 tsp water (eggwash)
2 large free-range eggs, plus
    1 extra egg yolk
100ml milk
300g crème fraîche
sea salt
$\frac{1}{2}$ tsp cayenne pepper
$\frac{1}{2}$ tsp freshly grated
    nutmeg
1 vine-ripened beef tomato,
    sliced, to garnish

rosemary potato galette

Serves 4

4 large potatoes, peeled

100g unsalted butter

4-6 rosemary sprigs, leaves
stripped, plus extra sprigs
to garnish

3-4 thyme sprigs, leaves
stripped

sea salt and pepper

Slice the potatoes very thinly. Melt half the butter in a 25cm cast-iron frying pan. Take off the heat and arrange a third of the potato slices in an overlapping layer to cover the base of the pan. Sprinkle with half the rosemary and thyme leaves and season well. Dot with half the remaining butter.

Repeat these layers, then cover with the rest of the potato slices, season generously and press well down.

Cook on a low heat (or bake at 180°C/Gas 4) for 40–45 minutes until golden brown underneath. Invert the potato on to a plate and then slide back into the pan (this isn't necessary if you are baking the galette in the oven). Cook for a further 10–15 minutes.

Scatter a few rosemary sprigs over the galette and serve, cut into wedges.

stuffed baby squash

Slice the top off each squash, and cut another slice off the base, leaving 2cm thick shells. Scoop out and chop the flesh; set aside. Heat the oven to 200°C/Gas 6. Put the squash shells on a baking tray, brush with oil and season well. Bake for 5 minutes; let cool.

Peel and thickly slice the artichokes and immerse in a bowl of water, with the lemon juice added, to prevent discolouration.

Sauté the onion in 2 tbsp olive oil until soft. Stir in the celeriac and drained artichokes, then add the wine and 200ml stock. Simmer for 8–10 minutes until the vegetables are tender but still have a bite. Drain, reserving the stock, and tip into a bowl.

Sauté the chopped squash in 1 tbsp olive oil and half the butter for 2–3 minutes, then add the remaining 100ml stock and simmer for 6–8 minutes until very tender. Strain into a small pan, discarding the squash. Add the reserved stock and bubble to reduce by half. Stir in the cream and reduce again by half. Check the seasoning and add half the herbs.

Sauté the mushrooms in the remaining butter for a minute. Add to the bowl of vegetables with a little of the sauce to bind. Spoon into the squash shells and heat through in the oven for 5–6 minutes.

Warm the sauce and add the remaining herbs. Lift the baked squash shells on to warm plates. Using a spatula, spoon the sauce over and around, then serve.

Serves 4

4 baby acorn squash

3 tbsp olive oil, plus extra to brush

sea salt and pepper

250g Jerusalem artichokes

2 tbsp lemon juice

1 small onion, finely chopped

1 small celeriac, finely diced

100ml dry white wine

300ml vegetable stock or water

100g butter

100ml double cream

1 tbsp finely chopped parsley

1 tbsp finely chopped chervil

125g mixed wild mushrooms

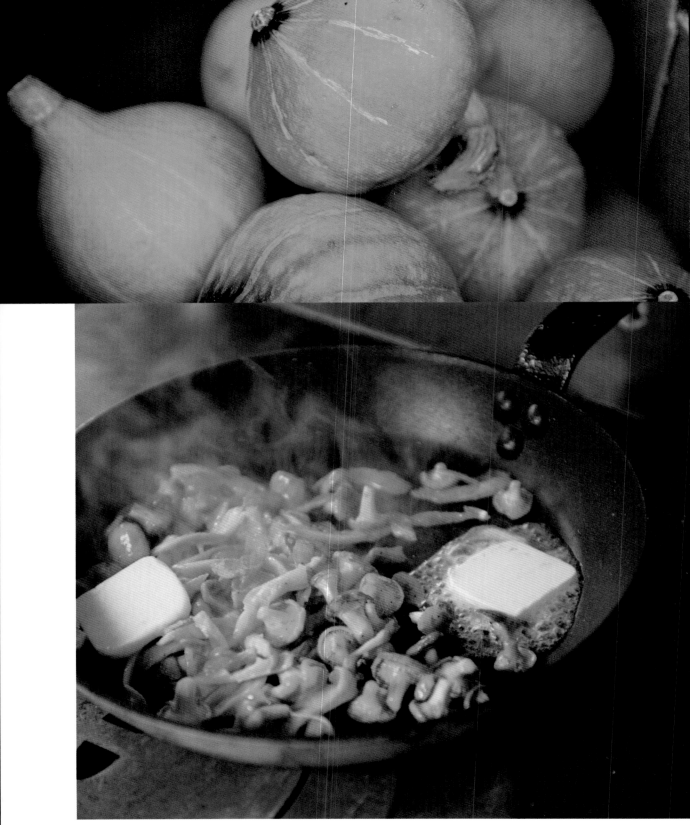

stuffed baby squash

"I first started to appreciate squash in Australia and the USA, where it has been popular for decades. This versatile vegetable is increasingly popular here, and you can now find a good variety of squash, including acorn, butternut and turk's head"

gordon's trifle

Serves 6

1½ tbsp cornflour

300ml milk

2 vanilla pods, seeds
   removed

40g caster sugar

2 egg yolks

225g strawberries

150g raspberries

130g Madeira sponge

300ml double cream

Mix the cornflour with a little of the milk in a pan until smooth, then add the rest of the milk with the vanilla pods and half the sugar. Slowly bring to the boil, stirring continuously, then take off the heat.

Whisk the egg yolks in a bowl, using an electric whisk, until pale in colour, then gradually whisk in the hot milk mixture.

Return to the pan and stir over a very low heat for 2 minutes; don't let it boil or the custard will curdle. Take off the heat, cover the surface with damp greaseproof paper and allow to cool.

Purée 100g strawberries and 40g raspberries in a blender or food processor with the remaining sugar and 75ml water. Transfer to a bowl and stir in most of the remaining berries, reserving some for decoration. Spoon into a glass serving bowl. Cut the sponge into 2cm squares and scatter over the fruit.

Whip the cream until softly peaking. Remove the vanilla pods from the cooled custard, then fold in the whipped cream. Spoon over the sponge and spread evenly. Chill for 1 hour or until ready to serve.

Scatter the reserved berries over the top of the trifle to serve.

steamed apricot pudding

Serves 4–6

10 fresh apricots

butter to grease

100g self-raising flour

125g shredded suet

3 free-range eggs

finely grated zest of
    $\frac{1}{2}$ lemon

$\frac{1}{2}$ tsp baking powder

60g fresh white
    breadcrumbs

Sauce:

30g unsalted butter,
    softened

65g light muscovado sugar

75ml apricot purée (see
    recipe)

50ml double cream

Halve and stone the apricots, then cut off a third of each half horizontally from the base to give a rounded slice. Butter a 1.2 litre pudding basin. Arrange the rounded apricot slices in the bottom of the basin and a little way up the sides.

Purée the rest of the apricots in a blender or food processor. Measure 100ml apricot purée for the pudding. Keep the rest (about 75ml) for the sauce.

Put the flour, suet, eggs and lemon zest in the food processor and process for 30 seconds. Add the baking powder, apricot purée and breadcrumbs, and whiz for a further 30 seconds. Carefully spoon the mixture into the basin.

Cover the top of the basin generously with a double layer of greaseproof paper, making a pleat in the centre. Secure under the rim with string. Place in a saucepan containing enough boiling water to come halfway up the side, cover tightly and steam for 2 hours, topping up the boiling water as necessary. (Or cook in an electric steamer for $1\frac{1}{2}$ hours.)

To make the sauce, gently melt the butter in a small pan, add the sugar and stir until dissolved. Increase the heat slightly and cook to a treacle-like consistency. Take off the heat and stir in the apricot purée and cream; keep warm.

Turn the pudding out on to a warm plate, pour over the apricot sauce and serve immediately.

pan-roasted apples and pears
WITH BRAMBLE SYRUP

Serves 4

2 large Cox's apples

2 large Conference or
   Williams pears

4 tbsp icing sugar, sifted

200g blackberries

250ml stock syrup (see
   page 248)

2 tbsp Poire eau-de-vie or
   Calvados (optional)

mint sprigs to serve

Core and slice the apples and pears, but don't peel them. Heat a large, heavy-based frying pan until you see a faint haze rising.

Toss the sliced fruits in icing sugar, then immediately put into the pan in a single layer. Leave for a few seconds until the undersides begin to caramelise, then turn and lightly caramelise the other side for a few seconds. Don't overcook – the fruit should still be firm.

Tip the blackberries into a large bowl and lightly crush with a potato masher. Add the caramelised apples and pears, pour the stock syrup and alcohol over, and toss gently. Leave to cool, then cover and chill for 2 hours.

Spoon the fruit and liquor into glass dishes and top with mint sprigs to serve.

"I use this technique for peaches, nectarines and mangoes as well. Caramelised fruit is also the basis of my tart tatins: Use an ovenproof pan for pan-frying, then cover the fruits with a sheet of puff pastry and bake at 200°C/Gas 6 for 10–15 minutes. Invert on to a plate to serve"

"There's something very satisfying about picking fruit from the hedgerows and transforming it into delectable desserts, jellies and jams, that is of course if you live in the country. Otherwise, farmers' markets and pick-your-own-fruit farms are a good source of seasonal soft fruits"

summer
barbies

When I'm relaxing at home in the summer, I invariably fire up the barbecue. It's such a great way to bring out the flavour of food and shouldn't be limited to burgers and sausages. Fish, meat, vegetables and fruit all lend themselves to barbecuing. Marinating food in advance adds flavour and keeps leaner cuts succulent. Use good sturdy tongs, long-handled forks and gloves to ensure that you don't burn yourself. Barbecues are an excellent way to entertain – especially if you get everyone involved in the cooking.

"I like to serve these juicy tiger prawns with a spiked vinaigrette for dipping. Just flavour 150ml classic vinaigrette with 1 chopped, deseeded red chilli, 1 finely chopped lemongrass stalk and a squeeze of lemon juice"

"This spice paste also works well with chunky fish fillets and chicken pieces. Remember that barbecue coals need to be white, with no flame, or you will scorch the food before it's properly cooked"

seared tiger prawns
WITH GARLIC, CHILLI AND LEMONGRASS

Serves 4–6

12 large, raw tiger prawns,
    peeled and deveined (tail
    shell on)
2–3 garlic cloves, peeled
2 red chillies, deseeded
2 lemongrass stalks
2.5cm piece fresh root
    ginger, peeled
4–6 tbsp olive oil
sea salt and pepper

Put the tiger prawns in a shallow dish. Pound the garlic, chillies, lemongrass and ginger together using a pestle and mortar, gradually adding the olive oil until you have a rough paste (or whiz briefly in a blender). Season with salt and pepper. Baste the prawns with the spice paste and leave to marinate in a cool place for 2–3 hours.

Cook the marinated prawns on the hot barbecue for 4–6 minutes, turning, until they turn pink and feel slightly firm to the touch – don't overcook. Serve at once, with a flavoured vinaigrette, soured cream or tomato salsa.

barbecued whole sea bream
IN BANANA LEAVES WITH CHILLI

Serves 4–8

4 sea bream, about
   500–600g each, scaled,
   gutted and cleaned
4 large banana leaves
olive oil to brush
a little sesame oil
4 red chillies, deseeded and
   chopped
2 lemongrass stalks
2–3 garlic cloves, roughly
   chopped
2.5cm piece fresh root
   ginger, sliced
sea salt and pepper
handful of coriander leaves,
   chopped
juice of 2 limes
600ml coconut milk

Slash the skin of the fish 3 or 4 times on both sides. Lay the banana leaves on a surface, brush lightly with olive oil, then sprinkle with a little sesame oil. Lay a sea bream across the centre of each leaf. (If you can't find banana leaves, use foil instead.)

Mix the chillies, lemongrass, garlic and ginger together, and press into the slashes in the fish. Season with salt and pepper, scatter the coriander over the fish and drizzle with the lime juice.

Wrap each fish in a banana leaf, folding in the ends like an envelope. Carefully pour the coconut milk into the parcel (find a gap to do so), then secure with string. (Should any of the banana leaves split, simply overwrap in foil.)

Place the fish parcels on the barbecue and cook for 25–30 minutes or until the flesh is opaque. Test by inserting a knife – the flesh should lift cleanly from the bone.

To serve, open out the banana leaf and carefully lift the fish fillets from the bone. Hot new potatoes and a simple green salad are ideal accompaniments.

lemon chilli chicken wings
WITH A COUSCOUS SALAD

Serves 4–6

8–12 chicken wings

juice of 1 lemon, skins
  reserved

9 tbsp olive oil

2 red chillies, chopped

2 green chillies, chopped

2 red peppers

2 green peppers

3 garlic cloves (unpeeled)

200g couscous

1 tsp ground cumin

sea salt and pepper

120g cherry tomatoes,
  halved

large handful of coriander
  leaves, chopped

Toss the chicken wings with half the lemon juice, 4 tbsp of the olive oil, the chopped chillies and spent lemon skins in a bowl. Cover and leave to marinate in the fridge for 2–3 hours.

Meanwhile, heat the oven to 200°C/Gas 6. Toss the whole peppers and garlic cloves with 4 tbsp olive oil and roast on a baking tray for 15–20 minutes or until the skins are scorched and wrinkled. Leave to cool on the tray.

Put the couscous in a bowl and pour on 200ml boiling water. Stir with a fork, then leave to stand for 20 minutes, forking through the couscous every 5 minutes or so, to ensure that the grains separate and the couscous is fluffy. Sprinkle in the cumin and add the remaining olive oil and lemon juice. Fork through, seasoning liberally with salt and pepper.

Peel the roasted peppers, then tear open, remove the seeds and chop the flesh. Squeeze the soft pulp from the garlic skins and mix into the couscous with the chopped peppers and halved cherry tomatoes. Mix in the chopped coriander to taste.

Cook the chicken wings on the barbecue, turning and basting regularly with the marinade until brown, crisp and cooked through. Serve in bowls on a bed of couscous salad.

wild boar sausages
WITH CHIANTI SAUCE

Serves 4–6

500g wild boar sausages

Sauce:

150g unsalted butter, chilled and diced

3 shallots, thinly sliced

1 garlic clove, crushed

few thyme sprigs

500ml Chianti or similar red wine

1 tbsp brown sugar

1 tsp Dijon mustard

splash of balsamic vinegar

sea salt and pepper

"There is really no excuse for serving inferior sausages when there are so many excellent quality butcher's sausages around now. Wild boar sausages are not as strongly flavoured as you might imagine, and they go brilliantly with a red wine sauce"

Have the sausages ready at room temperature, but don't prick them (as you want to keep the fat within to baste them naturally on the barbecue).

To make the sauce, melt a knob of the butter in a pan, then add the shallots, garlic and thyme. Cook over a high heat for a few minutes, then add the wine and sugar and bring to the boil, stirring to dissolve the sugar. Boil steadily until reduced by half. Discard the thyme.

Take the sauce off the heat and whisk in the mustard and cold butter, a piece at a time. Add the balsamic vinegar and season with salt and pepper to taste.

Barbecue the sausages slowly on a medium heat until nicely coloured and cooked through. Serve on a bed of herb-flavoured mashed potato, with the Chianti sauce and crusty bread on the side.

barbecued steaks
WITH A PIQUANT RED PEPPER SAUCE

Serves 4–6

4–6 sirloin or rib eye steaks,
   about 200g each

2 tsp paprika

2 tsp pink peppercorns,
   lightly crushed

1 glass red wine

6–7 tbsp olive oil

2 red peppers

4 garlic cloves (unpeeled)

2 lemons

sea salt and pepper

Lay the steaks in a shallow dish and sprinkle with 1 tsp paprika and the pink peppercorns. Pour on the wine and 2 tbsp olive oil, then cover and leave to marinate at room temperature for 1 hour.

Meanwhile, heat the oven to 200°C/Gas 6. Toss the whole peppers and garlic cloves with 2 tbsp olive oil and roast on a baking tray for 15–20 minutes or until the skin is scorched and wrinkled. Leave to cool on the tray.

Squeeze the garlic pulp out of the skins into a blender or food processor. Peel the roasted peppers, open and remove the seeds, then add to the blender with any juices. Whiz to a smooth paste.

With the motor running, add 1 tsp paprika, the juice of $1/2$ lemon and 2–3 tbsp olive oil, processing to emulsify. Season with salt and pepper to taste.

Cut the other 1½ lemons into fairly thick slices, removing the pips.

Cook the steaks on the barbecue over a high heat, along with the lemon slices. Allow 3–5 minutes on each side, then allow to rest on a warm plate for about 5 minutes. Serve topped with the lemon slices and accompanied by the sauce.

"Look for well-hung steaks with a good dark colour and a marbling of fat. Aberdeen Angus beef is my favourite"

barnsley chops

"These double loin chops from the saddle of lamb are ideal for a barbecue, because the fat is all around the outside of the chops and prevents them drying out"

Serves 4–6

4–6 Barnsley chops
1 tsp thin honey
1 glass red wine
pepper

Mint sauce:

2 tsp sugar
125ml white wine vinegar
1 shallot, finely chopped
large handful of mint leaves, finely chopped

Put the lamb chops in a shallow dish, drizzle with the honey, pour on the wine and grind over plenty of black pepper.

To make the sauce, combine the sugar, wine vinegar and shallot in a pan, bring to the boil and let bubble until reduced by half. Take off the heat, add the chopped mint and allow to cool.

Cook the chops on the barbecue for 4–6 minutes each side, basting with the marinade. Serve with the mint sauce.

barbecued fennel
WITH PERNOD AND STAR ANISE

"This dish is too good to be limited to the barbecue. To cook indoors, char-grill the fennel on an oiled griddle, then bake in a covered dish at 180°C/Gas 4 for around 30 minutes until tender and fragrant"

Serves 4–6

3 large fennel bulbs

2 celery sticks, finely sliced

2 star anise

sea salt and pepper

1 glass medium dry white wine

shot of Pernod

5 knobs of butter

2–3 garlic cloves, chopped

small handful of tarragon and parsley, chopped

Cut the fennel from top to root into thin slices and cut out the tough core. Have ready a large square of foil.

Char-grill the fennel slices briefly on the barbecue, turning once, then transfer to the middle of the foil. Scatter the celery over, add the star anise and season with salt and pepper. Pour over the wine and drizzle with a little Pernod. Dot with the butter and chopped garlic, then scatter the herbs over.

Wrap the fennel in the foil to make a parcel, then place on the edge of the barbecue. Leave to cook slowly for 20–25 minutes, then open up the parcel and serve.

grilled flat mushrooms
WITH MASCARPONE, BLUE CHEESE AND BASIL

Serves 4

4 large, flat field
   mushrooms
1 tbsp olive oil
125g mascarpone
75g Stilton or other blue
   cheese, crumbled
pepper
handful of basil leaves,
   chopped

Wipe the mushrooms with a damp piece of kitchen paper or use a soft brush to remove any dirt or grit, but don't wash them. Cut out the stalks.

Brush a large sheet of foil with the olive oil and place the mushrooms, gill-side up, in the middle.

Mix the mascarpone with the blue cheese and season with plenty of pepper. Fill the mushroom caps with this mixture and sprinkle with chopped basil.

Keeping the stuffed mushrooms flat, bring up two opposite sides of the foil and fold the edges together, then seal the ends of the parcel. Place on the edge of the barbecue to cook for 10–15 minutes (or you could cook in the oven at 180°C/Gas 4).

Serve as a starter with sourdough bread, or as an accompaniment to barbecued meats.

"I adore mushrooms, especially those gathered as they grow naturally in woods and fields. I often chat to the mushroom pickers who bring samples into the restaurant – it's as though they belong to a secret club. We buy their mushrooms and use them on the menu, but I know what we pay is a pittance for the time they take collecting them"

lemon tart

WITH A CARAMELISED TOPPING

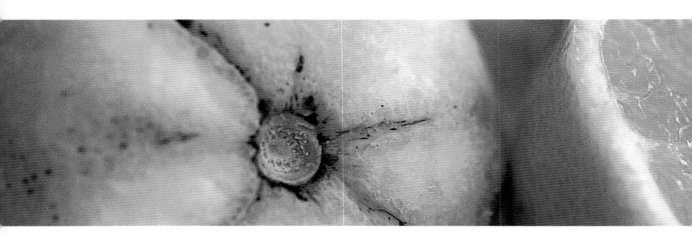

Roll out the pastry thinly and use to line a 20cm tart tin placed on a baking sheet. Press well into the edges and leave the excess pastry overhanging the edge. Line with greaseproof paper and fill with dried beans or rice. Chill for 20 minutes. Heat the oven to 180°C/Gas 4.

Bake the tart for 12–15 minutes. Remove the paper and beans and bake for a further 5 minutes. Allow to cool, then trim the pastry level with the top of the tin. Turn the oven down to 100°C/Gas 1.

To make the filling, put the lemon juice, caster sugar, egg yolks, double cream and 110ml water in a bowl and whisk with a fork to combine, but do not overwork.

Place the tart tin on the middle oven shelf and carefully pour in the filling. Bake for 45–50 minutes, then turn out the oven and leave the tart inside to cool very slowly. (The filling will be slightly wobbly when you turn the oven off.) When completely cold, chill the tart for 1–2 hours until set.

Dust the surface with icing sugar and caramelise with a cook's blowtorch. Leave until the topping is cool and crisp, then dust again and caramelise. Serve at once.

Serves 4–6

1 quantity of sweet flan
   pastry (see overleaf)

Filling:

juice of 1½ lemons

180g caster sugar

6 free-range egg yolks,
   beaten

150ml double cream

icing sugar to dust

Sweet Flan Pastry
is easy to make in a food processor – just take care to avoid overworking it.
Put 125g unsalted butter (at room temperature) and 90g caster sugar in the processor and whiz until just combined, then add 1 free-range large egg and whiz for 30 seconds. Add 250g plain flour and process briefly until the dough just comes together. Knead lightly on a floured surface, then wrap in cling film and rest in the fridge for 30 minutes before rolling out.

"Like strawberries, redcurrants are synonymous with an English summer. Counter their slight tartness by frosting in caster sugar, and use to decorate desserts and cakes"

summer strawberry salad
WITH CHAMPAGNE GRANITA

Serves 4–6
400g strawberries, sliced
few lemon balm leaves,
  shredded
125g redcurrants
caster sugar to coat
Champagne granita:
125g sugar
juice of 1 lemon
3 tbsp liquid glucose
250ml Champagne

To make the granita, put the sugar, lemon juice and liquid glucose in a pan with 250ml water and heat gently until the sugar has dissolved. Bring to the boil and simmer for 3 minutes. Allow to cool.

Stir the Champagne into the cooled sugar syrup, then pour into a freezerproof container. Freeze for 2–3 hours, forking the mixture every hour to break up the ice crystals.

Arrange the strawberry slices on a large platter and sprinkle with the lemon balm. Scrape shavings off the granita and scatter over the top. Dip the redcurrants into the caster sugar and arrange on the salad. Serve immediately.

just for
kids

Getting children involved in the kitchen from an early age encourages them to appreciate good food. It's amazing how much more a child enjoys eating food they've helped to prepare, or perhaps grow in the garden. Watching them make their own burgers and pizzas is so rewarding – matched by the pure delight on their faces as they later devour them. I get them to think about what they are eating and where it comes from. This year they are all growing tomatoes in the garden ... it could become competitive.

chunky vegetable soup

Serves 4–6
1.2 litres vegetable stock
4 celery sticks, finely sliced
1 onion, diced
2 carrots, diced
1 turnip, diced
1 sweet potato, diced
400g can butter beans, drained
sea salt and pepper
2 tbsp chopped flat-leaf parsley
olive oil to drizzle
freshly grated Parmesan to serve

Heat the stock in a large saucepan. Add the celery, onion, carrots, turnip and sweet potato, and bring to the boil. Lower the heat, cover and simmer for 20 minutes.

Add the butter beans and simmer for a further 10 minutes. Season with salt and pepper to taste. Whiz briefly, using a stick blender, to purée a little of the soup and thicken the liquor slightly, but keep a good chunky consistency.

Stir in the parsley and check the seasoning. Spoon the soup into warm bowls, drizzle with a little olive oil and serve sprinkled with Parmesan.

"Brimming with vegetables, this is the ideal food for hungry kids returning home from school. Even a child who hates veggies may be tempted. Plenty of crusty bread turns the soup into a meal in its own right"

tomato and mozzarella pizza
WITH VARIOUS TOPPINGS

Serves 4–8

Dough:

2 tsp fast-action dried yeast

250ml tepid water

600g strong plain (bread)
  flour

1 tbsp olive oil

Tomato base:

560g jar passata

knob of butter

1 garlic clove, crushed

sea salt and pepper

Toppings:

100g bocconcini (mozzarella
  balls), halved

300g cherry tomatoes,
  halved

small handful of basil
  leaves, roughly torn

100g pepperoni sausage
  (optional)

small jar or tub of olives
  (optional)

sea salt and pepper

freshly shaved Parmesan

To make the dough, add the yeast to the warm water, stir and leave to stand for a few minutes. Tip the flour into a food processor, add the oil, then with the motor running, pour in the yeast liquid. Process until the dough is smooth and leaves the side of the bowl clean. Transfer to a bowl, cover with cling film and leave in a warm place until doubled in volume.

To make the tomato base, place the passata, butter and garlic in a small pan over a medium-high heat. Bring to a simmer and cook until reduced by half. Season with salt and pepper to taste.

Put all the topping ingredients in bowls on the kitchen table. Heat the oven to 220°C/Gas 7. Cut the pizza dough in half.

Roll out the pizza dough, one portion at a time, on a lightly floured surface to a large round – making it as thin as possible. Place each round on a heavy baking sheet (or a large cast-iron frying pan suitable for use in your oven if you have one). Spread with the tomato base.

Top with the mozzarella, cherry tomatoes and basil. Add other toppings as you like, season and scatter over some grated Parmesan. Better, still, get the children to apply their own choice of ingredients.

Bake for 8–10 minutes, until golden, then cut each pizza into 4 wedges and serve.

"Pizzas are deceptively easy to make at home and healthier than a take-away. There's no limit to the toppings you can apply – seafood and pan-roasted vegetables are tasty options"

"I'm a great believer in getting children involved in preparing food, and homemade pizzas are a brilliant way of encouraging them to try different ingredients"

salmon fish cakes

Serves 4–8

600g floury potatoes, such as Desirée,
   peeled and cut into even-sized pieces

sea salt and pepper

large knob of butter

1 onion, finely chopped

2 tbsp olive oil

400g salmon fillet, skinned

1 free-range egg yolk

1 free-range egg, beaten

100g natural breadcrumbs

groundnut oil to fry

"To make these appealing to young children, make fish-shaped cakes. When cooked, add a little red pepper eye to each one ... guaranteed to raise a smile"

Boil the potatoes in salted water until soft, then drain and press through a potato ricer into a large bowl (or mash well). Beat in the butter and seasoning.

Fry the onion in the olive oil until soft but not coloured, then add to the potato mixture. Check the salmon fillet for small bones, removing any with tweezers.

Purée a quarter of the salmon in a food processor, then beat into the potato mixture with the egg yolk. Finely dice the remaining salmon and fold into the potato mixture. Cover and chill for 30 minutes.

Shape the mixture into 8 fish cakes. Dip first into the beaten egg and then into the breadcrumbs to coat. Place on a tray and chill for a further 30–40 minutes.

Heat a thin film of groundnut oil in a large frying pan, add the fish cakes and fry for 2–3 minutes each side or until golden brown. Drain on kitchen paper. Serve with halved cherry tomatoes and cucumber.

pasta with bacon
AND PEAS

Serves 4–6

200g dried fusilli or other pasta shapes

sea salt and pepper

3 tbsp olive oil

1 onion, finely chopped

1 garlic clove, finely chopped

100g bacon lardons

300ml double cream

100g frozen peas

1–2 tbsp chopped flat-leaf parsley

1–2 tbsp freshly grated Parmesan

Cook the pasta in a large pan of boiling salted water with 1 tbsp olive oil for 7–10 minutes until al dente (cooked but firm to the bite). Drain and rinse under cold water to remove excess starch. Return to the pan and set aside.

Heat the remaining olive oil in a deep sauté pan. Add the onion and garlic and fry, stirring, for 2–3 minutes, then add the bacon and fry until crisp. Add the cream and let bubble until reduced by half.

Add the peas, bring back to a simmer and cook for 2 minutes. Season with salt and pepper to taste.

Add the pasta to the sauce and heat through, stirring, for 1–2 minutes. Scatter with parsley and Parmesan, and serve in warm pasta bowls.

"Pasta is a great energy booster and children love it. You'll probably find you have all the ingredients for this simple recipe in the kitchen ... and what's more it is nutritionally well balanced"

cheese toasties

Serves 4

225g Lancashire cheese,
  cut into cubes
1 free-range egg yolk
2–3 tsp Worcestershire
  sauce
½ tsp Dijon mustard
1–2 tbsp single cream
8 slices good-quality white
  bread
olive oil to fry

Put the cheese, egg yolk, Worcestershire sauce and mustard in a food processor. Whiz until smooth, adding enough cream to give a thick paste.

Spread the mixture on to 4 slices of bread and sandwich together with the other slices of bread. Remove the crusts and cut the sandwiches in half on the diagonal.

Heat a thin film of olive oil in a frying pan and cook the sandwiches for a minute or two on each side until golden brown. Drain on kitchen paper and serve wrapped in paper napkins.

mini meg burgers

"All kids love burgers. They are so simple and quick to make that I fail to understand why parents ever buy processed patties packed with additives and preservatives"

Makes 6 mini-burgers

300g lean ground beef or minced rump steak

1 onion, finely chopped

pepper

2 tbsp olive oil

6 mini buns, split

1 tbsp mayonnaise

1 tbsp tomato ketchup

4 Cos lettuce leaves, shredded

10 cherry tomatoes, sliced

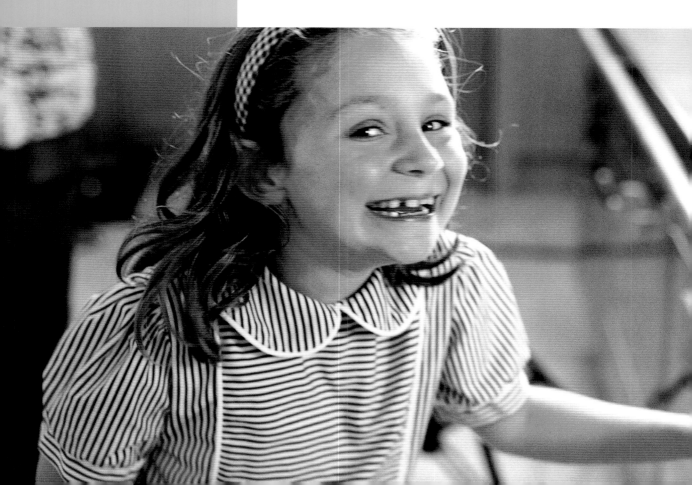

oven-roasted chips

To make your own chips, cut 2 clean, large baking potatoes into wedges, about 2cm thick. Add to a pan of boiling water and blanch for 4 minutes, then drain well. Return to the dry pan, add 2 tbsp olive oil and shake the pan to coat the chips in the oil. Spread the chips out on a baking tray and bake at 200°C/Gas 6 for 10 minutes. Shake the tray to turn the chips and bake for a further 10–15 minutes. or until crisp and golden brown. Drain the potato wedges on kitchen paper, season with salt and serve.

Put the ground beef and onion into a bowl and mix well, seasoning with pepper. Form into 6 balls, flatten slightly and wrap in cling film. Refrigerate for 30 minutes or until ready to cook. (This can be done a day ahead.)

Place a heavy-based frying pan (preferably cast-iron) over a high heat for 2–3 minutes and add the olive oil. When hot, add the burgers and press down gently. Cook for 3 minutes each side and then turn down the heat and cook for a further 5 minutes. Turn off the heat and leave the burgers to rest in the pan for 5 minutes.

Heat the grill and lightly toast the split buns on both sides. Mix the mayonnaise and ketchup together in a small bowl.

Put the shredded lettuce on the bun bases, top with the burgers, then cover with the sliced tomatoes. Spoon the ketchup mix on top, then sandwich together with the bun tops and press gently. Serve with homemade oven-roasted chips.

fruity yogurt lollies

Makes 4

1 large mango, 6 apricots or
   3 peaches, peeled, halved
   and stoned
65g caster sugar
500g natural yogurt

Whiz the fruit in a blender or food processor with 1 tbsp sugar until smooth. Pass through a sieve or mouli into a bowl, cover and refrigerate.

Tip the yogurt into a bowl, add the rest of the sugar and stir well to dissolve. Divide between 4 lolly moulds or strong plastic cups and place in the freezer for 1 hour.

Swirl the fruit purée into the semi-frozen yogurt (don't mix too thoroughly). Place a lolly stick or strong plastic spoon in the centre of each lolly and return to the freezer for 2 hours or until solid.

Store the lollies in a freezer bag (unless they are going to be eaten the same day). They will keep well for up to 2 months. To serve, allow to stand at room temperature for 5 minutes, then remove the moulds or cups. Watch the kids devour them!

fruit kebabs

WITH CHOCOLATE DIP

Serves 6–8

½ pineapple, peeled,
  halved and cored

2–3 bananas, peeled

3 kiwi fruit, peeled

12–16 strawberries

12–16 raspberries

12–16 blackberries

12–16 cherries, pitted

200g good-quality dark
  chocolate

Cut the pineapple, bananas and kiwi fruit into chunks and arrange them on a large platter with the various berries and cherries. Encourage the kids to thread their favourite fruits on to short wooden kebab skewers.

Melt the chocolate in a bowl set over a pan of gently simmering water. Stir until smooth, then pour into a couple of warm ramekins.

Serve the fruit kebabs with the warm chocolate for dipping.

banana split

Serves 4–6

750g strawberries

75g good-quality dark
    chocolate

4–6 medium bananas

300ml double cream

400g vanilla ice cream

Whiz half of the strawberries in a blender or food
processor to a purée, then pass through a fine sieve
into a bowl.

Break up the chocolate and put into a bowl set
over a pan of gently simmering water. Leave until
melted, then stir until smooth.

Halve the bananas lengthways and place, cut-side
down, in shallow serving bowls. Set aside a handful
of whole strawberries for serving. Slice the rest and
scatter over the banana, then drizzle with half the
melted chocolate.

Whip the cream until softly peaking. Place scoops
of ice cream on top of the bananas, then spoon on the
whipped cream. Drizzle with the strawberry purée
and remaining melted chocolate. Top with the whole
strawberries and serve.

"When I was a child we didn't eat out as a family very often, but when we did it was a huge treat. The best part for me was always the pudding and a banana split was my absolute favourite"

fruit and honey cereal bars

Makes 9 or 12

300g porridge oats

70g demerara sugar

3 tbsp thin honey

100g mixed dried tropical
    fruit, such as mango,
    pineapple and papaya,
    roughly chopped

100g unsalted butter

Heat the oven to 180°C/Gas 4. Line a shallow 20cm baking tin with baking parchment. Put the oats, sugar and honey into a large bowl, add the dried fruit and stir well.

Melt the butter in a pan over a low heat, then pour into the oat mixture and mix thoroughly. Tip into the lined tin and spread evenly. Press down firmly with the back of a spoon.

Bake in the oven for 20–25 minutes until golden brown. Leave to cool completely in the tin, then lift the baking paper to remove. Cut into squares or slices.

party biscuits

Makes 20–24

125g unsalted butter

125g caster sugar

1 egg, beaten

250g plain flour

$\frac{1}{2}$ tsp ground mixed spice

To decorate:

150g icing sugar

coloured sugar

silver balls (optional)

Cream the butter and sugar together in a bowl until creamy and soft. Gradually beat in the egg.

Sift the flour and spice together, then work into the mixture, using a metal spoon to begin with, then your hands. Gather the mixture together and knead for 1–2 minutes to make a smooth dough.

Wrap the dough in cling film and rest in the fridge for 30 minutes. Heat the oven to 180°C/Gas 4. Line a baking sheet with greaseproof paper. Divide the dough into 4 portions and re-wrap all but one.

Roll out the dough on a lightly floured surface to a 5–7mm thickness. Use biscuit cutters to cut out figures, stars or other shapes. At Christmas, use festive cutters (Christmas trees, etc.) and make a hole near the top with a skewer, so you can hang the biscuits on the tree. Place on the lined baking sheet. Repeat with the rest of the dough.

Bake for 10–15 minutes until the biscuits are pale golden in colour. Leave on the baking sheet for a few minutes to firm up, then lift on to a wire rack to cool.

To decorate the biscuits, mix the icing sugar with enough water to make a smooth, very thin glaze. Brush the biscuits with the icing glaze, using a pastry brush, and then sprinkle on the coloured sugar. Decorate with silver balls if you like. Leave on a wire rack until the icing is dry.

"Cooking with children is pure magic, I love to see the joy on their faces as they see the product of their work"

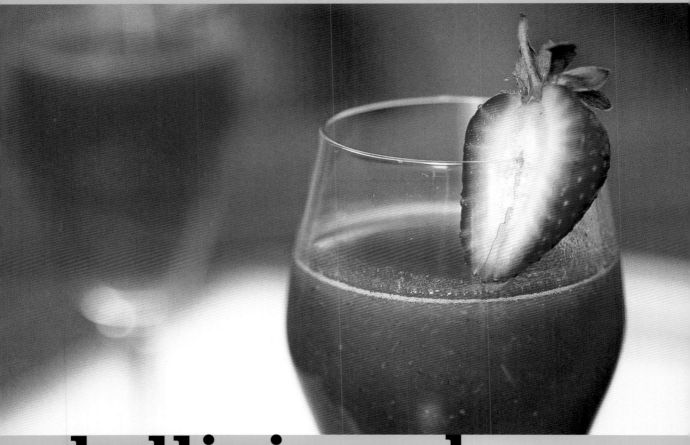

bellinis and blinis

When Tana and I throw a party, we never quite know how many we are catering for. Finger food with Champagne cocktails is an easy option. We make canapés in advance and treat ourselves as guests at our own party. We encourage friends to pass round trays of food and this gets them mingling. It never ceases to amaze me how much food is consumed. As a rough guide, I suggest you allow 7–10 canapés per person, depending on the time of day. Scatter bowls of olives and nuts around the room and keep everything relaxed.

hot-smoked salmon blinis
WITH CAPER BERRIES

Makes 25–40, depending on size

50g wholemeal flour
1 tbsp fast-action dried yeast
700ml tepid milk
125g buckwheat flour
125g plain flour
4 free-range eggs, separated
butter to fry

To serve:

200g kiln-roasted or hot-smoked salmon
125ml soured cream
caper berries

Put the wholemeal flour and yeast into a large mixing bowl and stir in 475ml milk. Stir well and leave in a warm place for 20 minutes.

In the meantime, flake the salmon along its natural contours, cover and set aside.

Add the buckwheat and plain flours, egg yolks and remaining 225ml milk to the yeast mixture and mix well until smooth. In another bowl, whisk the egg whites until softly peaking, then lightly fold into the yeast batter.

Cook the blinis in batches. Heat 1 tbsp butter in a blini pan or small non-stick frying pan. Drop small spoonfuls of batter into the pan, spacing them slightly apart. Cook for about $1\frac{1}{2}$ minutes until the surface is covered with tiny bubbles and the under-sides are golden brown.

Flip the blinis over and cook for another minute, then transfer to a warm plate lined with kitchen paper; keep warm while you cook the rest.

Spoon a little soured cream on to each blini and top with a piece of salmon and a caper berry to serve.

mini tart tatins

OF CARAMELISED RED ONION AND GOAT'S CHEESE

"Blinis are great canapés and you can vary the toppings as you like. Use crème fraîche instead of soured cream if you prefer. For a glamorous finish, spoon on a little caviar or lumpfish roe instead of the caper berries"

Makes 24

2 tbsp olive oil

2 red onions, finely chopped

1 garlic clove, finely chopped

1 firm, ripe goat's cheese, about 125g, in pieces

200g ready-made puff pastry

Heat the oven to 200°C/Gas 6. Have ready two 12-hole non-stick mini muffin tins.

Heat the olive oil in a small frying pan and add the onions and garlic. Cook slowly for 5–8 minutes until the onions begin to caramelise. Spoon into the mini muffin tins and dot each with a little goat's cheese.

Roll out the puff pastry, then scrunch it up and roll it out again (this will prevent it from rising too much, which you want to avoid here). Cut out discs that will fit snugly over the filling in the muffin tins.

Place the pastry discs on top of the onion and press down firmly. Bake for 5–7 minutes until golden brown. Allow to stand for 5 minutes, then carefully turn out the tarts on to a wire rack. Serve warm.

roasted pumpkin crostini
WITH PANCETTA

Makes 20

1 small French stick

¼ peeled, deseeded
pumpkin (about 150g
prepared weight), finely
chopped

2 tbsp olive oil

sea salt and pepper

100g diced pancetta

freshly shaved Parmesan

Heat the oven to 180°C/Gas 4. Cut the bread into 1cm thick slices, place on a baking tray and bake for 6–8 minutes or until crisp and golden brown. Allow to cool.

Scatter the chopped pumpkin on a baking tray, drizzle with the olive oil and season with salt and pepper. Bake for 10–15 minutes or until tender.

Meanwhile, put the pancetta in a heavy-based frying pan and cook over a medium heat until crisp. Drain on kitchen paper.

Spoon the pumpkin on to the crostini, sprinkle with the pancetta and arrange some Parmesan shavings on top. Serve immediately.

tempura onion rings

Serves 10
2 large Spanish onions
sea salt and pepper
3–4 tbsp flour to dust
groundnut oil to deep-fry
Batter:
80g self-raising flour
1 small free-range egg yolk
2 free-range egg whites
paprika to dust (optional)

Slice the onions finely and place in a bowl. Season with salt and pepper and add 3–4 tbsp flour. Toss the onion slices to coat in the flour.

To make the batter, sift the flour into a bowl and make a well in the middle. Add the egg yolk, then gradually beat in 150ml cold water to make a smooth batter. In another bowl, whisk the egg whites until softly peaking, then fold into the batter.

Heat the oil for deep-frying in a suitable pan to 180°C. Have ready a baking tray lined with kitchen paper.

Deep-fry the onion rings in batches. One by one, dip into the batter and then transfer to the hot oil, using a pair of tongs. Fry for 3–4 minutes until crisp and golden in colour. Transfer to the paper-lined tray to drain and keep warm while you cook the rest.

Serve the onion rings as soon as they are all cooked, dusted with a little paprika if you like.

pan-fried baby octopus

"If you can't find baby octopus, then use small squid for this recipe. Most fishmongers sell ready-prepared baby squid, with the pouches and tentacles separate. Don't overcook the squid or you will ruin the delicate texture"

Serves 10
500g cleaned baby octopus
100g plain flour
sea salt and pepper
olive oil to fry
lemon or lime wedges to serve

Cut the octopus into 3cm pieces. Put the flour into a large plastic bag and season generously. Add the octopus and toss around to coat thoroughly with seasoned flour. Have ready a baking tray lined with kitchen paper.

Heat a 2.5cm depth of olive oil in a small, deep frying pan. When hot, fry the octopus in small batches for 2–3 minutes until crisp and golden. Transfer to the paper-lined tray to drain and keep warm while you cook the rest.

Serve the deep-fried octopus as soon as it is all cooked, with lemon or lime wedges.

spring rolls with a soy dip

Makes 20

20g rice noodles

2 spring onions, diced

20g beansprouts

1 carrot, grated

5cm piece mooli, grated

1 tsp fish sauce

sea salt and pepper

130g packet dried spring roll
  wrappers

groundnut oil to deep-fry

Dipping sauce:

50ml soy sauce mixed with
  1 tsp wasabi

Soak the noodles in boiling water for 3–4 minutes. Drain and mix with the spring onions, beansprouts, carrot, mooli, fish sauce and seasoning to taste.

Plunge the wrappers into hand-hot water for 15 seconds until pliable, then lay on a clean surface. Put a spoonful of the mixture in the centre of each, fold in the sides and carefully roll up to secure.

Heat the oil in a suitable pan to 180°C. Deep-fry the spring rolls, a few at a time, for 3–4 minutes until crisp and golden. Drain on kitchen paper and serve hot, with the dipping sauce.

"Dried spring roll wrappers are available from supermarkets and Asian food stores. Vary the filling as you like – try prawns, chicken or duck – but don't overfill them or they will split"

king prawns in breadcrumbs

Makes 20

20 raw tiger prawns, peeled
and deveined (with tail
shell left on)

1 free-range egg white,
beaten

125g fresh white
breadcrumbs

groundnut oil to deep-fry

Hold each tiger prawn by the tail end and dip first into the egg white and then into the breadcrumbs. Gently shake off excess crumbs and place on a baking tray lined with greaseproof paper while you coat the rest.

Heat the oil for deep-frying in a suitable pan to 180°C. Deep-fry the prawns in small batches. Drop them into the hot oil, one at a time, and cook for 3–4 minutes or until they just turn pink. Drain well on kitchen paper. Serve warm.

"I love courgette flowers, but you can't always find them. Fortunately fine courgette slices – cut lengthways using a mandolin – work equally well"

wild sea bass

WRAPPED IN COURGETTE FLOWERS

Makes 20

250g wild sea bass fillet, with skin

20 courgette flowers, or thin strips of courgette

olive oil to drizzle

sea salt and pepper

Heat the oven to 200°C/Gas 6. Line a baking tray with greaseproof paper.

Cut the sea bass into small even-sized pieces. Carefully wrap each one in a courgette flower or thin strip of courgette and secure with a wooden cocktail stick or short kebab stick.

Arrange the sea bass parcels on the baking tray and drizzle with a little olive oil. Bake for 4–5 minutes, then leave to rest for a minute or two.

Season the sea bass lightly with salt and pepper, and serve warm.

"I only ever use scallops that have been hand-dived (rather than dredged from the seabed along with grit and sand) and I suggest you do the same"

scallops in parma ham
WITH MONKFISH AND ROSEMARY

Makes 20

10 scallops, shelled and cleaned

10 slices Parma ham

250g monkfish fillet, skinned

2–3 long rosemary sprigs

olive oil to drizzle

Heat the oven to 200°C/Gas 6. Slice the scallops in half horizontally. Cut the Parma ham slices in half lengthways. Cut the monkfish into small chunks. Break the rosemary stems into short twigs.

Wrap each scallop disc in a strip of Parma ham, top with a piece of monkfish and secure with a rosemary twig or two.

Carefully transfer to a baking tray and drizzle with a little olive oil. Roast in the oven for 3–4 minutes until just firm to the touch.

Allow to stand for a few minutes, then serve warm.

seared tuna with herbs

Makes 20
250g tuna fillet (mid-loin cut), in a squared log,
    about 10cm long and 3cm across
pepper
1 tbsp olive oil
4 tbsp chopped parsley
4 tbsp chopped chervil

Trim the tuna if necessary and season with pepper. Brush a 20cm square of foil with olive oil and scatter the herbs across the centre. Lay the tuna log on the herbs, then roll to coat on all sides.

Roll the herb-coated tuna in the foil very tightly and twist the ends to seal (like a Christmas cracker). Roll the tuna roll back and forth on the work surface to round off the squared edges. Refrigerate for 20 minutes.

Heat a cast-iron frying pan over a high heat, then put the foil parcel in the pan and cook quickly for about 15–20 seconds on each side. Remove the foil parcel and allow to cool.

Place the foil-wrapped tuna in the fridge and leave to firm up for at least 30 minutes, or up to 4 hours.

To serve, unwrap the tuna and cut into thin slices with a very sharp knife. Serve immediately.

"As this dish is served raw, only very fresh, sushi-grade tuna is suitable. Ask your fishmonger to prepare this for you"

steak tartare

"Prime fillet of beef is the key to this recipe and it is worth having it freshly minced by your butcher. Alternatively, this can be done in the food processor, but take care not to overwork"

Serves 10

250g minced fillet steak

1 tbsp minced red onion

1 tbsp finely chopped flat-leaf parsley

2 tsp Dijon mustard

freshly ground black pepper

1 free-range egg yolk

2 vine-ripened tomatoes, to serve

Put the minced steak into a bowl with the onion, parsley and mustard. Mix well, seasoning with pepper to taste, then bind the mixture with the egg yolk.

Immerse the tomatoes in boiling water for 20 seconds or so, then remove and peel off the skins. Halve the tomatoes, scoop out the seeds, then cut the flesh into small dice.

Serve small portions of the steak tartare on teaspoons, topped with the tomato dice.

pork satay

IN LETTUCE WITH PEANUT DIPPING SAUCE

Makes 10

1 pork fillet (tenderloin)

100ml soy sauce

25ml dry sherry

2 star anise

1 tsp coriander seeds

1 tsp grated fresh root
   ginger

2 tsp thin honey

oil to brush

Peanut dipping sauce:

1 tbsp sugar

100g unsalted peanuts

sea salt and pepper

To assemble:

1 round lettuce, separated
   into leaves

2 spring onions, finely sliced

handful of coriander leaves

Cut the pork into bite-sized pieces and put into a bowl. Add the soy sauce, sherry, star anise, coriander seeds, ginger and honey, and toss to coat the pork in the mixture. Leave to marinate for 2 hours.

To make the dipping sauce, dissolve the sugar in 125ml water in a small saucepan and bring to the boil. Add the peanuts and take off the heat. Whiz the mixture in a blender or food processor until fairly smooth. Season with salt and pepper to taste.

Heat a cast-iron griddle pan until very hot and brush with oil. Add the pork and cook quickly for 2–3 minutes, turning until golden brown on both sides and cooked through.

Place 2 or 3 pieces of pork in the centre of a lettuce leaf and scatter with a little spring onion and a few coriander leaves. Roll up and secure with a cocktail stick. Repeat with the rest of the pork.

Serve the pork satay warm, with the peanut dipping sauce.

bellini

Serves 2

60ml peach juice

200ml Champagne or
   Prosecco (sparkling wine)

Pour the peach juice into chilled flute glasses, top with the Champagne or Prosecco and serve.

strawberry champagne cocktail

Serves 2

60ml strawberry purée

200ml Champagne or
   sparkling wine

halved strawberry to finish

Pour the strawberry purée into chilled flute glasses, top with the Champagne or sparkling wine and decorate with the strawberry halves.

champagne alexander

Serves 2

2 sugar cubes

40ml brandy

200ml Champagne

Place a sugar cube in each of two flute glasses, add the brandy and top up with the Champagne.

pina colada

Serves 2

8 ice cubes

few drops of Angostura
  bitters

100ml pineapple juice

100ml white rum

150ml soda water

Place the ice cubes in tall glasses, add the Angostura bitters, and pour on the pineapple juice and rum. Stir thoroughly. Top up with the soda water, stir once and serve.

bloody mary

Serves 4

12 ice cubes

200ml vodka

600ml tomato juice

4 dashes of Worcestershire
  sauce

4 dashes of Tabasco

4 celery sticks

pinch of celery salt

Place the ice cubes in tall glasses, add the vodka and then top up with the tomato juice. Add a dash each of Worcestershire sauce and Tabasco to each glass. Pop in a celery stick, sprinkle with a little celery salt and serve.

"Champagne is so evocative of luxury, celebration and fun. Nothing can be easier than popping open a few bottles and making a few simple cocktails – it's the easiest way to get a party off to a great start"

posh

It's rewarding to create dishes that are a bit more special at home, and I think you will find plenty of inspiration here. Lobster thermidor is far easier than you might imagine, or for an impressive, inexpensive dish, try my pork fillet in prosciutto. Posh food that isn't time-consuming is the essence of this chapter. It's the kind of food Tana likes to cook, but her problem is that she never really knows when I'm likely to turn up for dinner. These recipes are ideal – simple to prepare and quick to finish.

frisée and potato soup WITH TARRAGON

"This soup is delicate and sensuous. To make it even more appealing, top with poached quail's eggs and a little caviar"

Serves 6
300g potatoes, peeled
1 leek, white part only, well washed
400ml chicken stock
$\frac{1}{2}$ tsp coriander seeds, or to taste, freshly ground
1 head of frisée, stem removed
sea salt and pepper
handful of tarragon leaves
120ml double cream
large knob of unsalted butter

Dice the potatoes and leek and put in a pan with the stock and coriander seeds. Bring to the boil, then simmer for 10–15 minutes until the potato is just tender. Strain through a chinois into a clean pan. Set aside half the leek and potato for later; add the rest to the pan. Slowly bring to a simmer.

Take the pale centre leaves from the frisée, roll them together and shred very finely with a sharp knife to make a chiffonade. Set aside for the garnish.

Tear up the remaining frisée and add to the soup. Season, then add the tarragon and cook until just wilted – no longer or you will lose the colour. Immediately pour into a blender or food processor and whiz to a purée. Strain through the chinois back into the clean pan. Stir in the cream and heat through. Check the seasoning.

Meanwhile, heat the butter in a small frying pan, add the reserved potato and leek and cook over a high heat to colour lightly.

Pile the sautéed leek and potato into the centre of warm soup plates, pour the soup around and top with the frisée chiffonade. Serve at once.

turnip soup
WITH LANGOUSTINES AND MANGO

Serves 6

900g turnips, peeled

large knob of butter

1 onion, chopped

450ml chicken stock

125ml double cream

sea salt and pepper

Mango garnish:

1 ripe, firm mango, peeled,
   sliced or diced and pitted

knob of butter (optional)

2 tsp sugar (optional)

Saffron langoustines:

1–2 tbsp olive oil

1 garlic clove, crushed

pinch of saffron threads

18–30 langoustines or tiger
   prawns (or more), blanched
   for 1 minute and peeled

To finish:

handful of sorrel leaves,
   shredded (optional)

olive oil to drizzle

Roughly chop the turnips. Melt the butter in a medium pan, add the onion and sweat for a few minutes to soften. Add the turnips and stock and bring to a simmer. Cook gently for 20–30 minutes until the turnip is very soft.

Caramelise the mango in the meantime if you like. Melt a knob of butter with the sugar in a heavy-based frying pan and cook to a light caramel. Add the mango and cook for a few minutes until lightly tinged brown. Remove and set aside.

Pass the soup mixture through a mouli. Return to the pan, add the cream and check the seasoning. Allow to simmer very gently while you cook the langoustines.

Heat the olive oil in a small frying pan, and add the garlic, saffron and langoustines. Sauté quickly for a minute or two on each side; do not overcook.

Pour the soup into warm soup plates and arrange the mango in the centre. Top with a little shredded sorrel if using. Arrange the langoustines around the mango and drizzle with a little olive oil. Serve immediately.

turnip
soup

"I love the heat and flavour of turnip and consider it to be a very underrated vegetable. I often use it to thicken soups in place of potato. Here turnip comes into its own, marrying perfectly with the sweetness of caramelised mango and plump, juicy langoustines"

carpaccio of beef
WITH ROCKET AND PARMESAN

Serves 6 as a starter

olive oil to brush

2–3 tbsp black
  peppercorns, freshly
  crushed

500g piece fillet of beef,
  well-trimmed

2 tbsp chopped flat-leaf
  parsley

Dressing:

1 tsp thin honey, warmed

juice of ½ lemon

1 tbsp white wine vinegar

1 tsp wholegrain mustard

150ml olive oil

To serve:

handful of rocket leaves

freshly shaved Parmesan

Brush a large piece of foil with a little olive oil and scatter the crushed peppercorns in the centre. Roll the beef fillet in the pepper to coat completely. Wrap the fillet in the foil and secure the ends tightly. Rest in the fridge for 30 minutes.

Place a heavy-based frying pan over a high heat and sear the foil packet for 20–30 seconds on each of the four sides. Allow to cool, then return to the fridge for at least 1 hour.

For the dressing, put the honey into a bowl and whisk in the lemon juice, wine vinegar and mustard, followed by the olive oil.

Unwrap the beef and roll in the chopped parsley, then cut into very thin slices, using a razor-sharp knife.

Toss the rocket in the dressing and arrange on individual plates. Pile the rocket into the centre and scatter the Parmesan shavings over. Serve at once.

"Classic carpaccio is finely sliced raw beef served with a light mayonnaise or dressing. I like to sear the outside of the fillet very briefly, which gives it an almost smoky finish, but you can omit this stage if you like"

lobster thermidor

Serves 6

3 live medium lobsters

250ml fish stock (preferably lobster stock)

250ml dry white wine

splash of Noilly Prat

250ml double cream

1 tsp Dijon mustard

sea salt and pepper

2 tbsp freshly grated Parmesan

First, put the lobsters in the freezer for about 30 minutes to make them sleepy. When ready to cook, make sure you kill them quickly: Lay stomach downwards and plunge the tip of a knife through the crossmark on the skull, then cut the head in half. (If you prefer you can plunge them into a pan of boiling water for 2 minutes.)

Split each lobster in half lengthways through the tail shell and twist off the claws; reserve the empty half-shells. Discard the head and carefully remove the meat from the tail shells, discarding the entrails. Wash the reserved tail shells. Crack open the claws with a nutcracker and extract the meat. Place the reserved tail shells on a large baking tray and pile the lobster meat into them.

Boil the stock and wine in a pan until reduced by half. Add the Noilly Prat and cream and let bubble until reduced to a sauce-like consistency. Stir in the mustard and adjust the seasoning.

Heat the grill to high. Carefully spoon the sauce over the lobster meat and scatter the Parmesan on top. Place the lobsters under the grill and cook for 2–3 minutes until the sauce is bubbly and golden brown. Serve immediately, with a green salad.

"Ready-cooked lobsters are never as good as those you cook yourself, so I recommend you get to grips with handling a live lobster! Their claws will be wrapped in thick bands so they won't nip you. With a ready-cooked lobster you might end up with a dry, rubbery texture rather than deliciously succulent meat"

Serves 6

1kg fresh razor clams or
   medium clams
300ml dry white wine
200ml fish stock or water
2 shallots, very finely diced
1 tbsp chopped tarragon
15g butter
300g girolles (golden
   chanterelles), trimmed
   and cleaned
50ml double cream
sea salt and pepper
2 tbsp chopped flat-leaf
   parsley

razor clams with girolles

To clean the clams, put them in a large bowl of cold water, leave for 5 minutes, then drain. Repeat twice more, replacing with fresh water each time. Pull away the beards and scrub the shells to remove any barnacles. Discard any open clams.

Pour the wine and stock into a very large pan. Add the shallots and tarragon and bring to the boil. Add the clams, cover with a tight-fitting lid and cook for 3–4 minutes to steam them open, shaking the pan twice. Drain in a colander over another pan to save the stock. Keep the clams warm in the colander over the hot stock, covering them with the pan lid. Discard any that do not open.

Melt the butter in a pan and sauté the mushrooms for 2–3 minutes. Add 200ml reserved stock and bring to a simmer. Stir in the cream, season and heat through.

Divide the clams between warm bowls, spoon over the mushroom sauce and sprinkle with chopped parsley.

"Confit is an old technique, once used to preserve meat such as duck. To 'confit' you simply poach the food in warm oil or fat, sealing in all the delicious natural flavours"

confit of trout
WITH SAUCE MOUSSELINE

Serves 6

6 large trout fillets, with skin

sea salt

500ml olive oil for cooking

3 small ripe avocados

large handful of rocket leaves

Sauce mousseline:

125ml double cream

125ml mayonnaise

3 tbsp lemon juice

sea salt and pepper

Check the trout fillets for small bones and remove any you find with tweezers. Scatter plenty of sea sea over the trout and leave to stand for 30 minutes. Rinse the trout and place in a dish of cold water. Leave to soak for 20 minutes, then drain and pat dry.

Heat the olive oil in a deep frying pan to 50°C (warm enough to cook the fish and cool enough to be able to place your finger in the oil without it burning). Place the trout in the oil and maintain the temperature for 10 minutes. Remove the fillets with a slotted spoon and allow to cool.

For the sauce mousseline, whip the cream until softly peaking, then fold in the mayonnaise and lemon juice. Season with salt and pepper to taste.

Halve and pit the avocados, then slice lengthways and arrange on serving plates. Flake the confit trout, arrange next to the avocado and spoon over a little sauce mousseline. Garnish with rocket and serve.

halibut bourguignon

Serves 6

125g shallots (unpeeled)

400ml red wine

125g bacon lardons

4 tbsp olive oil

6 garlic cloves (unpeeled)

125g button mushrooms

50g butter

6 halibut fillets, about 150g
  each, skinned

250g spinach leaves, well
  washed

sea salt

Blanch the shallots in boiling water for 2 minutes, then drain and peel. Meanwhile, boil the red wine in a pan to reduce by half.

Sauté the lardons in a heavy-based frying pan until crisp. Remove and set aside.

Add 2 tbsp olive oil to the frying pan and heat. Add the shallots, garlic and mushrooms and sauté until softened and the shallots are lightly caramelised. Stir in the bacon; keep warm.

Meanwhile, heat the butter and remaining oil in a large frying pan until foaming. Pan-fry the halibut fillets for 2–3 minutes on each side until just cooked. Remove to a warm plate and rest for a few minutes.

Cook the spinach in a large pan over a medium heat, with a little water and a pinch of salt, until just wilted. Drain well.

Pile the spinach into the centre of warm plates and place the fish on top. Spoon over the mushrooms, shallots, garlic and bacon. Add the reduced red wine to the shallot pan, stirring to deglaze, then drizzle over the fish and vegetables. Serve with new potatoes.

halibut bourguignon

"Other firm fish fillets, such as cod, brill or turbot can be cooked in this way. Cooking time may vary slightly, according to the thickness of the fish"

"The secret of cooking fish is mastering the 'cuisson' or the point at which it is ready but not overcooked. Fish firms up during cooking and, when it has reached 'cuisson', it will feel firm but give slightly if you press the flesh gently with your index finger"

bacon-wrapped chicken legs
STUFFED WITH PORK AND PISTACHIOS

Serves 6

6 boned-out medium
   chicken drumsticks or
   thighs
sea salt and pepper
24 rashers rindless streaky
   bacon (approximately)
3 tbsp olive oil
1 tbsp sherry vinegar
2 tbsp Marsala
ladleful of brown chicken
   stock

Stuffing:

350g good-quality pork
   sausage meat
handful of skinned pistachio
   nuts, roughly chopped
1 egg yolk
4 thyme sprigs, leaves
   stripped and chopped

To make the stuffing, mix the sausage meat with the pistachio nuts, egg yolk and thyme. Season well with salt and pepper.

Open out the chicken legs or thighs, season with pepper and divide the stuffing between them. Roll up to enclose. Lay about 4 bacon rashers on a board, overlapping them slightly. Put one stuffed chicken portion on top and wrap the bacon around to cover completely. Repeat with the rest of the chicken.

Cut 6 very large pieces of foil. Wrap each chicken parcel tightly in foil, twisting the ends to seal. Roll back and forth to even the shape.

Poach the chicken parcels, two or three at a time, in a large pan of boiling water for about 20 minutes, depending on size. Allow to cool completely, then remove the foil.

Heat the olive oil in a large frying pan and sauté the chicken parcels until the bacon is brown and crisp on all sides and the parcels are cooked through. Transfer to a warm platter and rest in a warm place.

Deglaze the pan with the sherry vinegar, then add the Marsala and stock. Let bubble to reduce by half, then skim off excess fat and check the seasoning.

Cut the chicken into thick slices and arrange on warm plates. Spoon over the jus and serve with rice.

"Speciality free-range chickens are probably one of the most exciting things I have featured on my menus this year. Quality birds, such as Label Anglaise, are bred for the size of breast and quality of flavour. They taste nothing like battery-farmed chickens"

bacon-wrapped chicken legs

guinea fowl with broad beans
GEM LETTUCE AND BACON

Serves 6

6 boneless guinea fowl
　breasts, about 175g each
300ml chicken stock
150ml double cream
sea salt and pepper
300g podded broad beans
150g bacon lardons
3 tbsp olive oil
75g unsalted butter, diced
3 Little Gem lettuces,
　quartered lengthways

"Poaching the guinea fowl breasts in cling film seals in all the flavours. If you don't like the idea, then poach them directly in chicken stock"

Wrap each guinea fowl breast tightly in food-safe cling film, twisting the ends to seal. Immerse in a pan of boiling water and poach for 5 minutes, Remove from the water and let cool, then chill for 30 minutes.

Boil the stock in a pan to reduce by half, then add the cream and let bubble until reduced by half again to make a creamy sauce. Season to taste.

Blanch the broad beans in boiling water for 2–3 minutes, then drain and refresh in a bowl of iced water. Slip the beans out of their tough outer skins.

Sauté the lardons in a heavy-based frying pan until crisp. Drain on kitchen paper and keep warm.

Heat the olive oil in the frying pan. Unwrap the guinea fowl and pan-fry skin-side down for 5 minutes. Turn and cook for a further 3 minutes. Remove from the pan and rest in a warm place for 5 minutes.

Over a low heat, gradually whisk the butter into the sauce, then bring back to a simmer and check the seasoning. Add the lettuce and broad beans and cook for 2 minutes or until the lettuce starts to wilt.

Slice each guinea fowl breast lengthways into three. Spoon the wilted lettuce and broad beans on to warm plates, using a slotted spoon. Place the guinea fowl breasts on top and scatter over the bacon. Spoon the sauce over the guinea fowl and serve.

oven-roast duck breast
WITH CARAMELISED SWEDE

Serves 6

6 Gressingham duck
  breasts, about 175g each

1 or 2 knobs of butter

handful of thyme sprigs

good splash of red wine

2 large ladlefuls brown
  chicken stock

sea salt and pepper

Caramelised swede:

1 large or 2 small swede,
  peeled

40g butter

2cm knob of fresh root
  ginger, peeled and grated

1–2 tsp thin honey

Heat the oven to 200°C/Gas 6. With a sharp knife, score the duck breast skin in a criss-cross pattern, taking care to avoid cutting through to the meat.

Cut the swede into cubes, roughly 2.5cm, and simmer in salted water to cover for 10 minutes or until barely tender, then drain thoroughly.

Heat a heavy-based frying pan over a high heat. Add the duck breasts, skin-side down, and sear for a few minutes, pressing down on the flesh to ensure an even colour. Turn the duck breasts over, add a knob of butter with the thyme sprigs, and cook for 30 seconds only. Transfer to a roasting pan, adding the thyme, too. You may need to do this in batches.

Roast the duck breasts in the oven for 8–10 minutes, then transfer to a warm plate and rest in a warm place for 10 minutes. Put the roasting pan over a medium heat and add the wine, stirring to deglaze. Pour in the stock, bring to the boil and skim. Let bubble until reduced by half. Check the seasoning.

Caramelise the swede, meanwhile. Heat the butter in a pan, add the swede with the ginger and honey, and sauté for 3–4 minutes until lightly caramelised.

Pile the swede into the centre of warm plates. Thickly slice the duck breasts and arrange on top of the swede. Spoon over the jus and serve with fondant potatoes (page 190) if you like.

"The secret of perfectly cooked duck breasts is to cook them quickly and rest them well before carving. The skin should be crisp and golden brown and the meat pink and succulent"

oven-roast duck breast

pork fillet in prosciutto

WITH BAKED COUSCOUS

Serves 6

80g prosciutto slices

2 pork fillets (tenderloins), about 350g each, well trimmed

sea salt and pepper

2–3 tbsp olive oil, plus extra to oil

4 thyme sprigs, leaves stripped

250g couscous

40g Parmesan, freshly grated

handful of flat-leaf parsley, finely chopped

knob of soft unsalted butter

splash of Marsala

ladleful of brown chicken stock

Lay half the prosciutto slices on a board, overlapping them slightly, then lay one pork fillet across at one end. Wrap the pork in the prosciutto and season with pepper. Repeat with the other fillet.

Cut two 40 x 30cm sheets of foil, drizzle a little olive oil down the centre and sprinkle with the thyme leaves. Place the pork fillet on top, bring the edges of the foil up and fold together over the pork, then roll to enclose, twisting the ends to seal. Rest in the fridge for 15 minutes. Heat the oven to 200°C/Gas 6.

Put the couscous in a bowl, pour on 400ml boiling water, cover and leave to stand for 10 minutes. Add the Parmesan and parsley, fork through and season liberally. Place 6 large individual ring moulds on a baking tray, brush with butter and then oil. Spoon in the couscous and press down with the back of the spoon.

Place the pork parcels on another baking tray and bake for 15–20 minutes, depending on the thickness of the fillets. Take the pork out of the oven and then bake the couscous cakes for 10 minutes.

Heat 2–3 tbsp olive oil in a large frying pan. Remove the foil from the pork parcels, reserving any juices. Add the prosciutto-wrapped pork fillets to the pan and pan-fry for about 10 minutes, turning until the prosciutto is crisp and brown all over. Remove to a warm plate and rest in a warm place.

Add the Marsala to the frying pan with the reserved pork juices, stirring to deglaze. Add the stock and boil until reduced by half. Check the seasoning.

Cut the pork into thick slices. Unmould a couscous cake on to the centre of each warm plate, pressing it out with the back of a spoon. Surround with the pork and spoon over the jus. Serve with a green vegetable or salad.

"The beauty of this dish is that it can be prepared ahead – ready to bake when you're ready to eat. The couscous cakes simply rest in the oven while you finish the pork"

aubergine gâteau
WITH CHERRY TOMATOES, BASIL AND PARMESAN

Serves 6

2 medium aubergines,
  thinly sliced
olive oil to drizzle
large knob of unsalted
  butter
600g cherry tomatoes,
  halved
1 garlic clove, crushed
handful of basil leaves
sea salt and pepper
75g Parmesan, freshly
  grated

Heat the oven to 200°C/Gas 6. Thinly slice the aubergines and lay the slices out on two large oiled baking sheets. Drizzle with olive oil and bake for 5–8 minutes until softened and lightly browned.

Line a 20cm round cake tin with greaseproof paper. Melt the butter in a large sauté pan and cook the cherry tomatoes with the garlic until soft and pulpy. Tear in the basil leaves and season with salt and pepper.

Layer a third of the aubergine slices over the base of the prepared tin, top with half the tomato mixture, then scatter over some Parmesan. Add another layer of aubergine, then the remaining tomato mixture. Cover with a final layer of aubergine and then sprinkle generously with Parmesan.

Bake the gâteau for 10 minutes until the topping is golden and bubbling. Allow to stand for 5 minutes, then turn out on to a warm plate. Cut into wedges and serve with crusty bread.

"Contrary to popular belief, I'm more than happy to cook for vegetarians. Fortunately, this stunning dish is equally appealing to carnivores like me"

"I use salted butter to sauté vegetables and fish, as it foams more quickly. Par-boiling the potatoes in stock before sautéing enhances a fresh stock substitute, such as bouillon powder, as the stock isn't

fondant potatoes

Serves 6

1kg floury potatoes, such as Maris Piper

1 litre chicken stock

75–100g salted butter

4–5 garlic cloves (unpeeled)

1 or 2 thyme sprigs

1 rosemary sprig

sea salt and pepper

readily and fries at a higher heat so the food caramelises very
the flavour. This is one instance where it is quite acceptable to use
an integral part of the dish"

Peel the potatoes and cut into chunky slices, about 2–3cm thick. Place in a
pan with the stock and bring to the boil. Turn down the heat and simmer for
10–12 minutes until tender when pierced with a knife but still quite firm and not
breaking up. Drain well (saving the stock for a soup or sauce).

Heat the butter in a heavy-based frying pan until it starts to foam. Add the
potatoes, cut-side down, with the garlic and herbs. Cook for 4–5 minutes, then turn
and cook for a further 3–4 minutes or until the potatoes are golden in colour.
Discard the garlic and herbs, season with salt and pepper and serve.

Serves 6

10 ripe passion fruit

6 large free-range egg yolks

75g caster sugar

25ml vodka (optional)

350ml double cream

passion fruit parfait

Halve 8 passion fruit and scoop out the pulp and seeds into a blender or food processor. Whiz thoroughly, then tip into a small pan and boil until reduced by half, to 60–70ml. Rub through a sieve into a bowl and set aside to cool.

Whisk the egg yolks in a medium heatproof bowl until smooth and fluffy, then set the bowl over a pan of very hot water and continue to whisk until doubled in volume, pale and stiff. Take the pan off the heat.

Dissolve the sugar in 50ml water in a small heavy-based pan over a low heat, stirring. Then stop stirring and boil until the temperature registers 110°C on a sugar thermometer.

Return the bowl of whisked yolks set over the pan to a low heat. Slowly add the sugar syrup, whisking constantly until the mixture is thick, glossy and mousse-like. Take the bowl off the pan and whisk off the heat for 5 minutes or until cooled. Fold in the passion fruit purée, and the vodka if using, then chill for 1 hour.

Whip the cream until softly peaking, then carefully fold into the passion fruit mixture. Pour into 6 individual moulds, such as darioles, or ring moulds set on a tray. Freeze for 12 hours, or overnight.

To turn out, wipe a hot cloth around the moulds (or dip darioles into hot water for a second or two). Unmould the parfaits on to plates and spoon on a little passion fruit pulp to serve.

chocolate pots
WITH GRAND MARNIER

Serves 6

200g good-quality dark
    chocolate (about 60%
    cocoa solids)
6 free-range eggs, separated
50ml Grand Marnier

Melt the chocolate in a heatproof bowl set over a pan of gently simmering water – take care to avoid overheating otherwise it will seize. Remove the bowl from the pan and cool, almost to room temperature.

Whisk the egg whites in a clean, grease-free bowl until softly peaking.

Beat the egg yolks into the melted chocolate, then stir in the Grand Marnier. Carefully fold in the whisked egg whites. Pour into 6 custard pots and chill for 3 hours before serving.

lime pannacotta
INFUSED WITH MINT AND TEQUILA

Serves 6

600ml double cream

150ml milk

8 mint leaves

4–5 sheets leaf gelatine

60g caster sugar

finely grated zest of 3 limes

1½ tbsp tequila

lime segments to decorate

Pour the cream and milk into a small saucepan, add the mint leaves and bring to a simmer. Let bubble for 5 minutes to reduce by about a third.

Meanwhile, soak the gelatine sheets in a bowl of cold water to soften for about 5 minutes.

Strain the boiling cream mixture into a bowl and stir in the sugar, lime zest and tequila. Take the gelatine leaves, gently squeeze out excess water, then add to the hot cream mixture and stir until dissolved.

Pour the mixture into 6 dariole moulds and allow to cool, then refrigerate the pannacottas for 2–3 hours or until set.

To turn out, gently tease the side of each pannacotta away from the mould, then invert on to a plate and shake to release. Arrange a few lime segments on each plate and serve.

dinner for
two

We should all make time in our lives for romance. Tana and I try to keep to this philosophy – it's dinner after the children are tucked up in bed, either at home or in a restaurant. Food is sensual and sharing a meal is so romantic. Slaving over a hot stove trying to master a tricky dish, however, isn't at all romantic. There's a reason why oysters and Champagne have long been the food of lovers. Try my oysters rockefeller for a twist on the classic, and follow with rump of lamb with a rosemary-scented jus ... divine.

oysters rockefeller

Serves 2

12 oysters

100g unsalted butter

1 small celery stick, finely
   sliced

1 slice of fennel, chopped

2 spring onions, finely sliced

1 garlic clove, finely
   chopped

1 tbsp chopped parsley

handful of watercress leaves

few drops of Tabasco, or to
   taste

dash of Pernod

2 slices white bread, crusts
   removed

lemon wedges to serve

Shuck the oysters (see below). Place them in their half-shells on a baking tray and set aside. Heat the grill to high.

Melt the butter in a sauté pan until foaming. Add the celery, fennel, spring onions and garlic, and cook for 2 minutes, then add the parsley and watercress and cook for 30 seconds.

Tip into a blender or food processor, add the Tabasco, Pernod and bread and whiz for about 30 seconds until you have 'green breadcrumbs'.

Spoon the crumb mixture on top of the oysters to cover them completely. Grill for 30 seconds or until the topping begins to colour.

Arrange the oysters on plates, add the lemon wedges and serve immediately.

"To shuck oysters hold rounded-side down in a cloth. Insert an oyster knife into the hinge and twist from side to side to sever the muscle and lift the top shell. Tip juices into a bowl. Slide knife under oyster to release it. Rinse oysters in their juice, check for shell fragments and return to lower shells"

clam soup with samphire

Serves 2

12 fresh medium clams, cleaned (see page 172)
75ml dry white wine
50g pancetta, diced
25g unsalted butter
1 onion, finely chopped
350ml fish stock
2 potatoes, peeled and cut into 1cm dice
2 thyme sprigs, leaves only
sea salt and pepper
large handful of samphire
100ml double cream
2 tbsp chopped flat-leaf parsley

Put the clams into a large pan, add the wine and 75ml water and bring to the boil. Cover with a tight-fitting lid and cook for 2–3 minutes to steam the clams open. Drain, reserving the liquor. When cool enough to handle, shell the clams, chop roughly and set aside.

Cook the pancetta in a dry pan over a medium heat until the fat starts to run, then increase the heat slightly and cook until crisp; remove and set aside.

Add the butter to the pan and sweat the onion over a low heat until soft and translucent. Gradually stir in the stock, then add the potatoes, thyme leaves and pepper. Simmer for 10–15 minutes until the potatoes are tender.

Ladle about a third of the stock and potatoes into a blender or food processor and whiz to a purée. Stir back into the soup to thicken it slightly.

Add the clams and samphire. Cook for a few minutes, then stir in the cream and pancetta. Heat through, stirring, and adjust the seasoning. Serve in warm bowls, sprinkled with the chopped parsley.

"Clams are not used enough in this country. They have a great meaty texture, which is particularly good in soups, such as this chowder"

steamed asparagus
WITH ORANGE HOLLANDAISE

Serves 2

1 bunch medium asparagus,
  trimmed

Orange hollandaise:

juice of 2 oranges,
  preferably blood oranges

70g unsalted butter

1 free-range egg yolk

sea salt

pinch of cayenne pepper

squeeze of lemon juice

To prepare the asparagus, break off the tough ends and peel the lower part of the stalks thinly, using a potato peeler.

To make the hollandaise, boil the orange juice in a small pan until reduced by half, then remove from the heat and allow to cool. Melt the butter in another pan and cool until tepid.

Put the egg yolk into a small bowl and whisk in 1 tbsp water. Set the bowl over a pan of hot water and slowly whisk in the orange juice – the sauce will thicken as you whisk.

Take the bowl off the heat and whisk for a few more minutes, then slowly trickle in the butter as you continue to whisk. Don't add the butter too quickly or the sauce will curdle. When all the butter has been incorporated, the sauce should be thick. Season with salt and cayenne, and add a little lemon juice to taste.

Steam the asparagus in the meantime for about 3–4 minutes until tender. (If you don't have a steamer, cook the asparagus upright in a tall covered pan about one-third filled with boiling water, so the tips cook in the steam.)

Drain the asparagus and serve at once, with the orange hollandaise.

"An orange hollandaise makes a great dipping sauce for freshly steamed asparagus spears. Blood oranges lend a superb flavour and colour to this sauce, so look out for them during their short season. Otherwise use the sweetest, fullest-flavoured oranges you can find"

crab salad
WITH PASSION FRUIT DRESSING

Serves 2

200g fresh white crabmeat

125g salad leaves, such as
rocket, watercress and
radicchio

100g yellow or red cherry
tomatoes, halved

2 passion fruit, halved

2 tbsp classic vinaigrette

Check that the crabmeat is free from fragments of shell. Arrange the salad leaves and tomatoes on individual serving plates.

Pile the crabmeat into the centre – using a ring mould to shape a neat cylinder if you like.

Scoop out the passion fruit pulp and seeds, and whisk into the vinaigrette. Drizzle over the salad leaves and serve.

tiger prawn salad
WITH MANGO AND AVOCADO

Devein the prawns if necessary. Whiz half the mango flesh in a blender or small food processor to a purée; set aside. Dice the rest of the mango.

Halve and slice the avocado, removing the stone. Arrange the slices around the outside of a small platter and drizzle over the lemon juice.

Heat the olive oil in a frying pan, add the ginger and garlic and cook for 30 seconds. Add the prawns and stir-fry for 2–3 minutes until they turn pink – don't overcook. Drizzle with the lime juice and take off the heat. Discard the ginger and garlic.

Add the diced mango to the prawns and toss together. Season with salt and pepper to taste.

Pile the prawns and mango into the middle of the platter and scatter over the parsley. Drizzle the mango purée around the edge of the plate and serve.

Serves 2

12 raw tiger prawns, peeled (heads removed)
1 large ripe mango, peeled
1 large ripe avocado, peeled
juice of $\frac{1}{2}$ lemon
1 tbsp olive oil
1cm piece fresh root ginger, peeled
1 garlic clove, peeled
juice of 1 lime
sea salt and pepper
1 tbsp chopped flat-leaf parsley

"I always look
for the largest,
freshest tiger
prawns in the
fish market.
They need little
cooking and
taste divine"

turbot fillets
WITH FENNEL AND LEMON

Serves 2

2 turbot fillets, about 150g each

600ml fish stock

¼ vanilla pod

2 lemongrass stalks

1 tsp coriander seeds

1 fennel bulb, trimmed (fronds reserved)

sea salt and pepper

large knob of butter, plus extra to grease

1 thyme sprig

1 tbsp Pernod

juice of 1 lemon

Check the fish fillets for small bones, then set aside. Put the stock, vanilla, lemongrass and coriander seeds in a large pan. Bring to the boil and boil to reduce by one third. Cool, then strain.

Slice the fennel very finely and blanch in boiling salted water for 2–3 minutes. Drain and refresh in cold water, then drain well.

Heat the oven to 190°C/Gas 5. Lay the fish fillets in a buttered small ovenproof dish. Bring the stock to the boil, pour over the fish and bake for 5 minutes.

Meanwhile, sauté the fennel slices in the butter in a large sauté pan with the thyme until lightly caramelised. Add the Pernod, then the lemon juice. Toss well and season with salt and pepper to taste. Discard the thyme.

Arrange the fennel on warm plates and top with the turbot. Add the fish liquor to the sauté pan, boil to reduce, then drizzle over the fish. Garnish with fennel fronds.

wild sea trout and baby leeks
WITH CRUSHED POTATO AND TOMATO BUTTER

Check the fish fillets for tiny bones, score the skin side deeply and set aside. Cook the potatoes in salted water until tender. Heat the oven to 190°C/Gas 5.

To make the tomato butter sauce, heat the olive oil in a small pan, add the tomatoes and cook over a low heat for 10 minutes. Transfer to a blender or food processor, add the sherry vinegar and sugar and whiz to a purée. Pass through a sieve back into the pan. Add the cream and simmer for a few minutes. Whisk in the butter and basil; keep warm.

Put the tomato halves, cut-side up, on a baking tray, drizzle with a little olive oil and sprinkle with salt. Bake for about 5 minutes (or slowly overnight at 100°C/Gas $^1/_4$). Steam the leeks until tender.

Drain the potatoes, toss with a little olive oil over heat, then crush lightly with the back of a fork. Stir in the spring onions and vinaigrette. Season to taste.

To cook the fish, heat a non-stick frying pan and add the olive oil. Fry the fish, skin-side down, for $3^1/_2$ minutes or until the skin is crisp, then turn and cook for 30 seconds only. Season lightly and rest in the pan for a few minutes.

Pile the crushed potato and leeks in the centre of two warm serving plates and top with the fish fillets. Surround with the cherry tomatoes and serve the tomato butter sauce on the side.

Serves 2

2 wild sea trout or salmon
   fillets, with skin, about
   150g each
250g new potatoes, peeled
sea salt and pepper
125g vine-ripened cherry
   tomatoes, halved
2 tbsp olive oil, plus extra
   to drizzle
125g baby leeks, halved
few spring onions, chopped
2 tbsp classic vinaigrette
tomato butter sauce:
1 tbsp olive oil
125g vine-ripened cherry
   tomatoes
1 tsp sherry vinegar
1 tsp sugar
50ml double cream
25g butter, diced
1 tbsp chopped basil

wild sea trout and baby leeks

"This is a great way to serve fresh wild sea trout or salmon fillets. For best results, cook the fish almost entirely on the skin side, without moving. To make the dish extra special, toss the crushed potatoes with some fresh white crabmeat and chopped coriander"

rump of lamb
WITH ROSEMARY SCENTED JUS

Serves 2

2 lamb rumps, about 200g each

6 tbsp olive oil

1 thyme sprig

3 rosemary sprigs

2 garlic cloves, chopped

sea salt and pepper

1 shallot, thinly sliced

1 baby aubergine, cut into wedges

1 courgette, sliced

½ red pepper, deseeded and sliced

½ yellow pepper, deseeded and sliced

1 tbsp sherry vinegar

1 large glass of red wine

Score the skin of the lamb rumps lightly with a sharp knife. Put 2 tbsp olive oil in a bowl with the thyme, 2 rosemary sprigs and the garlic. Season the lamb with pepper, add to the bowl and turn to coat in the oil. Leave to marinate for 3–4 hours, then remove the lamb, saving the rosemary sprigs for the jus.

Heat the oven to 200°C/Gas 6. Heat 2 tbsp olive oil in a wide pan, add the vegetables and remaining rosemary, toss to mix and sauté for a few minutes to soften slightly, then transfer to an oiled roasting pan and roast in the oven for 15 minutes.

Meanwhile, heat a cast-iron frying pan and add 2 tbsp oil. When very hot, add the lamb, skin-side down, and sear until well browned on all sides. Add to the roasting pan and roast for about 15 minutes, then lift the meat on to a warm platter with the vegetables and rest in a warm place.

Add the sherry vinegar to the roasting pan, stirring to deglaze, then add the wine and bring to the boil. Add the reserved rosemary and simmer for 10 minutes. Skim off any fat from the jus, season and strain into a warm jug.

Cut each rump into 3 or 4 slices. Spoon the roasted vegetables on to warm plates and arrange the lamb on top. Drizzle the rosemary jus over and around the plate, and serve.

"Rump or chump of lamb is an ideal cut when you are cooking for two. If possible, buy West Country lamb, which yields good-sized rumps. These lambs are weaned naturally and then fed on grass so the flavour of the meat is superb. Lamb should be hung for 2–3 weeks to maximise the flavour. Look for meat that's dark red in colour with a matt appearance"

rump of lamb

chateaubriand for two

Serves 2

500g piece fillet of beef

1 red onion, cut into thin wedges

4 garlic cloves (unpeeled)

3 tbsp olive oil

1 tbsp sherry vinegar

1 glass of red wine

sea salt and pepper

Trim the beef fillet of any fat or sinew. Wrap in cling film, twisting the ends tightly to secure, then roll the meat to even up the shape. Refrigerate for 24 hours.

Heat the oven to 200°C/Gas 6. Put the onion and garlic in a roasting pan and drizzle with 1 tbsp olive oil. Put into the oven for 5 minutes while you sear the beef.

Heat a cast-iron frying pan, and add the remaining olive oil. When hot, add the beef fillet and sear quickly on all sides over a high heat. Add the seared fillet to the roasting pan and roast for 10–15 minutes, according to how rare you like your beef. Transfer the meat and vegetables to a warm plate and rest for 15 minutes.

Meanwhile, deglaze the roasting pan with the sherry vinegar, scraping up the sediment, then pour in the wine and boil to reduce by half. Strain, season with salt and pepper to taste and keep warm. Carve the beef into thick slices and arrange on warm plates with the roasted garlic and onions. Drizzle with the jus and serve with oven chips (page 60) or flavoured mash, and a green vegetable.

calf's liver
WITH GREEN PEPPERCORN SAUCE

Serves 2

4 tbsp olive oil

2 large banana shallots, finely chopped

1 tbsp demerara sugar

1 thyme sprig, leaves stripped

1 tbsp sherry vinegar

1 tbsp green peppercorns in brine, rinsed

200g calf's liver, trimmed and cut into 1cm thick slices

sea salt

1 tbsp chopped parsley

Heat 2 tbsp olive oil in a pan and sauté the shallots for 5 minutes until softened. Add the sugar and thyme leaves and cook for 5 minutes, then add the sherry vinegar and green peppercorns.

Heat the remaining oil in a large, non-stick frying pan. Add the calf's liver slices and sauté quickly until they are browned on the outside, but still pink and juicy within, about 1–1½ minutes each side. Season lightly with salt.

Arrange the liver on warm plates, top with the pepper sauce and sprinkle with chopped parsley. Serve immediately.

peach melba

Pour the wine into a small pan, add 150g of the sugar and the honey. Slowly bring to the boil, stirring to dissolve. Lower heat, add the peaches and simmer for 10 minutes. Leave to cool in the wine syrup.

Gently cook the raspberries in a small pan with the remaining sugar until soft, breaking them up as they cook. Add a little of the wine syrup to make a sauce, then pass through a sieve to remove the seeds.

Arrange the peach halves on two plates, top each with a scoop of ice cream, drizzle with the raspberry sauce and serve.

Serves 2

¾ bottle dry white wine

190g caster sugar

60g thin honey

2 firm ripe peaches, halved and pitted

80g raspberries, plus a few extra to serve

4 scoops of vanilla ice cream

hot chocolate fondant

Serves 2

50g unsalted butter, plus extra to grease

2 tsp cocoa powder, to dust

50g good-quality bitter chocolate (minimum 70% cocoa solids),
   in pieces

1 free-range egg

1 free-range egg yolk

60g caster sugar

50g plain flour

Heat the oven to 160°C/Gas 3. Butter two large ramekins, about 7.5cm in diameter, then dust liberally with cocoa.

Slowly melt the chocolate and butter in a small bowl set over a pan of hot water, then take off the heat and stir until smooth. Leave to cool for 10 minutes.

Using an electric whisk, whisk the whole egg, egg yolk and sugar together until pale and thick, then incorporate the chocolate mixture.

Sift the flour over the mixture and gently fold in, using a large metal spoon. Divide between the ramekins and bake for 12 minutes.

Turn the chocolate fondants out on to warmed plates and serve immediately.

salt baked pineapple

Serves 2

1 baby pineapple

about 10 cloves

2kg coarse sea salt

1–2 tbsp Chinese five-spice
 powder

1–2 egg whites, lightly
 beaten

herby mascarpone:

2–3 tbsp mascarpone

small handful of shredded
 basil

Heat the oven to 190°C/Gas 5. Stud the 'eyes' of the pineapple with cloves. Season the salt with the five-spice powder, then mix with the egg whites. Pack the salt mixture around the pineapple to cover the skin completely. Put the remaining salt into a baking tin and sit the pineapple on top.

Bake the pineapple on the lowest oven shelf for 20 minutes. Meanwhile, mix the mascarpone with the basil. Leave the baked pineapple until cool enough to handle, then crack open the salt crust and remove it.

Cut the pineapple in half and then into quarters. Carefully cut each wedge away from the skin. Serve at once, topped with a spoonful of herby mascarpone.

cooking for a
crowd

When our extended family is around, we are cooking for a crowd. I usually opt for food that can be prepared well in advance, and needs little final attention. A big casserole or pan is the key here, one that you can both cook in and take to the table. Getting everyone to the table at once can be a challenge in itself, so casual service is imperative. Catalan of cod is an impressive dish that couldn't be easier. As you lift the lid, the amazing aroma stimulates appetites. Follow with a pecan pie and everyone will be more than satisfied.

fennel soup
WITH SPICY MERGUEZ SAUSAGE

Serves 10

6 tbsp olive oil

6 fennel bulbs, trimmed and finely sliced

2 celery sticks, finely sliced

3 garlic cloves, finely chopped

2 litres light chicken stock

handful of flat-leaf parsley, stalks and leaves separated

$\frac{1}{2}$ tsp freshly ground coriander seeds

2 bay leaves

sea salt and pepper

410g can cannellini beans, drained

500g Merguez sausages, finely sliced

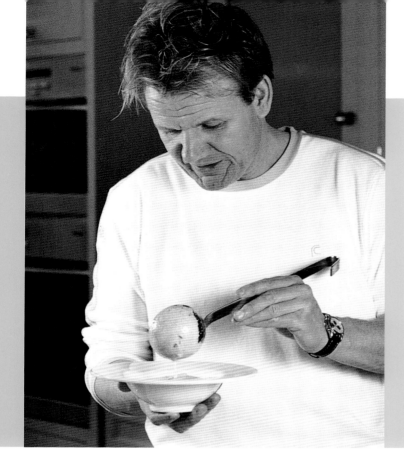

"Merguez is a French spicy beef sausage, similar to chorizo. As you pan-fry the sausage, it oozes a colourful, spicy oil – perfect to drizzle over the finished soup"

Heat 4 tbsp olive oil in a large pan. Add the fennel, celery and garlic, and sweat for 5 minutes over a medium-low heat until softened but not coloured. Add the stock, parsley stalks, ground coriander, bay leaves and seasoning. Bring to a simmer and simmer gently for 40 minutes. Discard the bay leaves and parsley stalks and let cool slightly. Chop the parsley leaves and set aside.

Whiz the soup in a blender until velvety smooth and return to the pan. Add the beans and heat through gently, stirring occasionally. Check the seasoning.

Meanwhile, heat the remaining oil in a large frying pan and fry the sausage slices for 3–4 minutes until crisp. Remove with a slotted spoon and drain on kitchen paper, reserving the oil in the pan.

Divide the sausage slices between warm soup bowls, placing them around the edge. Ladle the soup into the middle, scatter with the chopped parsley and drizzle with the reserved spicy oil. Serve immediately.

fennel soup

seafood bisque

Serves 10

3 tbsp olive oil

2 shallots, finely chopped

2 fennel bulbs, trimmed and
finely sliced

4 celery sticks, sliced

2 carrots, chopped

2 star anise

2 tsp cayenne pepper

pinch of saffron threads

6 beef tomatoes, deseeded
and chopped

100ml brandy

500ml white wine

3 litres fish stock

1kg fresh mussels

5 large potatoes, peeled and
diced

sea salt and pepper

500g monkfish fillets, cut
into chunks

500g red mullet fillets, cut
into 3cm pieces

Heat the olive oil in a large pan. Add the shallots, fennel, celery, carrots, star anise, cayenne and a few saffron threads. Cook, stirring, over a medium heat for a few minutes.

Add the tomatoes, lower the heat and cook for 5 minutes. Add the brandy and let bubble to reduce, then pour in the wine. Cook until the liquor has reduced down to a syrupy consistency. Stir in the stock, bring to a simmer and cook gently for 1 hour.

Meanwhile, clean the mussels. Scrub the shells thoroughly in cold water and pull away the beards; discard any open mussels.

Cook the potatoes in salted water with a few saffron threads for about 10 minutes until just tender; drain.

Whiz the soup until smooth, using a blender. Pass through a fine chinois into a clean pan and set aside.

Heat a third of the remaining stock in a large pan, add the mussels, cover tightly and cook for 3–5 minutes until they open; discard any that stay closed.

Poach the monkfish and red mullet in the rest of the stock in a shallow pan for about 2–3 minutes until just cooked.

Add the potatoes to the soup and reheat, then add the fish and mussels, and check the seasoning. Ladle into warm bowls and serve with crusty bread.

catalan of cod

Heat the olive oil in a very large, wide saucepan
(that has a tight-fitting lid). Add the chorizo and
garlic, and pan-fry for 3–4 minutes. Take off the heat.

Lay the cod on the sausage and season with pepper.
Cover with the tomatoes, season again and add the
thyme and bay leaves. Pour on the wine to cover, then
top with the mussels. Cover tightly, bring to the boil,
then lower the heat. Cook for 8–10 minutes until the
mussels open; discard any that don't. Check seasoning.

Scatter over the basil and ladle into warm bowls.
Serve immediately, with the olives and eggs on the side.

Serves 10

4 tbsp olive oil
2 small chorizo sausages,
    chopped
4 garlic cloves, chopped
10 cod fillets, 150g each
sea salt and pepper
16 beef tomatoes, sliced
2 thyme sprigs
4 bay leaves
1 bottle dry white wine
1kg fresh mussels, cleaned
handful of chopped basil
5 hard-boiled eggs, quartered
250g pitted back olives

tagine of lamb

> "I love the aromatic flavours in this Moroccan style dish. Use a tagine if you happen to have one, otherwise a heavy-based pan with lid, or flame-proof casserole will do fine"

Serves 10

6 tbsp olive oil

2kg boneless lean lamb, cut into 2–3cm cubes

3 large onions, finely chopped

4 garlic cloves, chopped

3 tsp Moroccan spice

1 tsp ground cumin

2cm piece fresh root ginger, peeled and finely sliced

4 plum tomatoes, skinned, deseeded and chopped

500ml medium dry white wine

500ml light chicken stock

200g ready-to-eat dried apricots

sea salt and pepper

Heat 3 tbsp olive oil in a large pan or tagine and sauté the lamb in batches over a high heat, removing each batch with a slotted spoon and adding more oil to the pan as necessary.

Lower the heat, add the onions and cook for a few minutes to soften, then add the garlic, Moroccan spice, cumin and ginger. Cook, stirring, for a further minute, then return all the meat to the pan.

Add the tomatoes, wine and stock and bring to the boil, then lower the heat, cover and simmer gently for 2 hours.

Add the dried apricots and check the seasoning. Cook for a further 20 minutes or until the lamb is meltingly tender. Serve with steamed couscous and a green vegetable or salad.

cold roast fillet of beef
WITH WATERCRESS AND BEETROOT FONDANT

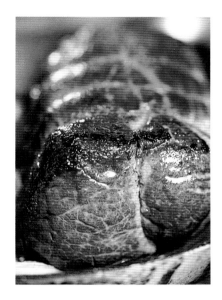

Heat the oven to 220°C/Gas 7. Trim the beef of any fat or sinew and season with pepper. Place a heavy-based frying pan over a high heat. Add the olive oil with the garlic cloves and rosemary, then add the beef fillet and sear on all sides. Transfer the meat and flavourings to a large roasting pan and roast for 15 minutes. Allow to cool.

Trim the baby beetroot tops, leaving on a little of the leafy stalks. Place on a large piece of foil in another large roasting pan and scatter with sea salt. Scrunch up the foil around the beetroot, leaving the top of the package open. Roast in the oven for 20–30 minutes.

Allow the cooked beetroot to cool, then peel. (You can prepare ahead to this stage – refrigerate the beef and beetroot, but bring the meat back to room temperature before serving.)

Heat the butter in a medium pan, add the beetroot and cook gently, stirring frequently, until well glazed.

Thinly slice the beef, arrange on a large oval platter and surround with the watercress sprigs. Spoon the warm glazed beetroot over the watercress and serve immediately.

Serves 10

1 fillet of beef, about 2kg
sea salt and pepper
4 tbsp olive oil
handful of garlic cloves
  (unpeeled)
few rosemary sprigs
large bunch of baby beetroot,
  washed
50g butter
3 bunches of watercress, trimmed

"I promise you this cold roast fillet will taste superb – as long as you've bought a good piece of beef. Superior butchers, small producers and farmers' markets are good sources of quality meat"

potage of ham hocks
WITH WHITE BEANS

Serves 10

4 ham hocks

1 head of celery, finely chopped

2 leeks, finely sliced

2 carrots, finely sliced

1 celeriac, cut into julienne

1 garlic bulb, halved crossways

2 handfuls of parsley, stalks and leaves separated

4 bay leaves

8 thyme sprigs

$\frac{1}{2}$ tsp freshly ground coriander seeds

sea salt and pepper

2 litres chicken stock

4 x 420g cans butter beans, drained

handful of chervil sprigs, chopped

A day in advance, place the ham hocks in two large saucepans and cover with cold water. Leave to soak overnight in a cool place.

The next day, discard the water and return the ham hocks to the pans. Add half the vegetables, garlic, parsley stalks, bay leaves, thyme and coriander seeds to each pan and season with pepper.

Pour half the stock into each pan and top up with water as necessary to cover the ham hocks. Bring to the boil, lower the heat and skim, then simmer for 2 hours. Allow to cool in the pans.

Lift out the ham hocks on to a board and carefully remove the skin. Discard the herbs from the broth. Strip the meat from the bone, cut into bite-sized pieces and return to the pans. Chop the parsley leaves.

Add the butter beans and bring to the boil, then lower the heat. Season to taste and simmer for about 10 minutes. Ladle into warm bowls and scatter with the chopped parsley and chervil to serve.

persian style aubergines

Serves 10

5 aubergines

200g basmati rice, rinsed

sea salt and pepper

2 onions, finely diced

400g cherry tomatoes, halved

120g pine nuts, lightly toasted

1 tsp ground allspice

2 tbsp chopped flat-leaf parsley

8 tbsp olive oil

Halve the aubergines lengthways, then score the flesh on the diagonal with a sharp knife, taking care to avoid piercing the base or edges. Carefully scoop out the aubergine flesh with a spoon, leaving 1cm shells. (Set aside half of the flesh; keep the rest for another recipe.)

Cook the rice in boiling salted water for about 15 minutes until just tender, then drain and rinse under cold water. Drain well and tip into a large bowl.

Dice the reserved aubergine flesh and add to the rice with the onions, cherry tomatoes, pine nuts, allspice and parsley. Toss together and season with salt and pepper to taste. Drizzle in half of the olive oil and mix well. Cover and leave the stuffing to stand at room temperature for 30 minutes to allow the flavours to blend. Heat the oven to 190°C/Gas 5.

Divide the stuffing between the aubergine shells, piling it quite high in the middle. Drizzle with the remaining olive oil and bake for 12–14 minutes or until the aubergine skins are glossy and the filling is beginning to brown. Serve hot.

boulangère potatoes

Serves 10

knob of butter to grease

8 tbsp olive oil

4 large shallots, finely
   chopped

8 large potatoes, such as
   King Edward or Desirée,
   peeled

sea salt and pepper

800ml chicken stock

10 smoked bacon rashers,
   (ideally Alsace), derinded

Heat the oven to 190°C/Gas 5. Cut ten 20cm squares of baking parchment and lightly butter the middle of each square.

Heat half the olive oil in a medium frying pan, add the shallots and cook over a low heat for about 12 minutes until softened.

Finely slice the potatoes. Arrange half the potato slices overlapping to roughly cover a 10cm circle in the middle of each parchment square. Scatter the shallots evenly over the potato rounds and season with salt and pepper. Cover with the rest of the potato, overlapping the slices again.

Transfer the parcels to a shallow baking tray, bringing the paper up and around the potato but leaving the top open.

Bring the stock to the boil and carefully pour around the potato. Brush the top of the potato cakes with the remaining olive oil. Bake for 25–35 minutes until the potatoes are tender and golden brown on top.

Meanwhile, lay the bacon rashers side by side on a baking sheet and place another baking sheet on top to keep them flat. Cook in the oven (on a shelf above the potato cakes) for the last 10 minutes, until crisp. Drain on kitchen paper.

Top each potato cake with a slice of crispy bacon and serve, in the paper.

pecan pie
WITH A CINNAMON CRUST

Serves 10

300g cinnamon shortcrust
   pastry (see right)

Filling:

2 sweet potatoes, scrubbed

50g light brown sugar

50g caster sugar

½ free-range egg, beaten

25ml double cream

25g soft unsalted butter

1 tsp vanilla extract

¼ tsp ground cinnamon

pinch of ground mixed spice

pinch of freshly grated
   nutmeg

Topping:

150g brown sugar

75ml golden syrup

1½ free-range eggs,
   beaten

30g unsalted butter

2 tsp vanilla extract

pinch of ground cinnamon

250g pecan nut halves

Heat the oven to 190°C/Gas 5. Bake the sweet potatoes for 30–40 minutes or until tender when pierced with a knife.

Roll out the pastry as thinly as possible and use to line a 5cm deep, 20cm flan tin. Press well into the edges and leave the excess pastry overhanging the edge. Line with greaseproof paper and fill with dried beans or rice. Rest in the fridge for 20 minutes, then bake for 10 minutes. Allow to cool. Turn the oven down to 160°C/Gas 3.

Halve the sweet potatoes and scoop out the flesh into a food processor. Add both sugars, the egg, cream, butter, vanilla and ground spices. Process until just smooth.

Trim the pastry edge level with the top of the tin, using a sharp knife. Pour in the sweet potato filling.

For the topping, whisk the sugar, golden syrup, eggs, butter, vanilla and cinnamon together in a bowl, using an electric whisk until smooth. Spoon the mixture evenly over the filling.

Arrange the pecans on top, pressing them down slightly. Bake for 1¾ hours or until a knife inserted in the middle comes out clean. Leave to cool in the tin.

Serve cut into small wedges at room temperature, with pouring cream.

cinnamon pastry Put 300g plain flour, a pinch of salt, $\frac{1}{2}$ tsp ground cinnamon, 15g caster sugar and 150g chilled diced butter into a food processor and process briefly until the mixture resembles breadcrumbs. Add 1 small free-range egg yolk and 1–2 tsp cold water and whiz for 30 seconds. Continue to add a little water and pulse until you have a smooth dough that holds together. Transfer to a lightly floured surface and knead gently until smooth, then wrap in cling film and rest in the fridge for 30 minutes before rolling out.

whole baked apples
WITH CRANBERRIES AND SULTANAS

Serves 10

10 large Bramley apples

125g dried cranberries

125g sultanas

finely grated zest of
  2 oranges

100ml Cointreau

125g demerara sugar

125g unsalted butter

300ml double cream

Heat the oven to 200°C/Gas 6. Using an apple corer or sharp knife, carefully remove the apple cores (you'll be removing a cylinder about 2.5cm in diameter). With a sharp knife, make a light incision around the circumference of each apple (to ensure that the apple skins don't burst in the oven).

In a small bowl, mix together the cranberries, sultanas, orange zest, Cointreau and sugar.

Place the apples in an ovenproof dish and fill the cavities with the cranberry mixture. Top each with a knob of butter. Bake the apples for 35–40 minutes or until golden brown and soft in the centre.

Pour a little cream into the centre of each apple and serve immediately.

"Bramleys are my first choice here, but you could use any other good tart, cooking apple. Experiment with different fillings, adding nuts if you like. Try dried mango and pecans, or dried pineapple and macadamia nuts"

my storecupboard
and equipment

The key to a really successful professional home kitchen is good quality equipment and a well-stocked storecupboard. You don't need a lot of items, but having the necessary basic tools and small appliances is really important. Similarly, a good storecupboard with all your essential dry ingredients to hand makes cooking quicker and easier. I regard my basics – stocks, vinaigrette and stock syrup – as essential standbys too. With the best ingredients and the right equipment, it is so easy to produce quality food.

my storecupboard

Freshly ground sea salt and pepper feature throughout my recipes and I cannot stress the importance of quality enough here. A dish can be ruined if you season it with bitter-tasting salt or harsh ground pepper. For its purity, we use French sea salt made from the foam of the wave rather than the seabed. Invest in robust salt and pepper mills, and freshly grind salt and pepper as required. Buy good-quality peppercorns – white, black and green – and experiment until you find the blend that you prefer.

Spices need to be kept fresh in sealed jars away from direct light. Buy spices as and when required – their flavour will deteriorate over time. Many Asian food stores and other speciality stores sell spices by weight, so you can purchase small amounts. In the restaurants, we use the following spices on a daily basis: coriander seeds (kept in a clean mill to be freshly ground), juniper berries, star anise, curry powder, smoked paprika (the Spanish paprika is my favourite), cardamom pods, caraway seeds, ground cumin, whole cloves, nutmeg (freshly grated), mace flakes, turmeric and, last but not least, saffron. When buying saffron, look for long threads with a strong colour and don't be put off by the price – you need very little to impart colour and flavour. Don't be tempted by the less expensive powder, as it is quite inferior.

Vinegars are used to deglaze pans, as well as to flavour vinaigrettes, dressings and sauces. We use sherry vinegar, balsamic vinegar (a good aged Italian variety), white wine vinegar and Cabernet Sauvignon vinegar – a red wine variety with a good, robust flavour.

Oils need to be chosen carefully, to ensure their depth and flavour is appropriate for any given recipe. The flavour of an oil must not overpower a dish, which is why I use groundnut oil to soften the flavour of extra-virgin olive oil in my vinaigrette. I like to keep a selection of oils for different purposes, including sunflower and groundnut oil. I use extra virgin olive oil for dressings and a light olive oil for frying. Hazelnut and sesame oils lend special flavours to dressings, while a drizzle of truffle oil will elevate a sauce or soup.

Sauces and condiments are used for flavouring. The most important are soy sauce (look for a good natural fermentation), Tabasco (a traditional chilli sauce), tamarind extract (from the Indian fruit of the same name), oyster sauce (for a Chinese twist), Worcestershire sauce (the stalwart of English cookery), mustards (wholegrain, Dijon and English), and tomato ketchup...no kitchen should be without it!

Rice is an indispensable ingredient and I always have several types in stock – for different purposes. For risotto, my preference is Carnaroli, but if you can't find it then use Arborio. I also like aromatic Thai Jasmine rice and Indian basmati rice. For the occasional rice pudding, there's short-grained pudding rice. It is essential to use the correct type of rice for a recipe.

Chocolate for desserts should always be of a very good quality – Valhrona is my favourite brand. When you are buying dark chocolate, look for a minimum of 70% cocoa solids. We also use milk chocolate and white chocolate, but to a lesser extent.

Spirits and liqueurs are used to enhance the flavours of my sauces and desserts and I would advocate keeping a good brandy or Cognac, Madeira, Noilly Prat and kirsch in the kitchen. Of course, I also use red and white wine for cooking, but I'm assuming you will have some freshly opened to hand. Don't use wine that's been left in a cupboard for days – it is liable to ruin the flavour of a dish.

Other storecupboard essentials are flours (plain, strong bread, buckwheat and pasta flours), arrowroot, sugars (caster, icing, Demerara and soft brown), honey, glucose syrup, maple syrup, dried fruits and leaf gelatine. We also have jars of capers, caper berries, good anchovies and olives to hand. Some ingredients considered to be storecupboard ingredients, such as nuts, are better bought as and when you need them, because they stale relatively quickly.

basics

These few standbys will make all the difference to the flavour of a dish – fresh stocks in particular. Make up these stocks in batches and keep them in the fridge (for up to 5 days) or freezer (up to 3 months) until required.

Chicken stock

Put 1 chopped carrot, 1 chopped onion, 2 sliced celery sticks and 1 sliced leek in a large pan with 2 tbsp oil and cook over medium heat until golden. Add a sprig of thyme, 1 bay leaf, 3 peeled garlic cloves, 2 tbsp tomato purée and 2 tbsp white flour, and cook, stirring, for a few minutes. Add 1kg raw chicken bones, cover with plenty of cold water and season lightly. Bring to the boil and skim. Simmer for 1 hour and then pass through a chinois. Adjust the seasoning. Makes about 1.5 litres.

Brown chicken stock

This is used for a greater depth of flavour. Follow the above recipe, roasting the chicken bones at 200°C/Gas 6 for 20 minutes before adding them.

Fish stock

This is quick to make, using fish trimmings, or you can use crab or lobster shells. Heat 2 tbsp oil in a large pan. Add $\frac{1}{2}$ chopped onion, $\frac{1}{2}$ sliced celery stick and 1 chopped fennel slice, and cook until soft but not coloured. Add 1kg fish trimmings (white fish bones and heads), a glass of white wine and water to cover. Bring to the boil, season lightly and simmer for 20 minutes. Pass through a chinois and adjust the seasoning. Makes about 1 litre.

Classic vinaigrette

Put 100ml extra virgin olive oil, 100ml groundnut oil, 3 tbsp white wine vinegar, a squeeze of lemon (to taste), 1 tbsp water, sea salt and pepper in a bowl and whiz using a hand-held stick blender. Refrigerate until required. Shake well before use.

Stock syrup

Put 550g granulated sugar, 1 litre cold water and the grated zest of 1 lemon in a pan. Dissolve the sugar over a low heat, then boil for 5 minutes. Cool, then pour the stock syrup into a jar, seal and refrigerate (for up to 1 month) until needed.

equipment

Good quality tools in the kitchen are important to the success of your cooking. When I'm buying equipment, I am primarily choosing on the basis of practicality and purpose. Every tool or appliance in our kitchen has a role – I'm not in favour of faddy gadgets. I also look for quality, durability and overall value for money – I don't necessarily buy the most expensive. Practicality of storage and style are other essential considerations. A beautiful granite pestle and mortar, for example, can be both a feature in the kitchen and a pleasure to use.

Knives are the first item of equipment I'm generally asked about. The most important aspect is that the blade is forged all the way through the handle, and that the knife has a good balance. One of the first tricks taught at catering college is to balance a knife on the forefinger of your working hand. It should balance at the part where the blade meets the handle – this indicates that the knife will have a good chopping motion.

There are three main types of steel: French, German and Japanese, and all have pros and cons. French steels are softer, which makes them easy to sharpen but also more vulnerable to damage and wear as they age. German steels are hard and require more skill to sharpen, but once you have a good edge to the blade it will last well. Japanese steels are similarly hard, much lighter in weight (which doesn't suit everyone) and very stylish.

The choice is a personal one, but the most important thing is that a knife should feel comfortable to handle. Buy good quality knives and they should last for ages. Over the years you will collect other knives for different uses but initially I would advocate buying the following:
• a paring knife, with a 5-7cm blade
• a chopping or cook's knife, with a 20cm blade
• a cook's knife, with a flexible 15cm blade
• a serrated knife, with a 25cm blade

Other useful specialist knives include an oyster knife, which has a short blade with a protective shield, and a small turning knife that has a curved blade used to shape turned vegetables.

Knives should be kept sharp. Blunt knives are dangerous as they have a tendency to skid off the food that you are cutting and into waiting fingers. Use a hand-held steel to keep the edge of the knife sharp and periodically sharpen them properly on a whetstone. Alternatively, find a good knife sharpening service.

Pans are the next most important purchase. In the restaurants, we use a wide range of pans, each for a specific purpose. Heavy-duty, non-stick pans are serious workhorses in the kitchen and we use these for all manner of dishes, from risottos to caramelised fruits.

A good starting set is a small 2-litre pan, a medium 3 to 4-litre pan and a large 6 to 8-litre pan, all with tight-fitting lids, plus an oval casserole that can be used on top of the stove as well as in the oven. You will also need a cast-iron frying pan or other good-quality frying pan – ideally one that can be used both on the hob and in the oven, up to 200°C/Gas 6.

Good pans should last a lifetime of cooking and come with a long warranty. The construction of the pan is the key here. Choose a heavy pan that has a good conductive base, such as copper or aluminium, with a stainless steel inner lining. Look for handles that are long and heatproof, well angled, and secured with stainless steel rivets.

Other pans I use regularly include a sautier – a saucepan with sloping sides – perfect for reducing stocks and sauces, and a pan that resembles a cappuccino cup, which is ideal for sauces that have butter or other ingredients whisked in. I'm particularly fond of my set of copper pans, which perform well and look attractive.

While vegetables and fruits can be sliced thinly with a knife, there are few chefs with the dexterity to slice with the precision and speed of the **mandolin**. We use this tool on a daily basis. You can buy stainless steel, wood or plastic mandolins and they vary in quality, the most important element being the sharpness of the blade. I am very fond of the Japanese mandolin, which has a plastic casing and isn't at all expensive.

The **chinois** is in constant use in my kitchen for straining stocks, sauces, etc. It is a strong conical sieve, perforated with small holes or made of mesh, available in various sizes. Look for a good-quality stainless steel chinois, with a long handle and a small balancing hook on the opposite side so that it can be balanced over a deep bowl or pan.

The **mouli** is another valuable straining tool, used for smooth pomme purée, soups and sauces. Made from stainless steel, the mouli comes with 2 or 3 perforated discs with different-sized holes for different uses. The mouli works by turning a handle attached to a semi-circular blade that forces the food through the perforated discs.

Another key tool is the **kitchen blowtorch** used for caramelising sugar, as for a crème brûlée, and also unmoulding frozen desserts. Apply the blowtorch to the outside of a ring mould and a dessert will be unmoulded effortlessly.

Essential small tools I wouldn't be without are: a **swivel vegetable peeler**, a **zester** (for finely paring strips of zest from citrus fruit), **stainless steel cutters** (for pastry and biscuits), at least two good **pastry brushes** (one for oiling, one for egg glazing) and strong **tweezers** (for removing the odd bone from fish, or a stray quill on a game bird).

For precision and accuracy, I would advocate a set of **digital scales**, which are easy to use and allow you to weigh ingredients directly in a bowl or pan. And I suggest you have at least two calibrated measuring jugs (in different sizes). You'll also need a **sugar thermometer** (for sugar syrups and caramel) and an **oven thermometer** to keep a check on your oven.

A good **food processor** is essential and I suggest you buy a powerful model with a magnetic drive belt situated directly beneath the bowl. I mainly use the processor for pastry and pasta dough.

A powerful **free-standing blender** is the key to velvety soups, fruit purées, frothy smoothies, etc. A hand-held **stick blender** is a convenient tool for soups and sauces, as it can be used directly in the pan or bowl. A strong, durable model is imperative, ideally one with at least two operating speeds.

A **hand-held electric mixer** is essential for whisking eggs for meringue, sponge mixtures, etc, though you may also want to invest in a free-standing mixer if you do a lot of baking. Other small appliances you may wish to buy are a **pasta machine**, an **electric juicer** and an **ice-cream maker**.

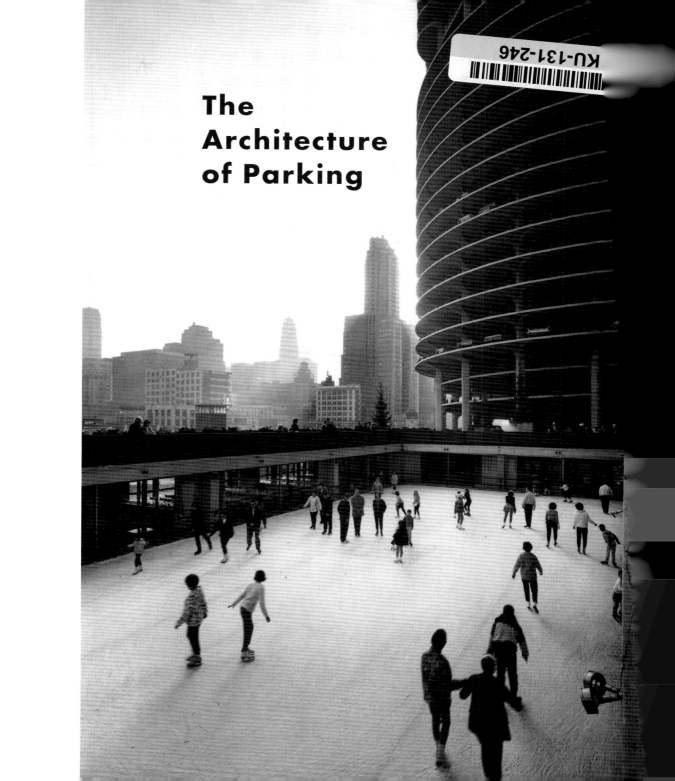

The
Architecture
of Parking

KU-131-246

Simon Henley

The Architecture of Parking

with photographs by Sue Barr

Thames & Hudson

To Eve and Tom

Any copy of this book issued by the publisher as a paperback is sold subject to the condition that it shall not by way of trade or otherwise be lent, resold, hired out or otherwise circulated without the publisher's prior consent in any form of binding or cover other than that in which it is published and without a similar condition including these words being imposed on a subsequent purchaser.

First published in the United Kingdom in 2007 by Thames & Hudson Ltd, 181A High Holborn, London WC1V 7QX

www.thamesandhudson.com

© 2007 Simon Henley

All Rights Reserved. No part of this publication may be reproduced or transmitted in any form or by any means, electronic or mechanical, including photocopy, recording or any other information storage and retrieval system, without prior permission in writing from the publisher.

British Library Cataloguing-in-Publication Data A catalogue record for this book is available from the British Library

ISBN 978-0-500-34237-4

Designed by Eggers + Diaper, Berlin Printed and bound in China by Everbest Printing Co Ltd

p.1: Marina City, Chicago
pp.2–3: Burda Parkhaus, Offenburg
pp.4–5: Zidpark, Upper Thames Street, London
p.6: Rut Blees Luxemburg, *Parkhaus 1*, London

READING BOROUGH LIBRARIES

Askews	
725.38	£24.95

Contents

The parking structure has captured the imagination of novelists, photographers and film-makers,[1] and yet it remains peripheral to our culture, best understood as a forbidding fictional setting or as an often imposing, silent building that we encounter on the way to work or shop. As a child I thought of these places as dynamic but secret, where the rules did not apply, and as an

introduction

adult I have grown to enjoy their mysterious, inhumane beauty, born out of an extreme obligation to the car. This book seeks to explain the unique aesthetic of these radical structures, and their uncanny ability to distil and project ideas about building. Above all, the culture of the car park seems to have made a lasting impression on contemporary architects.

Auguste Perret, Garage de la Société Ponthieu-Automobiles, Paris 1905 (interior)

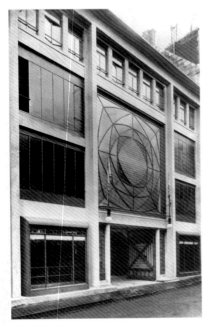

Auguste Perret, Garage de la Société Ponthieu-Automobiles, Paris 1905 (exterior)

Despite our dependency on the car (a trend that shows no sign of reversing), its physical by-products, in particular roads and multi-storey parking garages, have become increasingly unpopular. Somehow the very mobility of the car ensures that it largely eludes criticism. Criticisms of parking garages, unlike those of the car, are not abstract concepts, such as the impact of the combustion engine on global warming and the health risks of pollution, but concern the very real imposition that these structures place on our physical environment. For much of the last quarter of the twentieth century the environmental lobby sought to halt the influence of the car, and although the out-of-town shopping centre proliferated and acres of tarmac were laid for surface parking, the parking structure itself fell into disrepute. Then, in the mid-1990s, it re-emerged as a practical solution to the congested city, particularly in continental Europe. A new, more technically perfect and mischievous architecture of planes, ramps, spirals, folds and continuous landscapes surfaced. The sincerity of the 1950s and 1960s had been replaced by playfulness, or a search for the sublime.

Today there are two clear trends: the first emphasizing the importance of technique, and the second delirious in its search to create new typologies and to generate new landscape forms. But when and where did this definition of the car park as a distinct building type begin? Can we pinpoint the moment when the parking structure ceased to mimic other buildings, such as the warehouse, office block, or department store, and became identified in its own right? J.B. Jackson's description of the evolution of the domestic garage provides a good starting point. He identifies the car's role at the beginning of the twentieth century as that of 'a pleasure vehicle and a toy, costly, exciting, and of extraordinary elegance'.[2] It was driven and maintained by an expert, the chauffeur. In towns and cities the car was stored in livery stables, and in the suburbs and in the country, the stable or coach house. Initially, the expeditionary nature of motoring was a pastime, and an end in itself. This and the low numbers of automobiles limited the impact of the static (parked) vehicle on the city.

But when the vehicle became a tool rather than a toy, the need to park en masse arose. Only a few notable parking structures existed before the 1920s, the earliest examples in both Europe and the US predating World War I. These included Auguste Perret's garage in the rue de Ponthieu (1905) in Paris, Marshall & Fox's Chicago Automobile Club (1907),[3] and Marvin & Davis's garage for Palmer & Singer in New York, completed in 1908, a date that coincides with the launch of Henry Ford's Model T. At rue de Ponthieu, Perret employed his unique knowledge of concrete construction, although the internal order was concealed from the outside by a symmetrical façade with a central 'rose' window. This generation of buildings had appropriated the warehouse idiom, and indeed Jackson noted that the word 'garage' is derived from the French word for 'storage space', i.e., 'warehouse'.[4]

In 1925, the Russian architect Konstantin S. Melnikov forecast the three-dimensional internal landscape form to which we have grown so accustomed. The warehouse model was shattered by the abstract beauty that Melnikov brought to his designs for two unbuilt car parks, both for 1,000 vehicles, in Paris. The first, a bridge over the Seine, expressed the ramped decks and oblique geometry with a dynamic structure; the second, to be built on land, described a building in which the pure geometry of a cube was overlaid with the rotational dynamic of four ramps that wound through the structure. In each case, the car park would afford the driver both fantastic views over the city and a meaningful relationship with the immediately surrounding public space. It is hard to imagine the idealism with which these enigmatic proposals were conceived. Although technically flawed, they illustrate clearly the characteristics that would emerge in built form in the 1940s: the deep plan, compressed section, inclined planes and skeletal structure.

Built projects, however, remained stylized, or, at least in their external appearance, derivative of other building types. Buildings such as Robert Mallet-Stevens' for Alfa Romeo (1928) in the rue Marbeuf, Paris, which combined car park, repair shop, showroom and offices, had a symmetrical rendered façade with ramped access. By the late 1920s there were many such structures in the US, although there were less to be found in England and on the Continent. As was noted in *The Architect & Building News* of 1928, many garages in Paris were 'adaptations of existing buildings' (the same was true in London), but there were 'several schemes for circular ramp garages, a type which has also been favoured by German architects'.[5] In Venice, the gargantuan cream form of Eugenio Miozzi's 2,500-space Autorimessa (1931–34) established the model of the multi-storey car park as a terminus in the city, quite literally the end of the road for visitors arriving at the Piazza de Roma by car. Although Miozzi's scheme gave an idea of what was to come in its sheer scale and use of helical ramps, its symmetrical nature, together with the Art Déco façade, concealed an unusual interior (a deep open plan, with a low ceiling punctuated by columns), much as Perret's garage in the rue de Ponthieu had in 1905. Manned by attendants and often including chauffeur facilities, car parks of the pre-war period were designed with glazed façades, and in some cases heating, for internal environmental control; such conventional façades protected the oil-paint finishes on the cars. At the time, the harmful results of exposure to carbon monoxide were unknown.

The Great Depression and World War II halted the development of the parking structure. Low land values in the US and the availability of bombsites in England and on the Continent resulted in open land being used for surface parking by such companies as National Car Parks, founded in 1931. Then, as the car became more affordable after the war, particularly in the 1950s, the wider population took up motoring and the era of the car park began. From the late 1940s to the early 1970s, the parking structure

Konstantin S. Melnikov, drawing, car park over the Seine, Paris 1925

Eugenio Miozzi, Autorimessa, Venice 1931–34 (see p.158)

Louis Kahn, drawing, unbuilt city-centre proposal, Philadelphia 1947–62

E.M. Khoury, drawing, 'urban-future' amalgam

proliferated throughout the United States and Europe. Most famous of the American models was Louis Kahn's unbuilt proposal for downtown Philadelphia. Drawing parallels with a fortress, Kahn envisioned a city with a pedestrian centre protected from the car by walls and a collar of cylindrical parking towers. His studies covered a period of fifteen years, from 1947 to 1962, and in his models streets were variously described as 'rivers' and 'canals', and parking structures as 'docks', 'ports' and 'harbours'. Car parks were typically drawn as cylinders or spirals, and were shown forming the 'dark' core of mixed-use buildings, wrapped in an outer layer of shops, flats, or offices. Kahn's car parks divorced this abstract building type from the public realm. Unfortunately, the scheme remained unbuilt.

In Europe, the revolution in car ownership coincided with the devastation that wartime bombing had brought to our cities and opened the door to a new urban order, in which a pedestrianized centre was isolated from the surrounding city by a necklace of multi-storey car parks, linked by a ring road. At the heart of post-war planning theory was a debate over the accommodation of the pedestrian and the car without prejudice, which led to proposals for multi-storey circulation systems that would in turn be linked to multi-storey parking facilities, office buildings and retail structures. In England, the Buchanan Report (1963) forecast a new urban environment in which people would go to work and shop by car, and so the car park would become part of the destination. In 1950s America the situation was somewhat different; as a result of the car, the suburban population grew twenty-nine times faster than that in urban centres.[6] So significant was the impact of the car on the American way of life that the notion of a 'parking centre' emerged to describe the new out-of-town shopping malls that were being built to serve this new population.[7] In the end, the term 'shopping centre' prevailed. The potential for parking to change our environment radically is suggested in E.M. Khoury's undated drawing of an 'urban-future' amalgam of freeways and integrated car parks.

In 1940, Richard Neutra designed an 'Open-Air Multi-Storey Parking Garage'. His model suggests that, although the short elevations would be clad, the long ones would be open, exposing the ramped decks. Unfortunately, Neutra's project was not built, and car parks continued to be designed as warehouses.[8] So it was a radical departure when in 1948, in Miami, architect Robert Law Weed stripped the parking structure of its pretensions and broke the mould by exposing it quite literally for what it was.[9] Gone were the windows, the masonry, and any eclectic details associating such a building with a particular genre or type; in essence, the façade had been removed. Eliminating the façade lowered costs and allowed much-needed ventilation. It was constructed in concrete, with three floors cantilevered beyond the column grid and minimal perimeter barriers – an extremely efficient piece of engineering that could

Robert Law Weed, car park, Miami 1948

reasonably be described as beautiful, and indeed was described as 'a classic in the short history of garage design...unsurpassed by later attempts'.[10] Nearly sixty years later it remains paradigmatic for the lightness that the cantilevers bring to the form, something that Neutra had in no way predicted with his more rigid steel frame. What followed was a succession of skeletal, or 'section', structures; the pattern had emerged.

In the 1950s, attention turned to the car park's circulation systems, parking layouts and ramp design, which were intended to speed up parking in attended car parks and, later, to make parking one's own vehicle more straightforward. At this time the continuous-surface structure was developed to reduce the likelihood of stalling on steep ramps, and echelon parking (parking at an acute angle to the carriageway) was devised to make the parking manoeuvre easier. In 1952, the city of Chicago began an unprecedented programme to develop ten multi-storey parking structures in the downtown area, named, rather aptly, Parking Facilities Nos 1 to 10. This mix of ramp- and lift-type car parks produced a consistently high standard of design. Their scale and impact have only recently been matched by a programme of underground parking structures, commissioned since the late 1980s, in the French city of Lyon.

Over the next twenty-five years, the parking structure was to flourish worldwide. Remarkable examples included Bertrand Goldberg's Marina City twin residential towers (1962) in Chicago, in which parking for the sixty-storey buildings was integrated into the base of each tower in the form of a continuous, nineteen-storey helical parking deck, simply the most extreme piece of parking engineering. The car park would also form part of the 'megastructure', where, for example at Cumbernauld New Town Centre (1963–67) in Scotland, 'all the social facilities of a city, and all the commercial ones as well, [would be concentrated] in a single location'.[11] The architectural and social critic Reyner Banham noted how at the time the critical response to Cumbernauld was 'conspicuously approving', and that the project ultimately won an award for community design. By the end of the 1960s, with the demise of local government-funded planning projects and the rise of the historic conservation lobby, wholesale redevelopment in European cities became a thing of the past. Coupled with the fear that multi-storey car parks might harbour crime and blight the neighbouring streets, planning theory changed direction. The introduction of large, abstract structures alien to the fabric of the historic city was no longer considered welcome.[12]

In the UK, however, there is a significant heritage of private-sector parking structures built by companies such as NCP. These for-profit speculative ventures originated in the temporary use of flattened inner-city bombsites to provide parking at grade. NCP recognized the commercial value of developing these and similar sites for multi-storey parking, replicating the footprint of the site as many times as was permissible. The site was then divisible into 19 m² units – a parking space including half of the

Loebl, Schlossman & Bennett, Parking Facility No 5, Chicago 1952

//////////////// see case study pp.224–227

carriageway.[13] This unit of space, cheap to build, could be rented by the hour or by the day. When government-funded development ceased, NCP continued building car parks to serve hotels, shopping centres, offices, airports, ferry terminals and universities. These buildings and campuses contained such large concentrations of activity that multi-storey development was still considered appropriate.

In 1973, oil prices increased by 400 per cent, a situation that affected the whole of the Western world.[14] The 1970s also saw a string of oil-related environmental disasters, publicized by Greenpeace and other organizations. For many, these events spelled the end for the car as a sign of progress, but not to our addiction. The 1980s produced few new parking structures of note, with the exception of 60 East Lake Street in Chicago, designed by Tigerman Fugman McCurry. The façade of the twelve-storey building is formed by the image of a classic 1930s car, behind which is concealed a rectangular, continuous double-helix ramp. In total contrast to the 'section' structures that had appeared in the 1950s and 1960s, the elevation identifies the building as a car park without revealing either the ramps or the cars themselves. By the late 1980s, the alternative solution of 'park-and-ride', which enabled commuters to park their cars on the city fringes and take a shuttle bus into the centre, was being put into practice. Parking was again consuming vast tracts of land.

see case study pp.132–137 \\\\\\\\\\\\\\\\\\\

So with the above-ground parking structure largely consigned to history, and a plummeting reputation for those already in existence, car parks began to be recycled. In 1987, the offices of the French national newspaper *Libération* moved into the top five floors of a ramped multi-storey car park near the Place de la République, in Paris. Design firm Atelier Canal (Patrick and Daniel Rubin), the team behind the conversion, recognized an unusual asset of the parking structure: ramps bring continuity between each floor, giving otherwise independent floors uncharacteristically good connections.[15] The *Libération* scheme was followed by two London conversions: Wallis Gilbert & Partners' Daimler Car Hire Garage (1931), in Herbrand Street, was turned into offices for advertising company McCann-Erickson, and the Bluebird garage (1924) in the King's Road into a shop and restaurant for Terence Conran. In 1993, Birds Portchmouth Russum's unbuilt Croydromia project sought to utilize four multi-storey car parks that encircled the Croydon town centre, deserted when the shops and offices are closed, as the 'foundations' for a series of inflatable rooftop structures that would house a cinema, an auditorium, an art gallery and sporting facilities. The firm's proposal highlighted the potential of reusing such structures to regenerate our cities. In this instance, the parking structure was recognized as a catalyst and would have become the host in a symbiotic relationship between event and accessible destination.

Stirling Wilford & Associates with Walter Nägeli, Braun Headquarters, Melsungen 1986–92 (see case study pp.78–81)

Just when the car park seemed dead, a string of highly influential architects turned their attention to the type. The results are out of the ordinary and the projects do not conform to the idea of the generic, autonomous car-park form. In 1991, Stirling Wilford and Walter Nägeli completed the Braun plant in Melsungen, near Kassel, where the parking structure forms a central part of a large industrial campus in a rural landscape setting. Although relatively straightforward in isolation, it is the spiral silo ramps and bridges linking the car park to a continuous wall of stairs and the viaduct beyond that mark the Braun building out as both a pragmatic and picturesque evolution of the idiom. Dutch practices OMA, NL Architects, MVRDV, and UN Studio all began to explore the formal and spatial possibilities of parking structures, applying ideas about continuous landscapes and developing the type away from its mid-century model to create a new paradigm in which parking is integrated into housing, offices, shops, and, in the case of OMA's Souterrain in The Hague, into the very infrastructure of our cities. In the last decade, Kengo Kuma, TEN Arquitectos and Ingenhoven Overdiek Architekten have all built car parks, which, although simple in their interior spatial logic, employ sophisticated elevations that modify the interior using fabric and light as texture to engage the senses.

The demise of the modern project has undoubtedly altered the status of the car park. Once the icon of modern city planning, the height of convenience and efficiency, the car park has been largely relegated to urban blight. Its formal isolation from neighbouring buildings and its ability to isolate one part of a city from another is hard to condone. Instead, we have reverted to parking on the street or on wasteland sites, or building caricatures of vernacular architecture to conceal the bulk of the uninspired structure within. We have become ashamed of the scale and sculptural appeal of the multi-storey parking structure. As a result, parking structures are increasingly concealed underground, their abstract forms removed from the townscape. In existing cities, underground car parks are less likely to be situated beneath buildings, especially historic ones, and are instead built under parks, squares and streets. In occupying the ground beneath the public realm, or the 'white space' of Giovanni Battista Nolli's 1748 plan of Rome (for our purposes a particular map of an ideal city), the car park provides a foundation for what Michael Graves described in 1979 as the 'urban life and vitality' of cities.[16] Recent examples include I.M. Pei's Grand Louvre in Paris, the Museumplein in Amsterdam by Kees Spanjers, and Michel Targe, Jean-Michel Wilmotte and Daniel Buren's sinister spiral structure below the Place des Célestins in Lyon, each sharing the objectives of providing convenient parking, preserving the historic buildings and streets, and maintaining the status quo in our city centres.

Car parks could be explained as the cold realization of the engineer's criteria: the car is a certain size and is parked in a space with prescribed dimensions, with a predictable turning circle and ramps and floors that must not exceed a given pitch. But somehow these criteria do not give rise to the inevitable. Melnikov's experiments in the 1920s spawned a series of utilitarian, slab-like constructions that were repetitive, modular and skeletal, which weathered to great effect and overshadowed the historic remains of our city centres. The outright brutality of these engineered structures had given way by the 1980s to discretion, concealment and humour. Today the type has been rediscovered in the refined geometries of ascent and descent, in enclosure, in circular and linear geometries, symmetry, repetition and congruence. Enriched by being tied to other building uses, the aesthetic association or disruption sees multi-storey car parks evolving in their complexity and humanity, where the metanarratives of density, landscape, internal space and continuity with the public realm charge the abstract space of the structure as they fragment into didactic forms, or remain as isolated single-type buildings employing sublime technics.

Konstantin S. Melnikov, drawing,
car park over the Seine, Paris 1925

Birds Portchmouth Russum
Croydromia, Croydon 1993

Four existing car parks on the edge of Croydon
town centre are linked by a new loop and 'Central'
park, the latter bisecting the centre. The car parks,
or 'ports' (as termed by Louis Kahn, see p.12),
are reinvigorated by the addition of expressive
and colourful rooftop 'dromes' housing new
leisure uses. The car parks and public realm
connections made between them and the centre
transform these benign structures into civic
buildings.

In 1989, I came across Dietrich Klose's *Multi-Storey Car Parks and Garages*, a practical guide to car-park design and survey of 1950s and 1960s car parks. Photographed in black and white, it had an unfamiliar calmness. I found it intriguing and unfamiliar in the current context of High Tech, Postmodernism and Deconstructivism. The buildings were very simple, plain in plan, clever in section, graphic in elevation and

aesthetic influence

non-referential. Instead, they were made to respond dimensionally and anatomically to the module and trajectories of a moving car. The singular, straightforward requirement of arranging decks of parked cars led designers to seek the ingenious and elegant use of matter (concrete), form (inclined decks and helical ramps), and expressive and witty elevations.

see p.27 \\\\\\\\\\\\\\\\\\\\\\\\\\\\\\\\\\

The continuous surface

By 1996, when I rediscovered the book, the architectural climate had changed radically. Three years had already passed since OMA produced their Jussieu Library competition scheme, and MVRDV's Villa VPRO was on-site in Hilversum for completion the following year. Although the Jussieu project was not a car park, and Villa VPRO incorporated only a small amount of parking, both depended heavily on the ramp. In the last ten years, this preoccupation with the continuous surface has grown, and it has been used by architects around the world, including Diller + Scofidio, Foreign Office Architects and Zaha Hadid. The principle has been applied to museums and galleries, parks, offices, housing and a ferry terminal. It seems that it is the dynamic effect of human movement through the section that provides inspiration – a dynamic that is harnessed in the design of new and fearless, sometimes rhetorical, parking structures that meld the dark and somewhat grotesque car-park interior with the office, home, shopping centre, and, in the case of MVRDV's 'Z-Mall' (1997), in Leidschenveen, a new town centre.[17]

Alongside this trend for 'internal form' is a renewed interest in construction technique, and, in particular, in reinforced in-situ and pre-cast concrete, the primary material used to construct the post-war car parks. The multi-storey car park, designed for wheels rather than feet, is unique as a building type. Once a parking space has been elevated above street level, the architects must decide how to transport the car to its lofty position and then, once the car is in that position, in what environment do we, as motorists, expect to leave it. The resulting structures are designed on the understanding that we do not remain but instead come and go, and that our presence is transient – so it is in that split second that we begin to dwell in the space and experience such sensations as fear in the cold and damp. To what extent could light and dark, temperature and humidity, be affecting our physiological condition? The recent switch in emphasis from utilitarian efficiency to safety underscores an awareness that we spend enough time in these structures to appreciate their unfamiliarity. Unfortunately, this awareness has brought with it a new generation of bland parking structures.

So what are the enduring aesthetic qualities of a parking structure? Not surprisingly, these aesthetics are derived from the strategies employed in moving cars up and down the building, giving rise to what we will describe as a landscape type; pervasive in the interior, this type is also often demonstrated in its external form. Other qualities arise from structure, materials used and the way they weather, and the quality of light. Decks, ramps and lift halls characterize space. But where the link between movement and the oblique phenomenon is demonstrable, the others (matter, light and elevation) derive more subtly from the car. OMA's 1993 proposal for an urban extension of the *congrès vie sociale* for the two Jussieu libraries marked a radical change in architecture, in which attention was instantly turned to the floor plane and the idea of internal landscapes. According to the architects, this departure originated from their own design of

p.18: Robert Mallet-Stevens,
parking garage, rue Marbeuf, Paris 1927–28;
Albert Laprade and Léon Bazin,
parking garage, rue Marbeuf, Paris 1928–29

Euralille (1988–91) and from the issue of infrastructure. Of course, one could trace an interest in the 'oblique' to the Renaissance and the construction of spiral ramps for horses, including those at Bramante's Belvedere Palace (1504), in the Vatican, and *Il Cisternone* (the Citadel Reservoir; 1565–67), in Turin. But it seems more likely that the literal interest originates from the Futurists' enthusiasm for the car and the new human experience that was speed. In his preface to the catalogue for the first exhibition of Futurist sculpture in 1913, Umberto Boccioni said that he sought not pure form, 'but *pure plastic rhythm*; not the construction of bodies, but the *construction of the action of bodies*'. His ideal, therefore, was 'not a pyramidal architecture (static state), but a spiral architecture (dynamism)'.[18]

This dynamism did not materialize in Futurist architecture, however, but instead emerged in Russian Constructivism with Vladimir Tatlin's monument to the Third International (1919–20) and Melnikov's interest in all things vehicular. It also emerged in the ideas of Dutch architect Mart Stam and, most conspicuously, in the work of Le Corbusier, specifically the ramp at the Villa Savoye (1929–31), a device that was to recur in countless schemes including the Carpenter Center at Harvard (1961) and in Chandigarh, India (1957–65). Kenneth Frampton described how the car ramp on the outside of Frank Lloyd Wright's Automobile Objective and Planetarium for Gordon Strong (1925), for which the Tower of Babel and the spiral minaret of the Abu Dulaf mosque (849–51) at Samarra may have provided a precedent, became the inspiration for the helical ramped gallery at the Guggenheim Museum in New York.[19] In the same way that OMA's library proposed a continuation of the Jussieu campus, the Guggenheim suggested a spiral extension of the Manhattan grid, forty-nine years before. The experience of freewheeling out of control down the museum ramp is very much like that of being in a car, and the cause of some criticism of the resulting gallery in which works of art must be viewed from the incline of the ramp.

Frank Lloyd Wright, Solomon R. Guggenheim Museum, New York 1956–59

Just as the Futurists had fallen for the dynamic of the car, Claude Parent and Paul Virilio of Architecture Principe took their inspiration from ideas about ballistics and circulation. The same instability that we experience at the Guggenheim was for Parent and Virilio the reasoning behind their theory of the function of the oblique, in which they envisaged an architecture of inclined planes to replace the horizontal and the vertical. Virilio described the human body as being unstable and not in equilibrium, and how we 'effectively became locomotive, propelled by the (relative) disequilibrium created by the gravity of planet earth, the habitat of our species' – ideas that he contrasts with 'the horizontal order of the rural habitat in the agricultural era, and the vertical order of the urban habitat in the industrial era', but would have been able to experience in the 'space' of the ramp (of a parking structure).[20] Architecture Principe's full-scale prototype, 'Pendular Destabilizer No 1', was devised and built to test the

OMA, Bibliothèque Nationale, Paris 1989

see case study pp.244–247 \\\\\\\\\\\\\\\\\

see p.28 \\\\\\\\\\\\\\\\\\\\\\\\\\\\\\\\

'habitability of inclined slopes and to determine the best choice of angles for the different living spaces'. OMA would do the same nearly thirty years later with their 5m-by-6m test rig for the Jussieu Library, with which they aimed to prove the viability of inhabiting gentler gradients in order to answer the question: 'Could you live on a slope?' Yes, you could.

Virilio outlined further the need to 'discard the notion of the vertical enclosure, whose walls are made inaccessible by gravity, and to define habitable space by means of wholly accessible inclined planes, thereby increasing the useable surface areas'. This was, essentially, the 'principle of habitable circulation', and a fair description of the Jussieu model or a car park, both a grid of columns supporting a continuously ramped surface with little or no vertical enclosure. With Jussieu, the architects had established the limiting factor in the design of the continuous-surface type – the footprint of the building needed to be large enough to afford the changes in elevation necessary to link the inclined decks at a pitch that would still allow inhabitation. Here, the comparison with the integrated parking structure is unambiguous.

OMA broke free from the sandwich section to generate spatial qualities by manipulating the floor surface and avoiding interruptions between floors, most recently with the Seattle Library (2004). There, the spiral bookstacks proved a very pragmatic strategy for managing information. Not only was the continuity that the firm sought visceral, it also would arguably have a bearing on the functionality of the building for access, information management, adaptation and change.[21] OMA's self-confessed love of the car is evident in their work. The car park is an inspiration for many unrelated designs by the architects, such as the Bibliothèque Nationale competition (1989), and the cause of creative interference in integrating the actual use with another building type, the 'Souterrain' tram stations (2004), in The Hague. OMA recognized that infrastructure, because it was being devised in plan and not in section, was increasingly dividing the places it was intended to link. It is in their strategic shift to the section that the surface emerges as the generator for most of the work.

Order and construction

Whilst on the one hand an interest in the aesthetics of the continuous surface can be seen to coincide with the car park, the car and speed, it is more difficult to piece together a similar, literal interest in car-park order, matter and elevation as the inspiration for the other contemporary strand of architectural production popularized by Herzog and de Meuron, one of a constellation of protagonists that includes Peter Märkli with his rich and uncompromising use of concrete, Claus en Kaan with their revival of modern type-forms, and David Chipperfield, as seen in his America's Cup pavilion in Valencia. But a profession worldwide that is reflecting on Modernism, on the then new twentieth-century typologies, on the structural frame and claddings, their space, form and non-structural free elevation, could explain this coincidence of interest in the car-park form.

So in addition to what we might loosely describe as a Dutch interest in the 'oblique' (ramps), there is an equally compelling interest in construction. In 1995, Frampton set out a case for construction as a discipline. He described the legitimacy of 'craft technique' that arises from the recognition that a building is 'as much an everyday experience as it is a representation, and that the built is a thing rather than a sign', and went on to explain how a building is the product of 'the topos, the typos and the tectonic'.[22] But given the strong internal anatomy of the parking structure, the relation to topos, or location, rarely informs design. The result, of course, is that it becomes the product of typos (the 'static' or the 'oblique') and the tectonic (a combination of 'elevation', 'matter' and 'light'). Some buildings, therefore, derive their drama from the 'oblique' (surface), and others from the effect of construction, in which, largely due to the opportunity that the type affords, the narrative of construction is made explicit.

I suggest that we think of the parking structure not as an architectural anomaly, but instead as an architectural essential, as that which lies beneath; half made, half deteriorating, it is the abstract prototype, the syntax in building, for support and surface, of limitation and enclosure. It is the visceral antithesis of the natural world. Outside, their forms and elevations can surprise. Inside, the landscape, material and light into which one is immersed can be bewildering, sometimes terrifying, and occasionally beautiful. These extreme effects are not contrived. So what gives rise to these unfamiliar sensations? Compared to other buildings, the car park is autonomous, its shape derived from its own internal order and from that of the car. It is a type of warehouse or silo. Similar to Le Corbusier's Domino system (1914), in which structure is separate from enclosure, or to a deep-plan office, it is an array of columns supporting repetitive decks. In its purest form, the parking structure is a hypostyle and, although finite, gives the impression of being limitless. The disorienting nature of repetition suggests the notion that we are confronted with a labyrinth.

The unfamiliarity of this type of space is made all the more apparent by Archizoom's decision to use it as the model for their portrayal of 'No-Stop City; Residential Parkings; Climatic Universal System' (1969–72). In their revolutionary scenario, the public and private realms of the city are compressed into a single isotropic spatial and structural system, in which 'the house becomes a well-equipped parking lot'.[23] Inside it, there are 'no hierarchies nor spatial figurations of a conditioning nature'. Replacing the qualitative idea of place, this quantitative field provides a framework for home, work, leisure and parking, freeing them 'from all preconstituted cultural and social models, breaking the subtle intellectual links and hysterical linguistic knots which characterize architecture as the figuration of space'. Archizoom's conclusion is that the space is devoid of hierarchy, of cultural meaning, and of any spatial norms.

It is the module of the car 'body' that governs the shape of the car park,[24] and by repeating it, the building displays its own internal logic. Columns are positioned so that they do not obstruct the carriageway or parked cars, and provide a consistent rhythm. Floor-to-floor heights are designed to a minimum, homogeneous in plan and section. Difference is localized in the design of the entrance, stairways and ramps. If the ramps are integral to the parking surface, this furthers the homogenizing effect, as do perimeter safety barriers if they form a significant part of the design. There are few, if any, window and door components. Lighting, signage and surfaces (floors, walls and ceilings) are spare and utilitarian; there are no 'finishes' to mask crude construction. This vacuum leaves little to touch, and there is a lack of familiar detail. The process of construction is taken only so far, leaving little more than a skeleton of a building. Its composition, a static array of columns, beams, decks and barriers, and counterpoint of dynamic ramps, form the basis of the car-park syntax. This is the environment we encounter, an abstract and unique 'cosmos' remote from its site and from the city.

The narrative garage

In most cases, the journey on foot from car to street and back again is straightforward. But for some, this transition is what gives the parking structure its significance. It is the narrative journey, a journey that might also include the passage of the car. The forerunner to this type was Giancarlo di Carlo's executed plan for Urbino's Mercatale (1970–83), which introduced a two-storey underground car park beneath the square to manage the arrival of, in particular, tourist traffic. This was linked to the newly pedestrianized historic centre above by a 15th-century equestrian stair that di Carlo had discovered within a bastion. The scheme enlisted old and new elements to integrate the parking into the very fabric of this historic city.

see case study pp.78–81 \\\\\\\\\\\\\\\\\\\\\
see case study pp.166–169 \\\\\\\\\\\\\\\\\
see case study pp.228–231 \\\\\\\\\\\\\\\\\

Coincidentally, three projects, all designed in the late 1980s and built in the early 1990s, exemplify this pattern: Stirling Wilford and Nägeli's Braun plant, in Melsungen; Birds Portchmouth Russum's Avenue de Chartres, in Chichester; and OMA's L'Espace Piranésien, in Lille. In the first two cases, the illusory effect is to conjure the picturesque. The Braun campus, located in countryside, is in a vale that invites a bridge, with a small ornamental lake as a dam; the rest of the plant is concealed behind this bipartite device. The Chichester car park seeks to alter history, quite literally, by integrating a pedestrian bridge and bastion stair-towers into a fictional extension of the historic city walls. The city of Lille, however, is immersed in infrastructure, which makes its own context – a vast wedge of excavated ground and projecting building mass. Here, OMA conceived of L'Espace Piranésien, a single, subterranean volume of bridges, stairs, lifts and escalators linking Metro, train and car park.

The mechanical garage

Another type is the mechanical garage, in which an autonomous mechanism – whether conveyor belt, Ferris wheel, or lift – replaces the action of the driven car, the effect of which is to remove the car still further from the conventions of space. The conveyor-type uses a vertical loop of revolving parking decks (typically for one vehicle) that fill the available volume, useful in a constricted site. With the Ferris-wheel system, cars are again parked on individual decks, which are slung from the circumference of the wheel. This type does not use volume efficiently, but does lend itself to standardization and manufacture, thus enabling the parking structure to enter the prototyped world of industrial and product design.

Zidpark, Upper Thames Street, London 1961
(interior photograph: pp.4–5)

The lift-type, part building and part machine, is the precursor to the automated warehouses that sprang up at the end of the twentieth century. From the outside, there is little to see. At ground level, reception and delivery stalls mark the point where the machine consumes and later spits out vehicles. Inside, a great hall (hoistway) runs the length of the structure. The cars are delivered to a parking stall using an overhead crane or a dolly lift, both of which can move a car horizontally and vertically. On each side of the hall cars are 'parked', arranged on shelves. Inside the frame, the props and struts, which may be steel or concrete, that support the decks make explicit the industrial quality of these spaces. Various systems were devised. One of these was 'Zidpark', an eight-storey structure with sixteen lifts, which was used just once in the City of London.[25] On delivery, cars were conveyed sideways on roller conveyers into the lift hall, and then up. Upon reaching the correct level, the cars were transported again sideways from the lift into the stall – all of which was done remotely by a man at the arrival level. Because engines were switched off in the building, the risk of fire was negligible and the frame and decks, therefore, were made of steel. Zidpark was opened by Princess Margaret in 1961, but worked for just one day. What is interesting about the project, however, is that Archigram might have used the crane mechanism as a model for their 'Plug-In City' (1962–64).[26]

Mihai Alimanestianu, Speed-Park, 43rd Street, New York 1961

Another side-loading system, Speed-Park, in New York, was developed in conjunction with lift-manufacturer Otis. This fully automated facility for 270 cars, also built in 1961, could be manned by one person and could park or retrieve a car every twenty-two seconds. Other systems included the Wertheim-Autoparker (1957–58), in Neuer Markt, Vienna, and the Pigeon Hole (1957), in Temperance Street, Toronto. The Autoparker was fourteen storeys, including three basement levels, and the Pigeon Hole facility used a seven-storey lift cage (optimum ten-storey), mounted on rails.

Burlington Garage, London: lift-type

Both could deliver a car by lift to a stall in thirty to forty-five seconds, and both used a dolly to transfer the car onto the lift platform, but forwards rather than sideways. In each case, an attendant, who stayed with the car until it reached its parking stall, operated the lift. The Bowser Parking System, used for the fourteen-storey Parking Facility No 1 (1955), in Chicago, employed an overhead bridge-type crane mechanism. When reading contemporary accounts of these systems, it is evident that 'speed' was important. A mechanism for delivery and retrieval introduces the idea and relevance of time, superimposed on the spatial order and efficiency of the ramp-type car park.

In 1956, the search for solutions to the mechanized car park produced a circular lift garage, the unbuilt 'Rotapark', which employed a 25m-diameter revolving parking deck, or 'shelf', and would have occupied a compact 31 m-by-31m plot.[27] In the centre, a cruciform of four lifts delivered vehicles from the street to the 'shelf'. The parking deck would then revolve to receive the car in an empty bay. On the ground, a turntable adjacent to each lift enabled cars to be rotated on arrival. A contemporary account in *Builder* delightfully described Rotapark as 'a mechanical, fully automatic, push-button-operated parking machine'.[28] Almost half a century later, Henn Architekten built two nineteen-storey, steel-framed, glass-clad 'Car Towers' at the Autostadt, in Wolfsburg. The towers each employ a single revolving and lifting armature to stack cars manufactured in the nearby Volkswagen factory. At the Autostadt, cars are displayed in glass cabinets until retrieved for their expectant new owners, the very antithesis of the conventional dark store.

In contrast, when standing in a more typical lift-type hoistway, it is possible to appreciate how strange these spaces are. If a ramped car park seems an alien environment, then these gates, cages, cranes and rails are unfathomable, and the darkness that we associate with a conventional parking structure is far surpassed. With no need to light the decks for drivers there are few windows or openings. These secret halls are filled with cars but devoid of people – they are great machine cabinets in the city.

All ramp- and lift-type car parks exhibit a static structural order that reflects their roles as warehouses, and a second dynamic order of movement either in the horizontal, the vertical, or the oblique. The idea of the static and dynamic condition lies behind the two poles of contemporary architecture; perhaps this is the nature of expression and has always, to some extent, been the case. But right now the parking structure's essential characteristics, that it is pared down and utilizes the oblique, is reflected in one camp in the diagrammatic, crafted, even decorated work, and in the other in the continuous surface. The following chapters I hope help to evidence this thesis; the first three – 'Matter', 'Elevation' and 'Light' – address the ideas of diagram, craft and decoration, and the last – 'Oblique' – that of more complex geometries.

Office for Metropolitan Architecture
2 Bibliothèques Jussieu, Paris 1993

OMA describe how instead of floors simply being
stacked, they are 'manipulated to touch those
above and below', all connected to realize a
'warped interior boulevard'. The large-scale
model conveys a strong sense of what the library
would have been like to inhabit. A full-scale rig
was also made by OMA to prove it was workable
to arrange furniture on a gradient. The project
represents a unique extension of the public realm
within a building.

David Chipperfield Architects
Edificio Veles e Vents, Valencia 2005–6

The architects describe their building for the America's Cup as an array of 'stacked and shifting horizontal planes'. The overwhelming sense of reduction emerges from an architecture of cantilevered concrete decks, each designed to provide uninterrupted views and shade for spectators. Walls enclosing interiors are glazed and set far back from the perimeter. Simplified soffit and facia details give the impression that each level is a spare white platform.

Second-floor plan

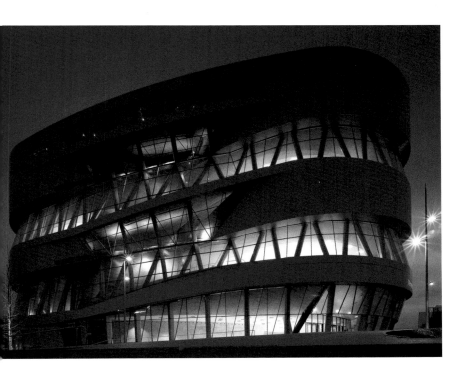

UN **Studio**
Mercedes-Benz Museum, Stuttgart
2001–6

Two pathways (a double-helix) spiral down through the building connecting the level galleries. The first spiral links a display of cars and the second contains exhibitions devoted to the history of Mercedes-Benz. Their paths cross at intervals.

plan - level 5

0 1m   5m   10m

matter
the plasticity of concrete

1

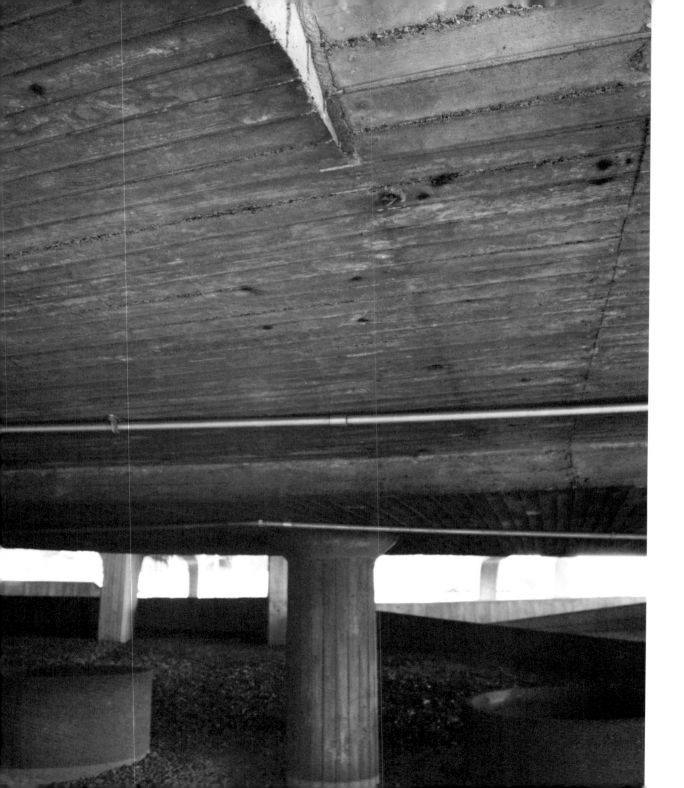

For a building that eschews the need for an envelope (vapour barriers, membranes and protective claddings) and finishes, the substance of a parking structure is largely in the superstructure, the material used in the frame and in the decks. During the high period of car-park design in the 1950s and 1960s, utility and fashion informed a generation of concrete structures, often clad in a kind of **matter** pre-cast concrete panel. Steel, although rarely considered in Europe, was used in the US where different building codes imposed less stringent requirements on fire-resisting structures, and timber has only recently made an appearance, notably in Norway and Austria.

It is no surprise, therefore, that our collective image of a multi-storey car park is one of concrete: rough textured, dark in tone, and ingrained with dirt. It is this bare surface – the deck, the soffit, the beam, the column – that we encounter when driving around inside these structures. The rudimentary construction and poor maintenance that many associate with such buildings mask the innate structural and constructional possibilities of concrete. When reinforced, it can span large distances uninterrupted and can resist fire. But still more remarkable is its plasticity; the liquidity of concrete lends itself to fluid surfaces – to the hyperbolic paraboloid and helical geometries of parking decks and ramps – and to the monolithic, allowing the structure and enclosure to be made as one. As the work of artist Rita McBride suggests, the resulting building can appear as if cast in a mould as a single, homogeneous form.[29]

In-situ, pre-cast or steel, flat-slab or framed, each of these has an impact on the layout of parking bays (the efficiency of the plan) or the floor-to-floor height (the efficiency of the section). Crudely put, perimeter columns ensure an efficient plan, and flat slabs an efficient section. Although efficiency plays a part in the design of these speculative buildings, it appears not to have been the science that it might have been. Of course, the car itself dictates dimension and, as a result, structure. In a linear plan, columns are spaced longitudinally on a multiple of the 2.4 m-wide European parking bay, usually at 7.2 m centres, efficient for flat-slab construction; any longer and spans need to be post-tensioned. But it is the transverse location of columns on the deck that dictates the structure, for which there are four basic options: an in-situ reinforced concrete flat slab, supported on a regular column grid (likely to generate four transverse columns); a balanced cantilever, supporting a reinforced concrete flat slab (two columns); a balanced cantilever frame (two columns); and a framed long-span beam and perimeter column (two columns, but no obstruction). Other engineering factors include the capital cost of the material used – Robert Law Weed's Miami structure of 1948 is a near-perfect balanced cantilever frame (1:5:1), and consequently used little material – and stability in an open-plan structure, which with few lift and stair cores, favours in-situ concrete.

In the 1960s, engineer E.M. Khoury devised an innovative model for the continuous surface, which consisted of four hyperbolic paraboloid quadrants. Where their four corners met at the centre of the plan – two folded up, two down – high and low corners fused to make a single, deformed surface. In effect, each deck was cut in the centre of the plan. At each cut, successive floors were joined up, the one rising up connected to the floor above folding down, with the resulting open mouth allowing a continuous route for cars from one floor to the next.

It is the initial liquidity of concrete that makes the shaping, curving and inclining of surfaces possible. Concrete – a mix of sand, cement, water and aggregate –

E.M. Khoury, hyperbolic paraboloid project

is 'formed'. The mould, or formwork, gives the concrete its shape and finish, and much of its character – steel or plywood for a fair-faced finish, or rough-sawn timber boards to create *béton brut* by marking the concrete with the wood grain. Just about any material can be used for formwork; in 1972, architect Miguel Fisac registered a technique known as 'flexible formworks', which employed trussed plastic forms to preserve the fluid origin of concrete. After the formwork has been struck, it is also possible to finish the concrete with a jet of water, air or sand, or by 'bush-hammering' the surface – all techniques designed to remove the sand/cement skin and reveal the aggregate. In its heyday the art of making exposed concrete finishes was well documented, with detailed advice on the mix, formwork, finishing techniques and weathering to achieve a particular colour, texture or pattern.[30]

The making of formwork and the mixing, pouring and curing (drying) of concrete all add up to a complex process that is part manufacture, part craft, and is therefore prone to defects, including grout loss, cracking (fine cracks), crazing, discolouration and spalling (chipping along an edge). In practice, the blemishes are in part what gives concrete the texture, depth of colour and character that distinguish it from plaster, render or paint. But these defects make concrete more vulnerable to the effects of weather, so that a material that should ideally be impermeable deteriorates from chemical imbalances in the aggregate or from water penetration. 'The modification to surfaces through erosion and the accumulation of dirt from weathering,' note David Leatherbarrow and Mohsen Mostafavi in *On Weathering: The Life of Buildings in Time*, are physical facts with 'ethical implications'. They suggest that this modification 'might be called "aesthetic" deterioration, as it can make buildings either "sightly" or "unsightly".'[31] The perception is that the weathering effect is unintentional and therefore 'unsightly'. Add the wear and tear of tyre marks and oil spills on the decks, and fumes and urine on any surface, and it is evident that these structures deteriorate in a conspicuous manner.

Inside, we encounter the rippling surface of a poured concrete deck and the dark expanse of concrete overhead, scarred with defects – these surfaces are unfinished and undecorated. Although they require little maintenance, after nearly half a century many have deteriorated; buildings that were only ever going to be mundane are now 'ruins'. With no windows or doors and few signs of life, they stand in limbo in our cities, half complete and half destroyed. Unloved and blackened by time, they chip and crack and are marked by stains of incontinence and stalactites that hang from the flat soffits. Decay is everywhere in this remote, grey place. Today these are the buildings that we encounter, their original brutish tectonic and simplicity muddled with a latter-day down-and-out demeanour. But all of this only emphasizes their unique ability to survive in increasingly sanitized cities that,

Roche Dinkeloo & Associates, Veterans
Memorial Coliseum, New Haven 1972
(see case study pp.70–77)

see p.51 \\\\\\\\\\\\\\\\\\\\\\\\\\\\\\\\\\

see p.50 \\\\\\\\\\\\\\\\\\\\\\\\\\\\\\\\\

see case study pp.78–81 \\\\\\\\\\\\\\\\\\\\\
see case study pp.174–181 \\\\\\\\\\\\\\\\\\

so we are told by politicians, have an ever-brighter future. Perceptions of matter make the car park extremely vulnerable to the collective psyche.

In contrast to the heavy, plastic and homogeneous order of concrete, steel transforms these buildings into relatively lightweight and apparently ephemeral structures; we see more of the cars and less of the building. Steel columns and beams support steel or pre-cast concrete decks, each structural component divisible from the next. Steel, which is as vulnerable to the weather as concrete, can be galvanized or protected with paint; untreated, the steel sections will rust. The alternative is to aestheticize decay in the design. In their design for the Veterans Memorial Coliseum (1972), in New Haven, Roche Dinkeloo used Corten, a steel that is designed to oxidize to the point where it protects itself from further atmospheric decay, lending the structure a deep, reddish-brown colour.

In the case of the parking structure, it used to be difficult to separate matter from elevation. But during the 1980s (and to a certain extent today), postmodernists and conservationists revealed a previously unrecognized and unexploited characteristic of the car park: that one could separate the appearance (both material and compositional) from the material and structural order. A car park can be designed to not look like a car park, or to appear utilitarian. These structures are often masonry-clad, and the concrete superstructure that is no longer visible from the outside is on the inside undisciplined. Poorly illuminated, its appearance is gloomy; up close, the encounter is even worse. Von Gerkan Marg & Partner's Hillman Garage is a rare exception where brick does not conspire to create an historic allusion. It is simply brickwork, a carefully crafted expanse of material that creates both a massive and abstract presence in the city, and incidentally disguises the cars parked within. Rarer still is the car park for Skidmore, Owings & Merrill's National Commercial Bank (1981–83), in Jeddah, where limited fenestration protects the interior from the intense sunlight, and the masonry used on the exterior reinforces the formality that pure circular geometry affords.

Since this nadir (excluding the examples above), we have entered a new age marked by a fascination for matter in building, for claddings and surface, and for new ways of building. Architects are interested in abstraction and many are recycling recent architectures; this brings with it a new interest in concrete, not for its efficacy but simply for its presence. Of course, the narrative of the construction is laid bare in the car park, and with thermal performance and condensation not an issue, construction can be unusually explicit. Equally, there are many more steel structures, including Stirling Wilford and Nägeli's Braun factory, in Melsungen, and Mahler, Günster, Fuchs' Parkhaus am Bollwerksturm, in Heilbronn. The latter is a long-span frame with perimeter steel columns and transverse beams supporting a pre-cast concrete steel deck. At each end, the final bay and helical ramp are cast in-situ to give the structure stability. The composite superstructure is then clad in fine timber laths and veiled in part with metal mesh; this is the antithesis of concrete's plasticity and monolithic nature. Instead, for each element a construction technique has been employed that denotes a scale of material application, which is refined. If there is a criticism, it is almost a critique of competence, of the inability to misjudge, to use a material at an inappropriate scale, to effect a dislocation between the individual and the building, and the building and the city. It is a bittersweet sense that one otherwise gets time and time again with these structures.

Daniele Marques and Bruno Zurkirchen's Marktzentrum Kirchpark, in Lustenau, uses a polycarbonate carapace that veils the roof, which extends out over a new public square. The sheet is marked by the shadows of fluting within the body of the material, its translucence giving depth to the flat surface. But for all its inventive-ness, the polycarbonate, which is itself a cheap material, accentuates through difference the uncompromising nature of concrete. This invokes a shift in mood from concrete as Le Corbusier used it – simply for its plasticity, damn the finish – to an approach that one might glibly associate with Kahn, that of surface with a degree of refinement that the budget for a car park does not tend to reflect.

///////////////////////////////// see p.164

TEN Arquitectos, Princeton Parking Structure, Princeton 1998–2000 (see p.107)

Along with purely architectural techniques of refinement, we can observe a shift in expectation to interiors, in which can be discerned detail or the idea of completion. Architects are being drawn into the commodification of the facility. In Princeton, TEN Arquitectos developed an urban design and cladding strategy for a generic structure that was designed by someone else. The position of the building is intended to frame a new public open space, and the building is clad in refined (think 'refined foods'), stainless-steel mesh. Designed to please the community, its outward appearance and utilitarian function are divided absolutely, just the kind of thing for a risk-averse, competent and sanitized world.

Existing concrete structures, such as Drury Street in Dublin, are being overclad.[32] In this case, architects Cullen Payne used perforated metal screens that conceal the horizontal strata of pre-cast concrete, exposed aggregate cladding panels and dark interior, casting a veil over the four parking decks above ground. Inside these structures, rippling surfaces of concrete are often covered with non-slip, colour-coded paint finishes that denote parking bays, carriageways, ramps and pedestrian areas. Most bear no relationship to the original. For some, like Antoine Béal and Ludovic Blanckaert's Euralille, painted surfaces form part of the original design and denote, in this case at least, the parking bay and number. Intriguingly, during the 2005 refurbishment the parking decks were coated with a high-gloss finish. This black-and-white realm has had the effect of changing the dimensions of the space, creating

///////////////// see case study pp.228–231

reflected depth in the floor, and radically changing one of the particular characteristics of the car-park structure, its horizontality. Whilst these retrospective changes produced unexpected results, for the majority of car parks the application of paint and protective finishes offers a short-term veneer of acceptability, a populist device in conjunction with more intense lighting to make these spaces brighter and jollier, and to appear safer and more intelligible.

In this depressingly pragmatic climate, Teresa Sapey's multi-coloured and playfully graphic walls in the Hotel Puerta de América underground car park in Madrid are a pleasure. Here, words and colours do not simply code and placate, but evoke an emotion. It is an idea that Rotzler Krebs Partner have used above ground for the Maag-Recycling car park in Winterthur, where a green-painted plane forms both parking deck and backdrop to a sculptural landscape that mixes plants and caged drums of recyclable materials to create a polychromatic rhetorical setting for useful activity. It is infrastructure, building and landscape, and is ethical and beautiful. In both cases, wit is ultimately a far more sophisticated response to the idea that people in a car park are longing for some humanity.

Function is a benign force in the multi-storey car park. It requires little, but in so doing makes for a homogeneous order, and for matter wrought sparingly and brutally. The haptic qualities of this matter and its distribution conjure uniquely unfamiliar places in our towns and cities, and create a degree of abstraction that is hard to find in other man-made environments. It is one with which we have become strangely familiar, and perhaps do not have the insight to recognize but for fear. Its abstract qualities are possibly best understood in the elevation of the car park – the subject of the next chapter.

see p.52 \\\\\\\\\\\\\\\\\\\\\\\\\\\\\\\\\\\\\

see p.53 \\\\\\\\\\\\\\\\\\\\\\\\\\\\\\\\\\\\\

'Floating' car park, Amsterdam

steel frame, pre-cast concrete deck

coffered concrete structure

steel frame, in-situ concrete deck

s l o w decay

unintentional weathering

in-situ concrete fins

sky viewed through concrete oculus

brickwork

concrete 'X' cladding (negative)
and structure (positive)

Architect unknown
Car Park, Penarth 1960s

Although we have grown accustomed to the
parking structure in our cities, here in Penarth,
on the edge of the Bristol Channel, it is a true
stranger. This bleak intervention conjures up
a stark scene that changes irrevocably our image
of the seaside. It is as if this brutal concrete urban
form has run aground, tethered only to the shore-
line by a ramp. Like the Normandy beaches used
for the D-Day landings, this is a beachhead rather
than a playground.

Alberto Pessoa and João Bessa
Car Park, Porto 1968

Emerging from a hillside in the centre of Porto, eight thick layers of boardmarked concrete stand one above the other, each separated from the next by a heavy shadow. Almost 70 m in diameter, the structure stands on a pair of concentric concrete drums and twenty-four perimeter columns. Between the inner and outer drum, a double-helix of paired ramps revolve. Cars are parked inside the inner drum and on the main parking deck between the outer drum and the perimeter columns. The driver gets a unique 360° view of the Porto skyline. The enclosure creates a rhythmic foil to the rich panorama that is visible from the carriageway between the deck and soffit above. Today, the top deck is a dance floor.

Skidmore, Owings & Merrill
National Commercial Bank, Jeddah 1983

The NCB's six-storey circular parking structure
(and triangular office tower) was architect
Gordon Bunshaft's last commission. The car
park bears a strong resemblance to his similarly
circular sandblasted concrete Hirshhorn
Museum (1974). Here, however, the concrete
drum, coloured to match the travertine tower,
sits firmly on the ground, a heavy structure in
a hot climate. A spiral of fine vertical windows
imprints the helical trajectory of the continuous
parking deck on the elevation.

Von Gerkan, Marg & Partner
Hillmann Garage, Bremen 1983–84

Brickwork walls enclose this seven-storey
structure, while a stair divides the long elevation
diagonally. Below, the brickwork is monolithic;
above, it forms a trabeated composition with
square apertures. These remain open where
used for access to the stair, otherwise they are
'enclosed' by a deep-set masonry lattice for cross-
ventilation. Below the stair, ventilation is achieved
by perforating the skin of brickwork in a hit-and-
miss bonding pattern.

Teresa Sapey Estudio de Arquitectura
Hotel Puerta de América, Madrid 2005

Mother and child, people in a lift and a giant hand
are a number of the many icons used by Teresa
Sapey in her design for the Hotel Puerta de
América car park. Inspired by the French poet
Paul Éluard's 'Liberté', most of the images are
intended to portray a free existence, some are
simply informative, though none are mundane.
Here, colour and text become 'matter', the
antithesis of a monochromatic darkness that one
expects from a basement car-park encounter.

Rotzler Krebs Partner
Maag-Recycling, Winterthur 2003–4

Concerned with 'artificial naturalness' and 'aesthetically ennobled recycling products', landscape architects Rotzler Krebs have divided the vivid green roof of a warehouse into an area for parking and what they describe as an 'outdoor lounge'. White graphics denote the ninety parking bays. Adjacent to this space, magenta seats (mesh drums filled with recycling materials) and circular planters dispersed across the surface of the 'lounge' form a didactic and poetic realm.

Gigon/Guyer Architekten
Museum of Transportation, Lucerne
1999–2000

The architects describe their 'Street Forum' building as suggesting 'movement on wheels'. Instead of stairs, they use enclosed ramps to link floors, encircling the simple, rectangular form. A language is derived from the exposure of the composite steel and concrete truss superstructure. When describing the rough concrete floors and soffits, the architects refer to roads. For them, the 'garage-like' aesthetic is tempered only by the expanse of glazing in the elevations.

Erdgeschoss +/- 0.00

Süd

Nord

Schnitt A - A

West

Ost

Schnitt B - B

Paul Rudolph
Temple Street, New Haven 1959–63

Home to Yale University, the town of New Haven has for the last forty-five years been a Mecca for those who enjoy *béton brut* and parking garages. In the mid-1950s, the local government began to replan a run-down district close to the city centre, New Haven Green. Predictably, a car park was to play a key role in this masterplan for a new commercial centre that would bring offices, department stores, a hotel and a bank to the area. Literally an extension of the road infrastructure, the intertwined entrance ramps at the southern end of the parking structure would form an umbilical cord between it and the Oak Street Connector expressway, linking the city centre with the Connecticut Turnpike. Commuting motorists would not have to set foot on Temple Street because of the series of integral pedestrian underpasses and bridges that would connect the car park to surrounding buildings, the kind of 'total' scenario that is today frowned upon because of the blight it causes to the public realm. The original intention was to extend the car park over the expressway; three times longer, the resulting megastructure would then have linked the two halves of New Haven. I do not intend to dwell on the urban plan, however. Instead, this 1,500-space, 270m-long, five-storey structure is about matter and light.

detail on corner of Temple and George Streets

'Most parking garages look like office buildings without glass,' Rudolph explained in 1961. 'I wanted to make [Temple Street] look like it belonged to the automobile and its movement...a system of bridges...of large open spans'.[33] The building is planned with an 'ABABA' rhythm. Nineteen paired columns, 3 m apart, which are in turn approximately 12m apart in three rows, support a six-deck, split-level structure; fifty-seven pairs in all. The module allows for one car to be parked between the paired columns, and three cars between each successive pair. The car park extends over two blocks and is bisected by George Street, where a deep beam transfers the load from the columns above onto a row of three columns on each side of the street.

The sheer length of the building creates a datum against which to measure topography, and the elevation reveals Temple Street's gentle incline. At the north end, there are four split-levels, but as the land falls away the section accommodates an additional mezzanine parking deck south of George Street. Below, an arcade of shops constitutes what Aldo Rossi would describe as an 'urban artefact'[34] – one that creates a place that elicits a response, a spatial element, which induces proximity to the fabric of the city and provides shade and shelter to which memory and body relate.

The Temple Street elevation describes accurately how the building stands up; the nineteen in-situ concrete cantilever structures are linked by short bridge sections to form a 'viaduct'. At each end, this is resolved with a 6 m cantilever. Columns are inset from the elevation. From the outside, this gives an anthropomorphic appearance – read columns as legs and deck as underbelly, fused by haunches. Column heads arch in all four directions to support the transverse vaults and integral spandrel barrier.

Light falling on the convex concrete forms of the barrier further accentuates the building's elephantine qualities. Each successive storey of columns emerges from the shadows of the deck below. Inside, columns and decks fuse into one monolithic, vaulted space. This is a cave for cars, illuminated by chandelier-like lights hung from the centre of each vault. The enclosure that the vault affords, and the warm pools of light cast on the pink boardmarked concrete, achieve an intimacy that is in stark contrast to the external expression.

Rudolph's use of boardmarked concrete seems to indicate the importance that he placed on matter. This is not a pragmatic use of concrete as a material best suited to civil-engineering projects and fire-resisting structures. In a sense, the brief seemed to envisage a 'port' for New Haven, much like Kahn's designs for Philadelphia. The reality could have been prosaic, however, simply the answer to a transportation question. But just as expressive form suggests that this structure was to transcend its purpose and fulfil a civic role, the 50 mm timbers used in forming the concrete throughout convey an idea about craft. The building is not machine-made and blemish free, the result of using fine ply or steel formers, but instead demonstrates that it is hand-made.[35] It therefore communicates by means of its haptic qualities through individual encounter. Textures and markings will over time be accentuated by weathering.[36]

below: detail of boardmarked concrete lights on roof deck

below: detail of haunch

The Owen Luder Partnership
Trinity Square, Gateshead 1967; Tricorn Centre, Portsmouth 1966

Trinity Square was immortalized in the 1971 film *Get Carter* by director Michael Hodges, a friend of Rodney Gordon, who was at the time one of the partners of the Owen Luder Partnership. In the film, Glenda and Carter speed to the top of the car park in her white, open-top Sunbeam Alpine, and then later, moments after Carter tips the developer Cliff Brumby to his death from one of the stair towers, one architect says to the other the now infamous line, 'I have an awful feeling we are not going to get our fees on this job' – a comic moment in a very dark film.

The real Brumby, Alec Coleman, won a competition to build a modern shopping centre on a sloping site that overlooked the Tyne, a scheme that the local council, who owned the site, hoped would help Gateshead rival neighbouring Newcastle. The centre was built over two levels, with fifty-three shops in all, including two supermarkets and a department store, serviced by an overhead road; above was a bowling alley. With no market for offices or luxury flats, the question was what to put on top. The answer was a car park. Car ownership had only really taken off in the UK in the late 1950s, so novelty would contribute to the parking structure's landmark potential. A nightclub on top of the tower would bring life twenty-four hours a day to the complex. Intriguingly, the punters would fill the parking tower from the bottom up by day and the top down by night, an idea that reappears in Birds Portchmouth Russum's unbuilt Croydromia (1993). Unfortunately the council, who leased the car park from Coleman, never sought a tenant for the nightclub and it remains a shell to this day.

Designed to take the weight of delivery vehicles, the service road necessitated a heavy concrete structure – a material strategy that, according to Owen Luder, provided a strong frame for the 'fairground' shopping centre below.[37] The inclined, 300 mm-thick, coffered parking decks above were cast with asbestos shuttering and the integral in-situ barriers were boardmarked. The barriers were also chamfered to reduce the dimensions of the parking decks. The seven-storey tower, planned for seventy-three cars per revolution (490 in total), is a continuous-ramp type, rectangular in plan, with oblique sections in the long elevation and flat 'landings' at each end.

detail of nightclub interior

parking deck

nightclub

ELEVATION FROM
LOOP ROAD PART I

230

charlotte st. portsmouth
OWEN LUDER ARCHITECTS
140 TACHBROOK STREET
LONDON S.W.1 Tel 01-834 2251

The Tricorn Centre, on the other hand, was the result of private negotiations between the same developer and Portsmouth Council, who were faced with replacing the wholesale market, the cost of which would result in a substantial annual deficit. Coleman acquired various pieces of land in addition to the market site, on which to build a 2,900 m²-department store, a supermarket and a further forty-eight shops, two pubs, a petrol station, flats, offices, a restaurant and market, and space for 500 cars. Again, the pedestrianized shopping centre would be served by an overhead service road. The parking here is spread over a series of six interlinking roof decks, accessed by helical ramps at opposing ends of the scheme – one up, one down – and used by lorries and vans to reach the service road. Unlike Trinity Square, the further three levels of parking that rise above the roof are split-level. The integral barriers are again boardmarked in-situ concrete, this time with a curved profile. In the service shafts, stairs and lift towers, there are clear signs of Le Corbusier and Luis Sert, especially in the half-hemispherical domes.

Trinity Square and the Tricorn Centre each has its genesis in the Partnership's Eros House (1959–62) in Catford, south London, in which a single-deck parking 'void' separates the shops below from the offices above. The scheme exposed the structure and services, and used formal expression to overcome any shortfall in the quality of construction. It was also designed to maximize the developer's profit. Both Gordon, in his 2002 article about the partnership in the 1960s, and Luder were keen to stress the commercial realities of constructing speculative buildings; the coarse concrete finishes that Le Corbusier had popularized could, of course, provide a medium for expressing construction, but could also leave the team a degree of latitude in execution.[38]

Trinity Square is angular, orthogonal, more literally ordered and tower-like. The Tricorn Centre, on its flat site, is bulbous, articulated by a skyline of towers – not exactly San Gimignano, but undoubtedly picturesque. Four hundred metres long,

it has a strong horizontal emphasis, in which only four elements (restaurant, office block and, most prominently, flats and parking decks) rise above a two-storey datum. Trinity Square, however, derives its drama from the site and the contrast between plinth and tower. It also has a fluidity that is read in the long, oblique elevations of the parking tower, a dynamic that culminates in the somewhat precariously placed nightclub and terrace. Tricorn is kasbah-like, with many vistas down narrow passageways, marked by shafts of concrete (think minarets and campaniles). The centre evokes other historic forms, no doubt made all the more plausible at the outset by the perspective of Gordon Cullen, architect and founder of the Townscape movement. Trinity Square is homogeneous, Tricorn heterogeneous, both are hard buildings and, like Warren Chalk and Ron Herron's contemporaneous Hayward Gallery and Queen Elizabeth Hall for London's South Bank, depend on the life that people and their ephemera (kiosks, shopfronts and signage) bring with them. The Tricorn Centre has now been demolished, and Trinity Square remains under threat. The latter has attained cult status, largely due to its association with *Get Carter*, but also because of its survival in such a prominent location, standing on the hill above Norman Foster's Sage Gateshead music building (2000–4) and Ellis Williams Architects' Baltic Centre for Contemporary Art (2001).

The Owen Luder Partnership was prolific, but Trinity Square and the Tricorn Centre, begun at a similar time, were the most accomplished of their many projects. Mixed-use schemes that incorporate parking are far from unique, but these two buildings both sought a heroic contribution from the strong order and dynamic that the car could bring. In both cases, parking transcends all else and is elevated 'high' above the city. In its final years before demolition, Tricorn was a forlorn, latter-day ruin that bore a strong resemblance to Hitler's French coastal fortifications: a city-centre Atlantic wall rejected as legitimate cityscape, and perhaps never the model popular place. When seen against a clear blue sky, it was bleak but fantastic.

ELEVATION FROM
PYE STREET PART II.

Roche Dinkeloo & Associates
Veterans Memorial Coliseum, New Haven 1972

Roche Dinkeloo's gigantic Veterans Memorial Coliseum, a three-storey steel table standing seven storeys above the ground, graced New Haven's skyline for just thirty-three years before demolition began in 2005. Underneath, an exhibition hall and street-level retail units (neither of which were ever completed) were planned for the site, along with a 9,000- to 11,500-seat arena for hockey, basketball and boxing. The clue to under-standing the extreme architecture of the Coliseum is in the area of the 3.44 ha site, in which a flat carpet of parking would have achieved just 1,300 spaces, fractionally more than half of the 2,400 required, with no arena, exhibition hall, shops or green space. Not only would it not 'fit', but the swathe of tarmac and cars that shopping malls, cinemas and sports stadiums bring with them, particularly in the US, would have blighted the scheme.

Rooftop parking was not unheard of. There was Victor Gruen's Milliron's store (1948) in Los Angeles, for example, and Arthur Ling's city-centre shopping scheme (1958) in Coventry. The obvious distinction here is that the Coliseum afforded no roof on which to park. Instead, the architects conceived of a 'table', 171 m by 110 m, raised 21 m above the street. This tabletop consisted of four steel decks for 600 cars each, suspended between ten 10 m-deep, 109 m-long steel trusses that spanned the short dimension of the table, which were in turn supported by twenty tile-clad concrete stanchions. Each truss spanned 59 m between the 6m-wide stanchions or table legs, and cantilevered nearly another 20 m beyond them at each end. The central span was divided into six structural bays and the cantilevers into two, and all were framed with diagonal struts. Two pairs of half-hexagonal trusses spanned over the arena, picking up the top chord of the fourth primary truss and transferring its load onto the two adjoining trusses and their stanchions, obviating the need for stanchions.

In placing the parking facility above the arena, explain the architects, 'the garage formed a shelter for the complex and allowed for easy pedestrian access to the facility from street level, as well as retail space'.[39] But in doing this, Roche Dinkeloo did

something quite remarkable to a public building. They chose to play down the arena and exhibition space, and to make the parking decks the primary element of expression. Each deck was divided into nine structural bays (19m by 110m), which without interruption could accommodate seventy-six cars. Just six parking bays were lost to the stair cores and one to the lift core. The remaining seventy-seven spaces were lost to longitudinal carriageways and access to the two helical ramps. In design, therefore, there was an exact fit between the module of the car (parking bay), the structural members and the plan, an achievement that is rarely possible with the usual site constraints on terra firma. Motorists ascended a helical ramp to the first parking deck, from which they would journey to the remaining three decks via two inclined sections, which were themselves 'park-on' ramps.

The resulting scheme was nearly three times the size of the site. At 1.9ha, each deck was more than three times the area of a soccer pitch, and nearly twice as long and twice as wide. The feeling of compression of space, therefore, that we associate with a parking structure finds its ultimate form in the Coliseum. The interstice between decks was about 3m, less than 1/36 of their width and 1/57 of their length. From the middle of one of these spaces, the outside world is but a brightly lit horizon. This strange construction, although briefly a reality, drew motorists seven or eight circuits up spiral ramps more than 21m into the air only to compress them, and made the individual intensely aware of the horizon that this elevated position afforded.

The contribution that structural steel made to this project must not be underestimated. The long spans of the table were only made possible by the deep trusses and their relatively fine sections, which generated a simple, strong and homogeneous graphic of thick and thin horizontal, vertical and oblique lines, beneath which the more heterogeneous masonry masses of the arena, exhibition space and shops stand. For the parking decks and trusses, the architects chose to use Corten,

a weathered steel, which is unusual in that it oxidizes, forming a layer of rust that protects the core. The tone of the steel further accentuated the dark interior, and the effect of this surface coating was to protect the section from further weathering. Having visited this colossal steel structure as it was being demolished and seeing the masonry base reduced to rubble, the choice of material adds a certain poignancy to its early fate.

Today, the language of the Coliseum lives on in the architects' adjacent Knights of Columbus office building (1968–70), a twenty-three-storey tower supported by four tile-clad concrete bastions, 9.1m in diameter, between which steel spandrel beams, 0.9m-deep, span the 22m between the towers. As if always intended as a memory of the Coliseum parking decks, the office floors enjoy the unobstructed views of the horizon made possible by this structure. After Eero Saarinen's death in 1961, Kevin Roche and John Dinkeloo inherited his office. The extreme character of first Saarinen's and later Roche and Dinkeloo's work is evident here in the scale, structural ingenuity and 'high drama' of the Coliseum parking decks.

Stirling Wilford & Associates with Walter Nägeli
Braun Headquarters, Melsungen 1986–92

Melsungen is a provincial medieval town, set in a valley some 30km from Kassel. Colourfully painted timber-frame buildings line the historic streets, where in 1839 Julius Wilhelm Braun bought the Rosen-Apotheke pharmacy. Having evolved into a global business, it is not surprising that Braun's presence is felt throughout the area.

Stirling Wilford's headquarters for B Braun AG lies just outside Melsungen in open fields, where the land forms a gentle vale framed by an escarpment to the south and a promontory to the north. The architects have conceived of an industrial cosmos that they suggest 'recalls the man-made objects in the landscape of the Roman *campagna*: viaducts, bridges, canals and embankments'.[40] It is easy to see why. A 200m-long concrete wall bisects the valley, and attached to it is a timber viaduct that appears to march across the site, linking the administration offices, laboratories, warehouse, dispatch and canteen. The masterplan is composed of closed (complete) and open (incomplete) elements, sketching out the anatomy of the processes and activities at Braun and articulating the dimension and nature of the landscape. The likelihood of future expansion greatly influences the function and position of certain buildings, each connected to the rest by a viaduct and an extended network of enclosed circulation decks. The ensemble, say the architects, is both evocative and functional.

The wall and viaduct provide both the order and the infrastructure for the site, to which the car park, a plain five-storey, steel-frame structure, is coupled. Although a 'section' building, it does not depend on visual abstraction, nor seeks refinement in plan, section, material or elevation. Instead, what is so unusual about the project are the conjunctions that it makes with the ground, the wall and the viaduct, and also the beauty that is derived from being incomplete. The masterplan creates a series of momentary encounters on a journey first by car and then on foot, an experience that both employees and visitors share (each employee has a designated space in the car park, whereas the open top deck is reserved for visitors).

The entrance to the site is west of the bisecting wall; from here, the journey to the car park crosses an idealized landscape. The road follows a sinuous canal that circumvents a lake, then drops into a cutting where it passes the end of the viaduct. Here, the scene changes abruptly as the motorist passes through an opening in the base of the heavy, concrete wall. The formal landscape is at once replaced by an informal one, dotted with industrial buildings, made all the more so by the open masterplan that sees a number of these elements being extended. In the foreground, the wall frames a view of the copper-clad computer centre and a pair of concrete silos, which are the in-and-out, up-and-down ramps to the car park. Inside each is a helical ramp in in-situ cast concrete, the structure cantilevered from the blind elevation. An apparently weightless form, the ramp revolves in the top light cast by an oculus overhead,

its progress tracked by a fine balustrade, otherwise uninterrupted by columns or downstand beams. With each rotation, the ramp arrives at a new level.

The next encounter comes on leaving the car park on foot. Concrete bridges and stairs span the chasm between parking structure and wall; angled and brightly painted, they accentuate the drama of departure and crossing the void to reach the wall. Pedestrians then step through a door and onto one of seven staircases traversing the long section of this strangely Egyptian structure. The staircases link the five parking decks with the viaduct level.

The 600-space car park is about half of its eventual size, which is dictated by the length of the viaduct and wall, and the position of the enclosed deck that links to the warehouse and loading bay. To the south of the car park, behind the wall, a no-man's land of roughly cut grass extends almost 100m. Here, the wall is punctuated by diagonally disposed openings inlaid with corrugated metal panels. These plugs mark the locations of future door positions and link bridges to the extended car park. The parking structure itself uses a steel frame braced by large, diagonal steel struts that support the five decks. Each deck, like an open book laid face down, is folded along its spine, with each half inclined towards the open edges (east and west). In section, the decks read as a stack of upturned Vs. From the outside, the long, eastern elevation is divided into fourteen structural bays; in each bay, the rainwater downpipe, two short gutters and the V-connection on each floor seem to mimic the building's structure and its use of steel props. Finally, seventy inclined concrete barriers complete the elevation. Like farm animals at a feeding trough, the cars line up behind the elevation, one to each barrier.

Glossed over in previous essays and articles devoted to the building itself, the drama of parking at the Braun headquarters has been largely overlooked. This is a sophisticated parking structure that derives its beauty from its unique relationship to site, uniting 'site-matter' with 'building-matter'. Pleasure comes from the devices employed to move cars and people through the section, from the light, and from the intimate encounters that particular situations afford.

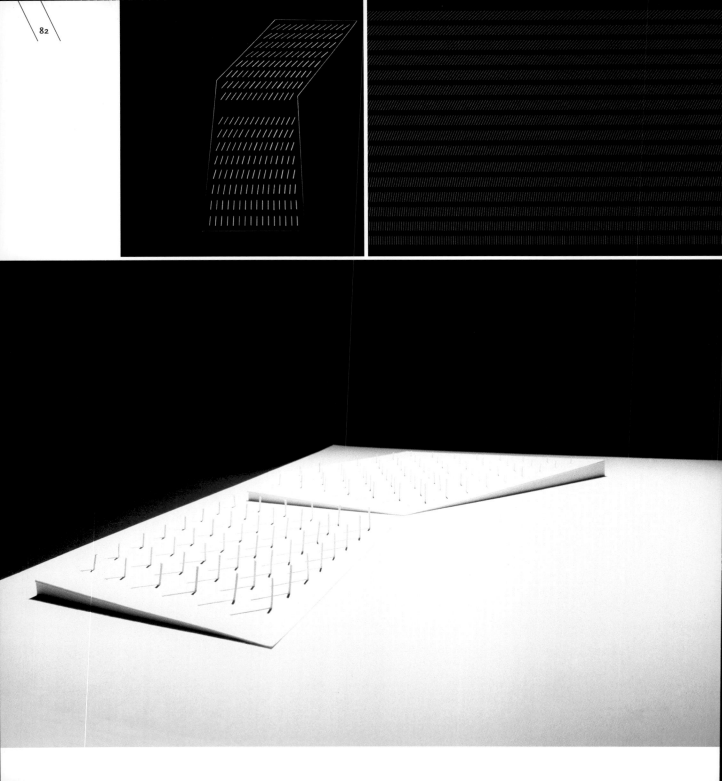

Zaha Hadid Architects
Hoenheim-Nord, Strasbourg 1998–2001

A field of white marks on a black background, the car park at Hoenheim-Nord is not a building, but rather a tilted canvas of tarmac laid out in a Strasbourg suburb at the northern extremity of a new tramline. Commissioned as an artist, architect Zaha Hadid did not have to contend with the conventional challenges that a parking structure presents; there were no ramps, no structure, no fire or ventilation regulations with which to comply, no elevations to design.

Hadid describes the concept as one of 'fields', where the 'patterns of movement [are] engendered by cars, trams, bicycles and pedestrians', each of which 'has a trajectory and a trace, as well as a static fixture'. It is, she explains, as though 'the transition between transport types…is rendered as the material and spatial transitions of the station, landscaping and the context'.[41] The 700-space parking lot is one component of a park-and-ride scheme, together with a tram terminus, and is tilted towards the terminus to emphasize a future connection to a train station planned to the immediate north of the site.

To express the site geometry, Hadid used conventionally prosaic media (the lines used to mark out the parking bays and lamp-posts) to synthesize a 'magnetic field'. Parallel lines of white paint, approximately 10m long, are arranged into fourteen bands and denote the space for two cars parked end-to-end. The bands are separated by a road and roundabout, with seven bands to the north of the road, and a further seven to the south. At the southern end of the site, the lines in the bands are orientated north–south, perpendicular to the carriageway, whereas the diverging geometry caused by the road resets the orientation of the seven bands to the north. Within each successive band, the lines gradually rotate and a head-on parking arrangement metamorphoses into an echelon one, described by an array of twenty-eight lines (twenty-seven parking bays) at the southern end of the site and twenty-five lines (twenty-four bays) to the north.

The car park is, therefore, effectively divided into two. The artificial topography created by the design superimposes two landforms, with the park forming a gentle valley with a low point where the road bisects the site and modified by a tilt from west to east. The resulting complex geometry generates high points in the northwest and southwest corners, and low points immediately north and south of the dividing road-way on the eastern edge, southwest of the tram terminus, where the tarmac surface is incised into the ground. By contrast, the scheme generates embankments along the south and west edges, and would along the northern edge but for an existing railway embankment. At every fourth parking bay is a vertical lamp-post, which are all set to a level datum at the top of the post. Their height and inclination relative to the ground provides a measure of the height and degree of tilt of the surface at that point. Finally, a large, white sweeping mark extends the geometries of the tram station roof and columns across the car park.

Simple and intuitive, the car park at Hoenheim-Nord brings the geometry of motion to the conventional parking lot. Like SITE's earlier 'Ghost Parking Lot' (1978) at the Hamden Plaza Shopping Centre in Connecticut, which submerged cars into a car park covered in a layer of tarmac, Hadid communicates a single strong idea about surface geometry measured against the module of the car.

elevation
order, construction and expression

2

Why is the elevation of a parking structure important? For reasons that might now be becoming familiar, the elevation of a car park 'functions' very differently from a conventional elevation, which gives the designer a certain freedom. It also communicates the building's order and its spatial and constructional logic, which is otherwise difficult to discern once inside. How does one

elevation

explain the elevation of a car park? The bleak, post-war buildings, with their geometric façades wrought in in-situ or pre-cast concrete, struck a note of discordancy in every provincial city in the developed world. These radically simplified elevations displayed their sections as elevations. However, this had not always been the case.

Before 1945, the multi-storey car park was still an unknown quantity. The requirements placed on the façades of parking structures seemed little different to those of any other building. Few understood the risk of fire, or that poor ventilation would result in dangerously high levels of carbon monoxide. With paint technology still undeveloped, cars, like people, needed to be kept warm and dry; Robert Mallet-Stevens' rendered elevations in Paris (1928) and Wallis Gilbert & Partners' Daimler Car Hire Garage (1931) in London's Bloomsbury both incorporated walls and windows. But with the advent of a new mass market of middle- and lower-income drivers, 'self parking' replaced attendant parking and the elevation was transformed. Income from each parking space declined, and the business of providing convenient and affordable parking became more competitive. Construction costs were slashed, codes governing ventilation and fire safety were introduced, walls and windows were discarded.

As multi-storey car parks began to proliferate in the 1950s, their elevations became rudimentary. Air was allowed to pass through the buildings, carrying away exhaust fumes and, more dramatically, smoke should there be a fire. Instead of walls, barriers were incorporated to prevent inexperienced motorists from driving off the decks. The simple frame-nature of the multi-storey car park was plain to see in Robert Law Weed's Miami structure, for example, and in that of Aeck Associates in Atlanta, where the interlocking split-level concrete decks allowed car boots and bonnets to dovetail one above the other. The convergence of architecture and engineering in a single design of columns and cantilevered slabs underlined the utility and efficiency of the car park. These constructions varied enormously, all using abstract patterns of essential elements in any number of geometric permutations.

One of the ten parking structures commissioned in Chicago in the early 1950s was Parking Facility No 1, designed by Shaw, Metz & Dolio and perhaps the purest graphic building with its pattern of thick horizontal lines (decks) and fine verticals (cables). The multi-storey car park could now be described as a naked, skeletal form consisting of columns, slabs and barriers, distinguished by the scale of the dark lift hall or the geometry of the ramps, and punctuated by passenger lifts and staircases. While the slenderness of Parking Facility No 1's elevation was perhaps only matched in the 1970s by Frank Gehry's Santa Monica car park, the idiom was established: spare, almost incomplete buildings, using only the most basic of structural materials, with little or no fenestration and no finishes. The patterning of the elevation and the internal slab-and-ramp geometry became the main features of a demonstrable design.

During the 1950s and 1960s, the dominant elevation pattern employed horizontal banding, or strata, in which floor and barrier were united in a single element

Aeck Associates, parking garage, Atlanta 1954

running the length of the building, a design that used in-situ or pre-cast spandrel panels – often with decorative concrete – to stiffen the cantilevered edge of the exposed floor slab. The panels were typically pared down to a simple, orthogonal shape. This type can be found in most American and European cities, and was used to great effect in such schemes as Jelinek-Karl's Rupert Street car park (1960), in Bristol, and Grenfell Baines & Hargreaves' bus station (1965–69) in Preston. The elevation is transformed into a pictorial surface of light (the barriers) and dark bands (the open storeys), an idea envisaged by Mies van der Rohe in his 'Concrete Office Building Project' of 1923.[42] With its continuous concrete spandrel panel, it could be easily mistaken for a post-war reinforced concrete parking structure but for the strip of glazing on each floor. This pattern also occurs in the historically and geographically remote seventh- and eighth-century Buddhist cave temples at Ellora, in Maharashtra, India.

Fitch & Phillips' Star Ferry Concourse car park (1957), in Hong Kong, employed a honeycomb elevation of rectangular and circular voids,[43] as did the Kaufhof in Dusseldorf, an idea reprised by Von Gerkan, Marg & Partner for their white-square concrete Regional Postal Directorate (1984–86), in Braunschweig, and by IaN+ for their Stazione Nuovo Salario (under construction) in Rome. The latter's supersized honeycomb, however, in a way more closely resembles the constructional technique of Michael Blampied's Debenhams car park (1970) on Welbeck Street in London's West End, which used a diagrid elevation structure of stacked pre-cast concrete arrowhead frames. Here one thinks of the geometric elevations of Marcel Breuer and Gordon Bunshaft, who combined an Escher-like interest for pattern-making with a greater structural order.

The heaviness of the elevation ended with Gehry's six-storey 'South Parking Structure' (1973–80). Poised at the north end of Main Street in Santa Monica, it uses blue chain-link fencing as the medium on which to write the name of the shopping centre. Each letter, in white chain-link, is nearly three storeys high, and the three words, 'Santa Monica Place', stretch some 100m across the length of the elevation. The material itself is held in tension between bars, top and bottom fixed back to the structure. The fine-grained material is transformed at close quarters into a dense surface, the absolute opposite of how it appears from afar; the words are 'simultaneously transparent and unmistakably legible'.[44] From a distance, the mesh becomes almost invisible; the text hangs on a veil over the parking decks and cars that are visible behind. Gehry achieved what architects Robert Venturi, Denise Scott Brown and Steven Izenour had observed in their 1972 book *Learning from Las Vegas*, and had previously tried out in their Fire Station No 4 (1965) and Football Hall of Fame competition (1967). Gehry treated the elevation as an advertising billboard,

Buddhist cave temples, Ellora, Maharashtra, India 7th–8th century

Frank Gehry, Santa Monica Place 1973–80

Frank Gehry, Santa Monica Place 1973–80

L.G. Farrant, ZCMI parking garage, Salt Lake City

//////////////// see case study pp.132–137

pure communication directed at the advancing motorist,[45] providing, as he explained, 'a unique, indelible graphic image that can be read at any speed'.[46]

Gehry had demonstrated that, in making a design or pattern, there is a suggestion that the face of a building can be reduced to, perhaps, one idea about material, one about shape, module, scale, joint, hue and tone. There is no need for comfort. The designer is not limited by a requirement to address issues such as cold bridging and insulation. The elevation demands the economic use of (structural) materials in response to evenly spaced parked cars, and the need for even distribution of daylight and air (i.e., openings) and, similarly, perimeter guarding. The figuration in plan is again prevalent in elevation. The elevation is functionally homogenized, and varies only when there is a conscious decision on the part of the designer to dehomogenize it. With no scruples and few regulations, the designer is in the enviable position of composer, indebted to an education in organizing and ordering. The potential for abstraction that the problem affords is unique.

There are, however, some notable exceptions to the homogeneous. The type that articulates the ramp (rather than the oblique deck), such as Gruen's scissor-ramped Milliron's store (1948) in Los Angeles, which plays on the dynamic. In the case of Melnikov's variant for an unbuilt Car Park for 1,000 Vehicles (1925), this otherwise homogeneous, cube-like structure has a clock at the centre of the elevation, in front of which the descending car must pass on a ramp. Another exception arises with the expressive potential of echelon parking. For the ZCMI structure in Salt Lake City, L.G. Farrant used the repetitive element of a steel cage to mark the line of each echelon parking bay. Each car is encased in the resulting saw-tooth elevation. But with Cabinet Genard's Place Victor Hugo bus station and car park (1958–59), in Toulouse, the plan is organized into two halves to accommodate first a carriageway, and then echelon parking. This is expressed first in a smooth white concrete spandrel, and then switches to a spandrel that is serrated in plan. On each consecutive floor, this motif is reversed with an overlapping section in the centre of the plan.

Postmodernism brought an end to the abstraction; overnight, the technique changed to that of representation. Concealment became the name of the game; derided for its grotesque appearance, the car park had to change. The superstructure was suppressed behind a variety of more palatable forms and façades, some comic, others earnest historic facsimiles. Bad examples abound. Two rare exceptions were Tigerman Fugman McCurry's parking structure in Chicago, which, in a twelve-storey, two-dimensional composition, replicates a mutant pre-war roadster's radiator grille. Instead of architectural expression that relied on 'distortion and over-articulation',[47] such as the continuous surface and echelon parking inside, the architects made a 'decorated shed'.[48] The second, Birds Portchmouth Russum's

Avenue de Chartres car park (1991) in Chichester, rewrote this small city's third dimension by extending the city wall to conceal a new parking structure.

/ / / / / / / / / / / / / / / see case study pp.166–169

Today, the makers of the parking structure have rediscovered the art of the elevation. A new generation of refined buildings is emerging that capitalizes on the uniquely simple demands of the type in a search for the material and sculptural sublime, such as Hentrich-Petschnigg & Partner's bamboo-clad structure for the Parkhaus Zoo Leipzig. Their decision to use bamboo seems to signify two things,

/ see pp.110–111

both represented by its natural state: one is the broader, ethical dimension of zookeeping, the other is the more direct contrast that is derived viscerally from the irregular but congruent shafts of bamboo as a setting in which to arrange cars. Occasionally concrete but more often timber, metal, cast glass and polycarbonate, arranged in fine sections or stretched tight as a skin, these forms are predisposed to an architecture of the single surface. If there is a significant difference between the post-war generation and the current one of elevations, it is that the first was generally modular whereas the latter is more skin-like.

The brutish, heroic structures of the post-war era conveyed a simple marriage of decoration and engineering. Abstract and geometric, they openly investigated a number of the technical challenges associated with the parking structure. Their elevations could be characterized as incomplete – frames without glass, devoid of reflection – and have more in common with the mosques, temples and palaces of the Indian subcontinent, which used finely perforated stone screens to combine visual privacy with good ventilation, and to protect those within from direct sunlight and women from the eyes of men. The elevations of the post-war car park were poured, cast or woven, and, like the *jali* screens, sieved the light that fell on the rough, oil-stained concrete surfaces and the shiny automobile bodies. Darkness is broken.

The Amber Palace, Rajasthan, 16th century

The elevation is often the means by which the multi-storey car park is judged. But how matter is then disposed in elevation, and the effect that the elevation has on a daylit interior, are all interlinked. An anonymous example on the Ratingerstraße in Dusseldorf illustrates that there is an effect on the pattern of light in the interior. The parking decks are cast with clerestorey and floor-level daylight, which in this instance appears to play a part in supporting the building. Each car park has a different emphasis. With some, the space can be experienced as an incline judged by the inner ear and in others as a world of rough surfaces, but with most it is the strong contrast between dark deck (soffit and floor) and the bright band of light seen around the perimeter dividing each deck from the next. Here in the Ratingerstraße structure, the grain of the elevation transforms that otherwise binary condition, filtering the natural light source into any number of patterns and intensities: direct, reflected and diffuse.

Multi-storey parking garage, Ratingerstraße, Dusseldorf

The best elevations depend for their originality on the functional and economic eccentricities of the parking structure. Equally, they can afford to be the reason for introducing abstract decoration into the city. Perhaps the greats were the brave new structures of the post-war years, which illustrate the original contribution that the multi-storey parking structure could make to the composition and design of the architectural elevation, a paradigm that is, with the work of Mahler, Günster, Fuchs in Heilbronn and IaN+ in Rome, once again on the move, in part due to renewed interest in housing the car.

Bath, bus station

Preston, bus station

Pavilion Road, London

Seattle

Kaufhof, Dusseldorf

Prince Street, Bristol

The Triangle, Bristol

Ratingerstraße, Dusseldorf

Reading

Young Street, London

Bordeaux

Swindon

Taunton

New York

Kaufhof, Dusseldorf

Santa Monica Place, Los Angeles

Fatehpur Sikri

Cabinet Genard
Place Victor Hugo, Toulouse 1958–59

The Place Victor Hugo site stacks parking over offices, restaurants and a covered market. Framed by double-helix up/down ramps at each end, this 100m-long, cream-painted, reinforced concrete structure is distinguished by the expression of its echelon parking bays. These are manifest in the zigzag barriers that stretch out over half the length of the building before flatlining to the end of the elevation. The composition is reversed on each subsequent level.

Von Gerkan, Marg & Partner
Regional Postal Directorate, Braunschweig 1984–86

This split-level parking structure uses a non-loadbearing honeycomb of pre-cast concrete elements in an elevation that meets the need for natural ventilation and daylight to the interior. Outside, one is largely unaware of the cars concealed by the elevation and is instead acutely aware of the building's strange scale and the effect of light and shadow in the openings.

Brian Healy Architects
Lincoln Street, Boston 1999

Recently renovated and reclad, this 'hybrid'
sandwich of a building, originally dating from
the 1950s, stacks an office on top of two parking
decks, a restaurant and a Chinese supermarket.
In a sense it is mundane, but it is also fantastic
with its motley collection of uses one on top of
the other. The elevations are also experimenta-
tions in cladding and lead to the idea of typologi-
cally derived elevations, a revelation here because
of the unprecedented juxtaposition of type.

TEN Arquitectos
Princeton University, Princeton 1998-2000

This parking structure is located on the southern edge of Princeton University, where a large parking lot existed previously. By positioning the structure opposite an existing tower and next to a building that houses the hockey rink, this new building completes a public space that will eventually become a campus plaza. The project reskins a mundane, pre-cast concrete parking structure (20,000 m²), already erected on the site. The stainless-steel wrap ensures good daylight and natural ventilation. Although it has the ability to change its appearance from one that is transparent, translucent or opaque depending on the time of day, the incidence of light or position and the material richness, cannot deny the silhouette behind.

Henn Architekten
Autotürme, Wolfsburg 1994

Theme park or car park, the Autotürme in
Wolfsburg, home of Volkswagen, is a strange
mix of science fiction and marketing genius.
A pair of elliptical, nineteen-storey towers stands
alone in a reflecting pool and forms the backdrop
to a complex of pavilions, set in a garden landscape, that celebrate the Volkswagen family of car
manufacturers. Although the towers are more
than 50m high and create quite a spectacle from
the outside, it is the futuristic interior, stacked
with the repetitive presence of the car but otherwise uninhabited, and enlivened by the activity of
the automated arm, that is disturbing. This is a
car park, but one that can only be experienced
remotely, and as an object rather than as a space.

Hentrich-Petschnigg & Partner
Parkhaus Zoo Leipzig, Leipzig 2002

The five parking decks of the steel-framed
Parkhaus are each divided into two parallel
carriageways, with a pair of spiral access ramps
at the end. The architects then wrapped a
bamboo veil around the structure, generating
both convexity and concavity. The bamboo,
110mm in diameter with 75mm gaps, screens
the cars and permits ventilation and dramatically
shadowed daylight. These bamboo walls suggest
a strong association with the natural world, and
therefore with the premise of the zoo itself, being
both exotic and inviting of ethical interpretation.
The allusions to conservation disassociate the
structure from the CO_2-emitting cars that it was
designed to accommodate. Brilliantly, Parkhaus
Zoo Leipzig leaves a lasting impression of a primitive, idyllic and natural prototype for a parking
structure. It is both beautiful and didactic.

IaN+
Parcheggio Nuovo Salario, Rome 2001

Inspired by naturally occurring cellular forms, the building's elevation is constructed from variously sized hollow concrete blocks, which project beyond the line of the parking deck above that they support and thus create a series of heterogeneous 'rooms' within an elevational 'zone'. The project challenges the conventional wisdom that presumes repetition in a parking structure. Instead, the car park is clearly a medium for decoration, in which the module of the car and the economics of construction in no way influence the picturesque order of the elevation.

Paul Schneider-Esleben
Parkhaus Haniel, Dusseldorf 1953

A glass case encloses a heavy concrete frame. Outside, a straight ramp the length of the building stretches up to the third floor. Next to this, a single-storey pavilion balances on a row of nine concrete columns. Parkhaus Haniel, designed by Paul Schneider-Esleben in the suburb of Flingern Nord, was the first multi-storey car park to be completed in West Germany after the war. The main four-storey structure originally housed a service station, office and stores on the ground floor, and 500 parking spaces on the three floors above, while the pavilion contained a small hotel and staff accommodation, with petrol pumps, control booth, entrance and exit underneath.

Today, the main building has been converted into a showroom for BMW, with a McDonald's replacing the ground-floor service station. The smooth glass surfaces of the façade depicted in black-and-white photographs from the 1950s survive, but the window sections now stretch a fishnet of turquoise over the building. A worse fate for such an historic building of its type and time is hard to imagine. It is tempting to picture a more forward-thinking conversion that would have placed the drive-through McDonald's on the top floor of the main building, demanding its clientele to drive up the long roadside ramp to the third floor, collect their burgers, and return to street level down the identical ramp to the rear.

More than fifty years of traffic planning, commercial development and signage makes it difficult to read the sculptural and material clarity of this structure today. But at night, without the foreground distractions, the in-situ concrete frame is revealed: three parking decks and a butterfly roof supported on three rows of rectangular columns, forty-five in all. The columns are positioned 2.5m in from the gable elevations,

and more than 3m in from the street and rear elevations. The skeleton of columns branch out under the projecting roof to support fifteen cantilevered, tapering downstand beams, which in turn support the up- and down-ramps suspended from the roof on 28mm steel hangers – a very clear diagram.

Parkhaus Haniel illustrates well both its structural logic and its skin. By day, the reflections of the neighbouring buildings and passing clouds conceal the interior and structural frame. At night, the picture reverses. The glass disappears, leaving only the fine black lines of mullions and transoms in silhouette, through which the greater order of the concrete skeleton is illuminated under artificial light.

Shaw, Metz & Dolio
Parking Facility No 1, Chicago 1955

Parking Facility No 1, a sixteen-storey, lift-type garage on Wacker Drive, is one of ten parking structures commissioned in Chicago in the 1950s. Like the majority of lift-types, this car park, designed by Shaw, Metz & Dolio, has a central lift hall with two flanking multi-storey parking 'towers'. The building is divided in section into three parts, the first of which is a three-storey plinth designed to connect at the upper and lower levels to the Upper- and Lower Wacker Drive decks. These reception and collection floors – arrival on the right, departure on the left – include customer waiting rooms and enough space for motorists to queue off-road on arrival and for attendants to pool cars awaiting collection. The intermediate of these three floors is a parking deck, three cars deep on each side of the hall. Above the plinth rises the eleven-storey body of the car park, in which cars are parked two deep on open-sided decks, again on either side of the hall. The final two-storey element houses the five overhead cranes, from which the Bowser System lifts are suspended.

plan of reception and collection floor, Lower Wacker Drive

plan of reception and collection floor, Upper Wacker Drive

Inside the 44m-long, 6.5m-wide, 45m-high hall, five lifts shuttle left and right, up and down, each guided by an attendant who works the mechanism from the lift within the car. This central space is, in effect, five separate but contiguous lift shafts. There is a stark contrast between the hall and the flanking parking decks. The hall, which is of cathedral-nave proportions, is inhabited by five steel truss structures suspended from the roof, guided by a single rail at the base. At intervals, 'clothes-hanger' elements project from the body of the truss. Steel dominates, the section sizes are small, associations with dockyard and rocket launch pads are inevitable; there is a literalness about it. The ends of the hall are closed off with high masonry walls, which incorporate stairs and bridges between the two wings, and the interior, therefore, is not visible from the street. Each of the eleven-storey blocks is supported by a dozen columns. Beams span the column lines, with a shallower pan section in between. The concrete floors are cantilevered and taper towards the perimeter. Vertical cables, 9mm in diameter and stretching eleven storeys, act as the guard. Each cable is restrained at the top with a turnbuckle to adjust the tension, and at the bottom with a coil spring to keep the tension. The cables are threaded through 7.5cm tubes in each slab.

As a composition, the elevation is beautiful. It simply superimposes a pattern of thick horizontal lines (the cantilevered concrete floor slabs) over one of fine verticals (the tension cables). Hundreds of parallel vertical lines cascade behind the heavy horizontal lines of the eleven concrete parking decks. The architects' composition is a careful one, in which the verticals, set out 20cm apart, form the backdrop, thus allowing the thicker 30cm deck edges to dominate (each spaced about 3m apart). The cables are immersed in the shadowy background. The long elevation is illustrated on the jacket of Klose's *Multi-Storey Car Parks and Garages*; in the photograph, cars are lined up behind the 'bars'. The picture demonstrates just how pared down the building was, and how abstract the elevation. The graphic lines that form the elevation in the foreground provide a simple measure against which to judge both the scale and complex forms of the cars.

typical floor plan

Michael Blampied
Debenhams, London 1970

Michael Blampied's structural elevation for his car park for Debenhams, in central London, illustrates beautifully the convergence of tectonic matter and geometric composition. Contemporary accounts of the building stressed economy and practicality in the face of public indifference, noting the prejudice against car parks that were seen as 'a necessary evil and should be screened or disguised in some way'.[49] Screened yes, but not disguised. The paper from which this quote is taken gives us an unprecedented insight into the design and construction of a generation of city-centre parking structures, buildings to which we rarely give any thought – and if we do, it is to vilify. Although abstract, the car park's elevation communicates what it is; Kenneth Frampton summarized Umberto Eco's observation by stating that 'as soon as one has an object of "use", one necessarily has a sign that is indicative of that use'.[50]

The plan is an irregular polygon, the result of imposing a module of the conventional 15.7 m parking deck upon a truncated, triangular site. This shape is replicated over ten levels, utilizing a split-deck section. But it is the elevation, not the plan or section, that generates the design. Highly permeable elevations on three sides were required to achieve the necessary natural ventilation; the fourth side was a party wall. Economy led the team to reject the initial scheme of structural columns and non-structural cladding, and to develop a system of pre-cast concrete, load-bearing Y-columns that would support the building perimeter. The Y, which required additional horizontal restraint mid-storey at the apex, evolved by degrees into a V that would span and support successive floors.

As the shape evolved, so, too, did its modular dimension in plan, which was reduced in the built unit to 2 m to fit all three elevations. Geometric rules and construction techniques and tolerances played their part in a design that evolved through the use of models at 1:12, 1:4, and a full-scale polystyrene mock-up, the latter left outside to test weathering and marking. The V is in effect an equilateral triangle, with the top two corners chamfered to form a cleft between each pair, into which each successive V fits and generates a diagonal array. The V is repeated on all three elevations, except where on alternate floors a non-standard component turns the corner, and at every level, apart from the ground floor where a sequence of T-components and interlocking keystones forms a base storey. The elevation is marked by shadows, the result of chamfering the face of each component and of 25 mm construction joints between each, a device that appears to deny the load-bearing quality of the elevation. The aggregate is white and the concrete is acid-etched.

T-column and keystone detail

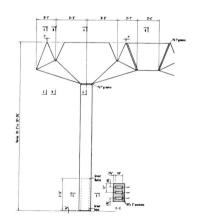

Behind the Vs, a second filigree screen of vertical 5mm stainless-steel tension cables at 24.5cm centres protects pedestrians and motorists. Like those used at Parking Facility No 1, in Chicago, the cables span from the top deck and pass through each successive deck to anchor at first-floor level. Finally, behind the cables is a

300 mm-deep plastic barrier. Inside, a 9.5 m-wide, in-situ concrete fin wall and slab core anchor the structure. This element runs the length of the building, incorporating lift, stair cores and ramps that link the split levels. Pre-cast concrete beams span the in-situ core and perimeter load-bearing Vs, which are set at 1m centres, half of the 2 m V-module and offset from the V-joints. Together, the pre-cast planks and in-situ floor is just 10cm thick. Steel bolts connect the beams to the Vs. The structure is made into one monolithic whole by pouring concrete into the head of the T and V and over the pre-cast beams and planks.

The effect of this myriad of pre-cast components on the soffit and in the elevation, the low reflectance of their grey surfaces, and the shadows cast by the elevation and the electric lights between the beams, is to suggest the tectonic (although not the space) of a compressed medieval hall with masonry walls and closely spaced, heavy timber beams. The muscular haunches of the concrete fin walls that stand either side of the ramps accentuate this. Around the perimeter, the view is bleached out by the contrast in light levels, but the glare does not mask the impression that each deck is supported off the one below by a continuous vertical truss with diagonal members, an illusion brought about by the masking of the horizontal chord of each V-section by the parking deck section.

From the outside, each V-form is hollow, the cables behind making it possible to carve out the centre. This diagonal array creates a diamond pattern, in which each diamond consists of a part-solid triangle below (the structural V) and an inverted empty triangular void above (the space between two structural Vs). The pattern conceals the conventional section to portray the structure as a single, wicker-like

frame (21 m high, 36 m wide and 40 m long). At the corner, the special pre-cast components used at two-storey intervals link the regular pattern of V-sections. Each is again a V, but realized in three dimensions. The result is a building that is, quite simply, sculpture – a field of tessellating forms and faceted surfaces wrought in a multitude of different tones. The pattern of the elevation is not derived directly from wall, column or barrier (the cables). Invisible to the naked eye, from the street, it is the barrier that allows for the abstraction. Similar structures in Bristol and Reading in the UK employ an X-component instead of the V.

above: elevation studies

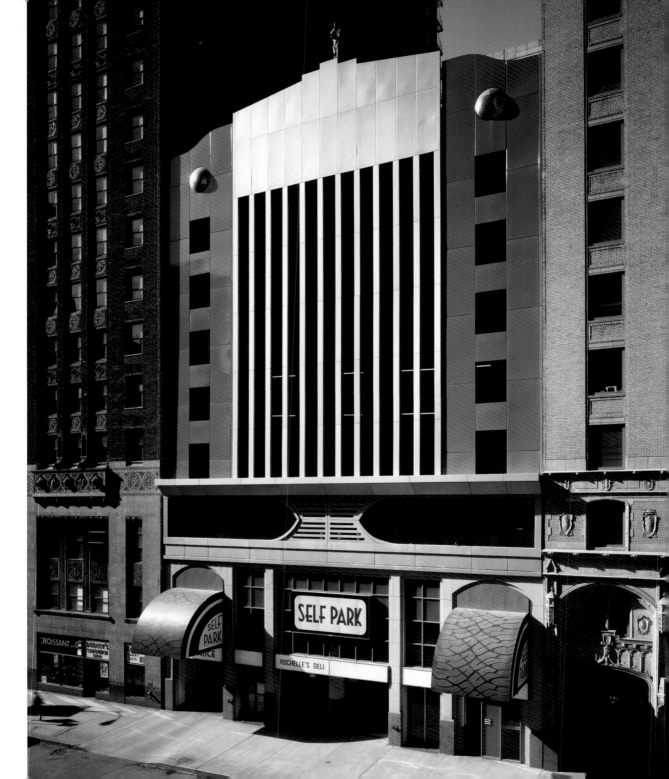

Tigerman Fugman McCurry
60 East Lake Street, Chicago 1984–86

Chicago's programme in the 1950s of building forty-four car parks demonstrated the impact that these structures could have on a city.[51] It was employment numbers and shopping patterns, traffic studies and infrastructure re-engineering plans (in short, statistics) that gave rise to these utilitarian buildings. Although at the time this had nothing to do with appearance and everything to do with how parking cars fitted into the bigger picture of convenience and efficiency, their other great impact was to be physical. Long and low, set amongst their rather stocky neighbours – office and apartment 'building blocks'– these buildings created strange voids in the city. Unquestionably modern, they expressed their construction clearly, early textbook examples of the mature parking structure. Today these techniques have been refined and modified, and we have returned to the same abstract explicit constructions. But for a time, doubts about car-park design led to such structures being disguised.

Thirty years later, the 1980s produced one fine example of masquerade, rather than disguise. The client's instruction was specific: 'I want it to look like a garage, not the Baths of Caracalla'.[52] The resulting building at 60 East Lake Street shows no outward signs of construction (it is a 'car', not a 'car park'), and the history to which it refers is not that of buildings but of cars. And for all the problems the small plot size (about 21.5m by 42.8m) raised, there is no sign of its internal workings. A 'schematic flow diagram' produced by the architects illustrates most prosaically its practical nature. There are no floors as such. Instead, a steep, rectangular helix (continuous surface) intelli-gently segregates the parking decks into an 'up' and 'down' flow (in effect, a double-helix) to create a single ramp that winds up twelve storeys before descending back down to street level. At a number of points (the third, fifth, seventh and eleventh levels), crossovers provide the means to short-cut a journey that would otherwise lead to the roof and back. One hundred and ninety-nine parking spaces, just twenty per floor, hug the centre of the plan and the East Lake Street elevation. Equally sophisticated is its post-tensioned, in-situ concrete structure. Unlike its predecessors of the 1950s, the plot has been 'filled' due to the pressure to develop, giving rise to a building 'block' more akin to its neighbours.

Outwardly, the elevation conceals its spatial order, that of the oblique, and its structural matter. Instead, the elevation is modelled on a 'classic touring automobile circa 1930 seen from the front. The twelve-storey car is complete with chrome-plated grille, headlights, bumper, stylized fenders painted a 1957 Chevy shade of turquoise, and awnings which mimic the tyres...clearly establish[ing] its identity as a parking garage'.[53] There are undoubtedly shades of Robert Mallet-Stevens' Art Nouveau garage for Alfa Romeo (1928) in Tigerman's design. But whereas Mallet-Stevens' symmetrical elevation reflects a symmetrical car entrance and exit diagram on the same street, this is not the case with Tigerman's amalgam of aluminium, baked enamel and

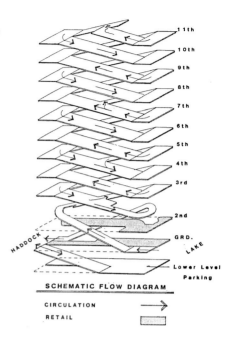

SCHEMATIC FLOW DIAGRAM

CIRCULATION ⟶
RETAIL ▭

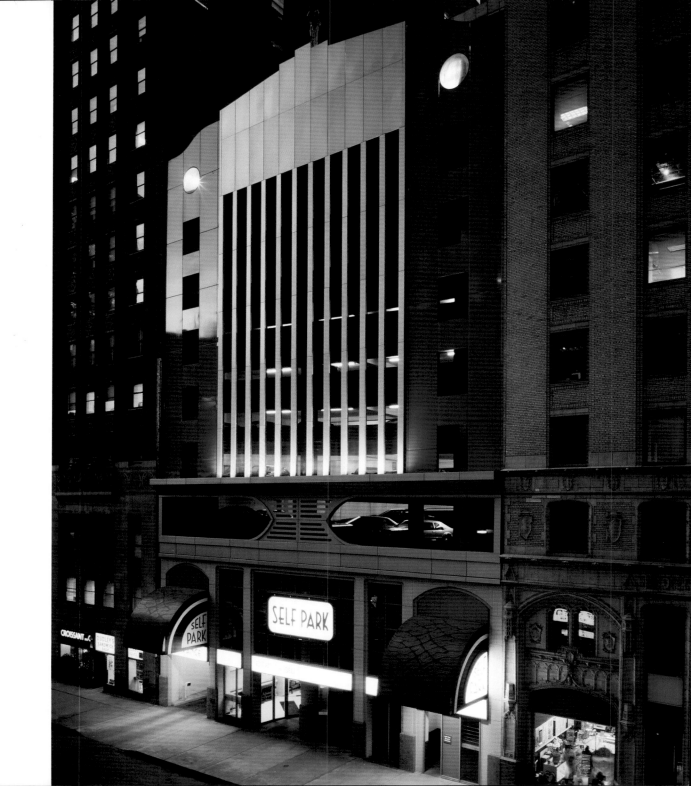

chain-link fencing. Instead of a homogeneous elevation patterned to achieve the necessary ventilation, the elevation, in mimicking the car, wilfully introduces significant expanses of cladding that do not allow the free passage of air, which is relieved only by a super-scale engine grille incorporated into this cartoon of a car.

The car park at 60 East Lake Street raises an interesting question: to what extent was the prolific period of car-park building (the 1950s to the 1970s) producing carefully conceived architectural forms, or simply accidents of utilitarianism? Were they intended to be things of beauty? Tigerman Fugman McCurry's building, the exception to any rule about car-park design, was the interval between two acts, which in radically distancing itself from the first arguably functional generation, gave it a certain legitimacy and the hindsight with which to look back on the previous generation as generically intentional, rather than accidentally aesthetic.

Kengo Kuma & Associates
Takasaki Parking Building, Takasaki 2001

The Takasaki Parking Building was perhaps the ideal commission for Kengo Kuma, an architect who has sought to 'de-emphasize the solidity of architecture',[54] and who has made a shift from the 'fragmentary' Small Bath House (1988) and the collaged historicist forms of the M2 Building (1991) to working with 'neutralized forms rather than fragmenting [ones]'.[55] This move towards minimalism was at the time unsurprising. What is relatively unusual, however, is Kuma's persistent use of the metal or timber slat and bamboo for screening interiors. Here is a building type, therefore, that does not require a conventional façade to keep out moisture and keep in heat, and for which a distributed elevation, a form of abstraction in itself, is a functional necessity, ensuring natural ventilation and mitigating the risk of carbon monoxide inhalation and, in extreme cases, fire.

This is a gargantuan 150m-long, 35m-deep, seven-storey structure for 1,000 cars that reflects the commissioners' request that the building reflect the city colour of Takasaki: brick. Kuma veiled the steel frame in pre-cast concrete louvres, and the result is a brown box interspersed with translucent glass louvres arranged at different angles to the elevation. When louvres are occasionally perpendicular, it is to keep clear the views of the sky; the glass louvres are used in front of the lifts and stairs to

improve natural illumination. The structure's louvres illustrate well the concepts of repetition and syncopated rhythm, regularly distributed but irregularly orientated. The louvre module is a standard dimension, and the array is also a standard dimension, imbuing the building with a singular character.

Whilst the louvres are literally fragments in the elevation, their intense regularity gives the structure presence, not as the frame, the non-building or engineered infrastructure that it might be, but as a solid. Furthermore, the authority's second aspiration that Kuma devise 'an architecture that doesn't make a parking lot look like a parking lot' is a total failure. But this observation is a compliment. Admittedly one can hardly see the cars and the building is not a heavy concrete structure, but Kuma has made the archetypal car-park elevation – a critique of a previous generation and at home with his present peer group. Gregg Lynn, in a 1997 article for *Space Design*, has compared Kuma's work to Pointillism.[56] Kuma himself uses the word 'particlization' to explain the repetition,[57] a term that might be applied to a great many multi-storey car parks that rely heavily on the abstract use of matter to make a carefully crafted response to ventilation, daylight and concealment.

left: detail at corner of building of pre-cast concrete louvres and ramp

right: detail of elevation

animating the utilitarian

3 light

Inside a parking garage, we experience an architecture of compression, of partial enclosure, of the horizon. The commercial pressure to minimize cost fixes the clearance between decks close to the head height of a car, yet the floor plates are typically 16-, 32- or 48 m wide, creating extremely deep spaces that can be as wide as a football pitch. In these seams of **light** space, it is no wonder that we sense this compression between the concrete strata, a sensation further heightened by fluorescent light. In addition, the low reflectance of the grey concrete surfaces, together with the often distant perimeter band of bright light visible outside, creates a strong contrast to the eye, causing glare. The mind plays tricks on the disabled eye.

We wonder what lurks in the shadows and become prey to imaginations fuelled by all-too-vivid scenes in books and movies that use the car park as the setting for illicit exchanges or violence. The dereliction and emptiness of these cavernous spaces only add to this feeling of unease. It is an experience for which none of us are prepared, being more comfortable in inhabited and evenly lit spaces, of which the interior of a car park is the very antithesis. Light is a strong component in constructing its unique reality.

The key variables in the design of a car park that affect the amount and distribution of light are the depth of the plan, the type or pattern of the elevation's cladding and the distribution of apertures. In the middle of a deep-plan structure, the contrast between the unremitting darkness and the lines of light on the horizon is so extreme that the eye cannot compensate, which bleaches colour and tone from the context. With simply banded claddings, this condition translates on the interior into a binary system of light. A more sophisticated cladding, whose geometrical order divides the light source, may temper this with vertical lines, triangles or polygons.

An elevation of storey-high, rectangular GRP (glass-reinforced plastic) hoops between decks in Roy Chamberlain Associates' Young Street car park (1970), in London, filters the incoming daylight in a manner reminiscent of a Hepworth sculpture. In effect, each pair of louvres is conjoined to create a void, the space described by these primitive forms suspended within the façade. The elevation, therefore, comprises a multitude of these voids, which cast a pattern of empty spaces on the interior surfaces. Similarly, concrete and glass baffles in the elevation characterize Kengo Kuma's Takasaki Parking Building, where the differently oriented baffles create patterns of light and dark across the surface. The otherwise nondescript Pavilion Road car park, also in London and clad in metal louvres, achieves a uniquely strange effect. With the split-level parking decks and the accent of columns distributed across the interior, all one can see is a barcode pattern suspended in an otherwise blackened field of vision. As one moves, the opposing parking deck and columns move, creating interference and continually changing the pattern of the barcode.

The role that light could play became particularly apparent with Albert Kahn Associates' car park for the Henry Ford Hospital in Detroit, in which each vertical concrete louvre, a hyperbolic paraboloid, performs a 90° rotation between deck floor and soffit above. Cast in white concrete, the light and subsequent shade shape each panel body. Across the whole, the effect is to generate interference patterns in the elevation. In car parks, the effect of illumination is reversed at night, these daytime clusters of darkness are transformed into luminaires the size of a city block. The homogeneous order of structure and distribution of light render the interiors purposeless. At night, artificial light invigorates buildings, varying in response to inhabitation. This is not the case with a car park: no windows, no furniture, no people, just a lantern of light.

Roy Chamberlain Associates, Young Street, London 1970

see case study pp.138–141 \\\\\\\\\\\\\\\\\\

Pavilion Road, London

The construction of Eduardo Souto de Moura's single-storey, underground car park below the seafront esplanade in Matoshinos in Portugal is wrought in light. A trough with two long retaining walls, the road deck above is constructed on a series of transverse concrete beams that span from wall to wall. Standing in the space, the effect of the foreshortening is to compress this multitude of beams into a Bridget Riley-esque pattern of receding black-brown horizontal lines, each separated from the next by a fine line of white-orange light. Downlight between the beams casts a warm hue in contrast to the unremitting order of the beam structure overhead. No doubt a car park, but at the same time the articulation of trabeated construction and the effect of light could equally be that reserved for an art gallery. Although the above- and below-ground car parks differ, one common characteristic is the dearth of light.

///////////////////////////// see p.159

Not surprisingly, some architects have sought the opposite effect. In Lustenau, Marques + Zurkirchen Architekten's car park is on the roof of the Kirchpark supermarket and is therefore the beneficiary of some daylight. An illuminated polycarbonate soffit transforms the whole ceiling into one large lamp, a variation on the 1960s opal glass-inlaid office ceiling. Instead of unremitting darkness, the interior is washed with light. The cast-glass cladding of Gigon/Guyer Architekten's car park, beneath their extension to the Museum of Art in Winterthur (1994–95), generates even light. Closely spaced to allow air to pass between the translucent vertical planks, the interior gives the impression of immersing the motorist in a tank of water. Whiteness reaches an unusual intensity in Von Gerkan, Marg & Partner's parking rotundas at Hamburg Airport, both in the circular decks and particularly in the central spiral ramp, where the light falling on the concrete conjures up images of Stanley Kubrick's space station in *2001: A Space Odyssey*. This pursuit of the light must in part be a functional response to 'lighting', but it also seems to recognize the huge potential of light to affect our emotions: dark equals fear, light equals happiness. This whiteness that we experience has a spiritual dimension, one that can be taken to a different plane with the use of the helical ramp.

Gigon/Guyer Architekten, Winterthur Museum of Art, Winterthur 1994–95

///////////////// see case study pp.186–189

Of the two spatial norms, the deep-plan flat or oblique linear deck and the helical ramp, the latter lends itself to spiritual interpretation. The decks of Miozzi's split-level, linear Autorimessa (1931–34) in Venice are joined by two helical ramps. Each six storeys, their geometry is reflected in the circular glazed roof overhead. Here, the concrete and light fuse. Lying on your back at the base of one of these drums, you have been transported to the floor of a Baroque church, the space and ceiling a 'sculptural rise to a single climax'.[58] Many have followed this early example, with most revolving around an enclosed, covered or open well (Braun Factory, Hamburg Airport, Parkhaus Saas-Fee), while others are cantilevered from a central trunk (Tricorn Centre). The regular geometry of turning circles and car dimensions ensures that each helix is similar.

///////////////////////////////// see p.158

But it is the light source, be it from above or from the side, which radically alters the quality of these spaces.

The chiaroscuro effect is perhaps most extreme in Wilmotte Targe Buren's Parc des Célestins (1994), in Lyon. This circular underground car park built beneath the Place des Célestins comprises two helical ramps, one revolving around the other, at the centre of which is an internal well lit from above and below around the perimeter. At its base, a circular inclined mirror revolves. The well is lined with pre-cast concrete panels, each punched with an arched window. From the parking deck, the outer helix, the shapes of light cast on the floors and walls are continually on the move, where strands of bright light and long shadows track across the inclined and vertical surfaces of the interior. Others have sought to bring daylight into the heart of these largely subterranean structures. OMA have used daylight as a point of orientation (first at Euralille with L'Espace Piranésien, and more recently with Souterrain in The Hague), as have UN Studio with their V-shafts incising the section of their bus garage and car park at Arnhem Centraal. In each case, there is little direct illumination but simply a variation in the hue and intensity of light and the potential to capture the effect of the weather overhead.

Vaulted parking garages are rare, with two examples in the US of interest because of the light. In Paul Rudolph's Temple Street car park (1962), the elephantine legs that support each successive deck arch out to form vaults, which run in a transverse direction across the plan, creating small-scale 'rooms'. In each, the suspension of large circular pendant fittings casts a warm light across the curved soffit, which is broken up into lines of light and shade by the boardmarking of the concrete. Steven Holl used a vaulted structure to form the 'roof' of a two-storey underground car park built along with extensions to the Nelson Atkins Museum of Art (2002), in Kansas City. The car park, beneath a new reflecting pool, is the result of a collaboration with artist Walter de Maria. Into the floor of the pool are set thirty-four glazed oculi that transmit daylight into the 4.6 m-high vaulted parking deck below. At night, the effect is reversed as artificial light emerges from the bottom of the pool to illuminate the public open space in front of the original museum portico.

In the shopping centre in Euralille, Jean Nouvel devised a way to disorient the public by constructing an architecture of reflections and coloured light. The centre's section is tiered; the shopping mall and parking decks overlap with only a glazed screen at the interface between the two, separating shopping and parking. As with Dan Graham's art installations, the subject (viewer) and object are superimposed in a single image. Cars and shoppers intermingle in the same virtual space, the bright space of the mall projected on to the dark space of the car park. At a civic scale, Birds Portchmouth Russum's Avenue de Chartres (1991), in Chichester, uses brick and glass-block

see case study pp.170–173 \\\\\\\\\\\\\\\\\

see case study pp.228–231 \\\\\\\\\\\\\\\\\
see case study pp.244–247 \\\\\\\\\\\\\\\\\

see p.215 \\\\\\\\\\\\\\\\\\\\\\\\\\\\\\

see case study pp. 56–61 \\\\\\\\\\\\\\\\\\\

see p.163 \\\\\\\\\\\\\\\\\\\\\\\\\\\\\\\\\\

Jean Nouvel, Euralille, Lille 1995

bastions in their extension to the city wall to house staircases. Inside, these are decorated a specific colour: red, yellow, green and blue. At night, the spiral of glass blocks become coloured beacons.

In future, the uniquely low light levels to which we have become accustomed will not be acceptable. The best will have to devise more ingenious ways to illuminate these deep spaces without sanitizing the interior. Already the worst flood the interior with harsh, flat light that falls onto often brightly painted surfaces. In these synthetic environments, the distant line of light that is the world outside is obliterated, marking the end of the car park as a uniquely dark place in the modern world. The decorative pattern of daylight in the car-park interior is a thing of exceptional and singular beauty, which can only survive if the next generation of structures for which more light will be a requirement can harness the matter, elevation and light. The recent work of architects in Germany, Austria and Switzerland illustrates the importance of technique in this respect.

binary system of light

lines of light contrast with unremitting darkness

daylight

sodium light

fluorescent light

Eugenio Miozzi
Autorimessa Comunale, Venice 1931–34

Today numerous car parks vie for motorists arriving in the Piazzale Roma, but the most substantial is Miozzi's Autorimessa, a white-render Art Déco building with strip windows. The split-level decks are linked by helical ramps that are lit by magnificent skylights. This almost symmetrical building was constructed in two phases, with the northeast deck and helical ramps being the first. The decks enclose a 'canyon' and vaulted parking space below.

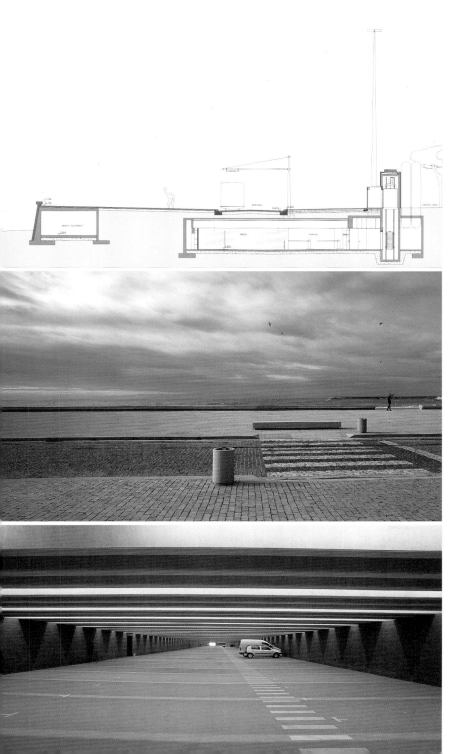

Eduardo Souto de Moura
Car Park, Marginal de Matosinhos
1995–2002

Behind the beach, a 740m-by-19m granite esplanade marks the line between the Atlantic and the land. Underneath is a long, thin concrete room about half that length for 250 vehicles. Heavy concrete beams supporting the road are lit to create a striated and highly figured ceiling, in contrast to the floor. Above ground, steel boxes (lifts), drums (vents) and glass screens (balustrades) mark the benign presence below.

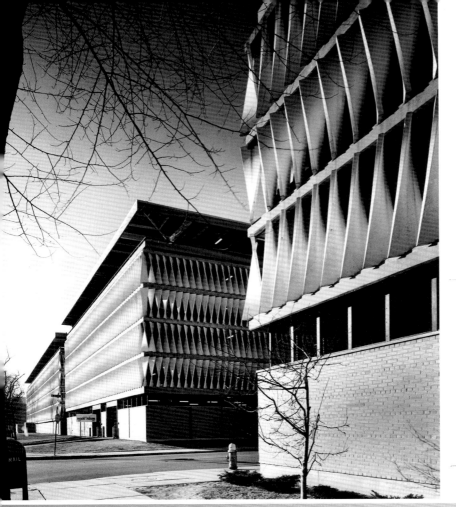

Albert Kahn Associates
Henry Ford Hospital, Detroit 1959

Concrete hyperbolic paraboloid panels enclose
this four-storey car park. Non-structural, each
is 2.25m by 0.6m and spans from deck to deck.
The interference pattern of light and shadow on
these revolving forms resembles psychedelic
designs from the 1960s and particularly the work
of English artist Bridget Riley. The concrete
included quartz to heighten the light intensity.

FIRST FLOOR PLAN

Ingenhoven Overdiek Architekten
Burda Parkhaus, Offenburg 2000–2

Built in an office park, a steel structure supports circular prefabricated concrete parking decks. The central drum and helical ramps are in-situ concrete, while the elevation and roof canopy are fabricated using tensile cables to support the silver-grey Oregon pine timbers. Just as Albert Kahn did forty years before, the architects employ a repetitive pattern to striking optical effect. Here, the screen's grain is finer and is applied to the surface of a drum.

Steven Holl Architects with Walter de Maria, Nelson Atkins Museum of Art, Kansas City 2002

An underground car park over two levels for 453 cars, above is the J.C. Nichols Plaza and new reflecting pool. Thirty-four oculi connect the vaulted upper parking deck, flooding the car park with light by day and uplighting the pool by night.

Marques + Zurkirchen Architekten
Marktzentrum Kirchpark, Lustenau 1990

Marktzentrum Kirchpark incorporates a supermarket, shops and car park adjacent to Daniele
Marques and Bruno Zurkirchen's new town
square. A projecting roof that is similar to, but
apparently designed before, Jean Nouvel's in
Lucerne protects both the weekly market in the
square and the cars parked on top of the supermarket. The elevations of Kirchpark and the
underside of the canopy are clad in polycarbonate. At night in particular the canopy takes on
the appearance of a single civic light fitting.

Birds Portchmouth Russum
Avenue de Chartres, Chichester 1991

Chichester, a medieval walled city near the south coast of England, has main streets running on a north–south, east–west axis. In the twentieth century, the walls could no longer contain development and buildings spilled out to the south towards the train station. Won in competition in the late 1980s by Birds Portchmouth Russum, the Avenue de Chartres car park revises the history of Chichester with a new city wall that extends to 'redefine the city', once again containing development.

The project is one of few contemporary parking structures that reflect a concern for the morality of the car, as opposed to the conventional car park, which Michael Russum has described as a 'deification of the car'. In 'the Thatcherite era, when no public buildings were being built', he continues, the proposal to build a car park was a rare commission to design a 'public building to house private cars'.[59] Russum notes the paradox. The architects' intention was to make a structure with the 'dignity and status of a public building, one that transfers the benefit of driving to the pedestrian'. Typically, the motorist cannot walk in comfort to and from the car without 'competing' with it, he cannot find his way out, and he cannot remember where he left the car on his return. At the Avenue de Chartres, matters are different.

The building is conceived in two parts, a sinuous city wall linking a coach park to the town centre with a three-storey parking structure. The building is made using what the architects describe as a 'tailored element' and an 'engineered element'.

'engineered element':
pre-cast concrete parking decks

The latter comprises standard pre-cast concrete parking decks, which fan out behind the wall in a gentle arc, joined by tapering 'glue' pavements that provide the motorist with his route to the wall. Each of the four paths are colour-coded (red, yellow, green or blue) to remind him where he parked. At the wall, each path is linked to a tower containing a spiral staircase: the historical 'bastion'. Here, ascending or descending the stair, the motorist can join the walk into the city. The colour of each aisle is revealed by the spiralling glass-block surface of each tower. It is apt that one of the competition drawings, made in the style of a medieval projection, illustrates a view from the parking structure looking towards the cathedral, city wall and moat.

Employing local tradition, the wall is made from soft, orange bricks with an inlaid pattern of burnt blue bricks. The architects used this combination to continue the theme of perforations required to ventilate the lower storeys of the building, creating a honeycomb of brickwork that appears to move along the wall towards the portal. In the upper storey, this reverts to the burnt-brick pattern, which finally spirals up the surface of each tower. The wall is punctuated with a variety of openings, ranging from the 'civic tailored' bridge to the more mundane punched square opening that allows a foot- and cycle-path to pass through the wall. The former peels away from the car park, opening to form the new portal into Chichester; another traditional arch allows the passage of a stream. Another punched opening, with its own miniature column, forms the entrance to the car park. The mythological is also present in the detail: benches were 'designed' for the giant, depicted in a medieval drawing, who walks around the city walls, and gargoyles were cast with the faces of the three partners.

Russum recognizes that the Avenue de Chartres project was designed at a time when society, at least in the UK, was ashamed of engineering structures that imposed their brutality in sensitive locations, and this car park, therefore, was conceived first and foremost as a public building performing a public function. The rhythmic nature of the regimented bastions and trees evokes the approach to Rome along the Via Appia. This is a ceremonial route and it invites a new mythology for Chichester, for in redefining the city it redefines the history of the city. Where the walk peels away from the car park and crosses the road, the bridge forms a portal to the city. Here, a single concrete column, like Trajan's Column in Rome, bears witness to the battle of building this car park. Parking is subordinated to the notion of civic improvement.

Michel Targe, Jean-Michel Wilmotte and Daniel Buren
Parc des Célestins, Lyon 1994

For more than a decade, the city of Lyon has been burying its thousands of cars beneath its many squares and quays. And for every new car park, the corresponding square above has been rejuvenated at the hand of a landscape architect or artist. This wave of construction is part of a broader green transport policy that includes public bicycle pools, electric buses and refuelling stations for electric cars.

More than twenty underground car parks have been constructed in the city, always with complex engineering challenges, but only one, the 435-space Parc des Célestins beneath the Place des Célestins, is fantastic. When searching for this particular car park, it becomes apparent that the policy is a success; the network of parking structures, a great infrastructural intervention, is invisible. Eventually, a straight ramp leads down from the narrow street, and the surface plateaus out at the head of a large underground chamber. Here, the plan begins to revolve, taking the car on a helter-skelter voyage into the underworld to bury it 22m below the city. Circular in plan, the parking ramp is wide enough to accommodate the carriageway and the echelon parking bays on each side. Around the perimeter (53m in diameter) is the first of three concentric concrete drums, which work in structural unison. A second, intermediate drum separates the parking ramp from the exit ramp, which spirals up in the opposite direction. Beyond is the third, inner drum.

But it is not the circular geometry or the scale of excavation that is arresting, both of which had been seen before in the early 1960s in the double-helix parking structure under Bloomsbury Square, London. Instead, it is the theatrical play of light and shadow over the surfaces, the views framed by overlain arches, and the spiralling incline of the ramps weaving between concentric structural layers that make Parc des Célestins a grotesque place. At the centre is a seven-storey cylinder of space shaped by the inner drum, which is divided in plan into fourteen segments, each a pre-cast concrete panel with an arch in the middle. As the plan revolves, the panels step up,

one above the other. The intermediate drum is similarly divided into twenty-eight panels, which also step up. On paper, the arches seem mannered, postmodern, over-designed. In reality, their relentless presence makes for a dramatic and macabre encounter worthy of Piranesi's *Carceri d'invenzione* (1745).

But it is through memory and experience, rather than through engineering, that the physicality of the building is felt. The central space, largely artificially lit from above, seems like a well open to the sky. Steel bars in the arched openings of the intermediate drum prevent motorists from stepping out onto the exit ramp, and stand between them and the light, imprisoning the eye only to free their gaze once they have begun their ascent. At the base of the central drum, a circular inclined mirror slowly revolves, modifying the patterns of light falling onto the surfaces. Inside the building, the motorist is completely unaware of the mirror. It is only the inquisitive passerby, stopping in the Place des Célestins above and peering into the periscope, who sees directly down into the central drum and the effect of the revolving mirror.

Parc des Célestins is an anti-Babel, frightening and at the same time pleasurable. It is the congruency of geometry in plan (the circle) and in elevation (the arch), coupled with light and dark, and one's awareness of depth and ultimate sense of incarceration, that makes this car park a total distraction from the mundane act of parking a car. In this respect, the result is a uniquely strange product of reason and the imagination.

Mahler, Günster, Fuchs
Parkhaus am Bollwerksturm, Heilbronn 1997–98

Long and thin with a five-storey timber and mesh-clad façade, the monolithic, 500-space Parkhaus am Bollwerksturm, which takes its name and form from a historic bastion on the site, approaches a sort of geometric perfection. Linear in form, cladding and illumination, the building has three unmistakable characteristics: its dimension, its finely clad elevations, and the light that generates from within. The anatomy of the 137.5 m-long plan is key to the structure's transcendent simplicity. It has just one central carriageway, with parking bays on either side, and is 18.5 m wide, the same dimension as that of the helical ramps, which complete the form with semicircular ends. The building is clad in larch sections, 4 cm wide at 6 cm centres, and the interior is dark but evenly lit by the vertical lines of light between the larch, resulting in a tonal field of brown-and-white stripes. The fine section softens the form of the exterior.

The architects have rejected the heavy, and more typical, modular order of the post-war buildings. The parking structure stands beside a dual carriageway, close to the centre of Heilbronn; to park, the motorist drives around its circular west end. Here, away from the road, the entrance mimics a rustic farm building with its heavy timber sliding doors, a detail that is replicated at the other end in the main pedestrian entrance and pay station. The south side is otherwise a plain accordion of timber. The north, roadside elevation of larch is overlaid with a linear stairway, which is in turn overlaid with chain-link metal fencing similar to that used by Frank Gehry at Santa Monica Place, in Los Angeles. From each parking level, a single, domestic-scale door bolted in the open position provides the means of reaching this stairway and leaving the building. Although the external concrete steps and mesh screen are well detailed, the mesh remains a literal, industrial material that fails to achieve the abstract beauty of the larch screen. By contrast, the long, plain expanse of the south palisade elevation is enigmatic, its density and material are such that there is nothing in the external appearance of the building that reveals its function. Whilst the dimension is an indicator of type, the construction is not.

Inside, a row of twenty-three steel-frame portals support pre-cast concrete planks, which span the width of the parking deck. The post-and-beam structure gives the interior an order, interrupted only by two in-situ concrete escape stair cores on the south side of the plan. At each end, in-situ concrete helical ramps, which brace the steel frame, glow in the top light, a light turned green by the planting in the void at the centre of the helix. Parkhaus am Bollwerksturm is disconcertingly simple; as the architects point out, 'the quiet, easy and disciplined form of the building shows and supports the contrast to the natural, moving structure of the trees on the site'.[60] In terms of technique, the structure gives the impression of being a highly evolved car-park type. Its dimensions seem the absolute, engineered result of the size and turning circle of the car, and the fine, louvred façade the result of the need for good cross-ventilation.

LAGEPLAN

Von Gerkan, Marg & Partner
Car-Park Rotundas, Hamburg Airport, Hamburg 1990–2002

Flying is a disorienting experience, involving in the first leg of the journey making one's way to a 'port' on the outskirts of a city, or to a remote patch of countryside where the idyll has been supplanted by frantic activity. There are acres of tarmac for planes and cars, and at the centre of all this, some great winged structure: the terminal building. Hamburg Airport appears to be no different but for the appearance of two silos – one small, one large – designed to house nearly 3,000 cars altogether. The Small Rotunda and the Large Rotunda, designed by Von Gerkan, Marg & Partner, stand in a socle of cars in front of the new terminal buildings.

The use of the concentric plan alludes to what architectural historian Alberto Pérez-Gómez terms the 'symbolic geometry' in the theoretical and idealized work of Etienne-Louis Boullée and Claude-Nicolas Ledoux.[61] The nine-storey Small Rotunda, completed in 1990, is 61m in diameter and has 800 spaces for cars. Twelve years later, the ten-level, 92m, 2,115-space Large Rotunda followed. From afar, the galvanized steel grillages set in square steel frames unite the floors and disguise the radial concrete frames that conceal the internal order.

The Small Rotunda employs a single, one-way access road with parking spaces both inside and outside of the carriageway. In the centre of this doughnut, the entry and exit ramps are entwined in a highly refined double-helix, marked by the ascending lines of the balustrade. Between the helical ramps and concentric parking decks is an in-situ concrete drum, from which a concrete slab spans onto twenty columns disposed at 18° intervals. The columns have been located about 3m in from the perimeter, achieving an efficient cantilever structure. The column intervals of approximately 7.5m coincide with the module of three parking bays. In the main, the decks are lit with a diffused light through the perimeter grills, conveying strong reflected light on the deck soffits. On the opposing side to the lift core, the metal screens have been omitted to reveal the repeating section of slab–void, slab–void. Here, the only feature on the elevation is a balustrade with vertical posts and close-centred horizontal rails.

By comparison, the Large Rotunda ('Big Brother') is planned with a 35m-wide concentric parking deck, wrapped around the 23m-diameter helical ramps at its core. The deck is wide enough to accommodate two carriageways, with parking on each side. So while it is only possible to park two cars end-to-end between core and perimeter in the Small Rotunda, in the Large Rotunda it is possible to park four. The Large Rotunda consequently has more columns: a ring of trapezoidal ones at the core, with an intermediate and outer ring of circular columns disposed at 12° intervals, two parking bays about 5m apart in the intermediate ring, and three bays about 7.5m apart on the perimeter. Here, the outer columns are located much closer to the perimeter and are thus more visible from the outside, day and night. These support in-situ radial beams that in turn support in-situ slabs, varying in thickness from 13cm to 17cm. The downstand beams vary in width from 27cm to 74cm, giving the effect of a folded soffit that is dramatized further by their convergence on the columns encircling the central drum. Between the trapezoidal columns and the concrete drum that houses the ramps is an exhaust stack. The architects placed great emphasis on the structural economy of means and bright interior surfaces, which improve security. The experience is compelling; unlike the Small Rotunda with its exposed concrete and dark deck surfaces, the Large Rotunda is washed white. This is a heavenly reality, reminiscent of a black-and-white Hollywood dream scene by Dalí.

Inside the inner drum, the horizon and reality have been excluded, and with them anxious passengers and their experiences of flying. The motorist has been removed to another place, an extremely tall, circular room, open to the sky and visible through an oculus, which describes the diameter of the void in the middle of the ramps. These revolve, and with them the fine lines of the guard rails. There are many things here to evoke a reaction, from the sense of the scale and geometry of Boullée's unexecuted memorials, to the total nature and scale of space that is Gilliam spoofing Orwell, to that felt in one of James Turrell's skyspaces. In reality, the latter can only be experienced by the most inquisitive traveller, who drops his bags on the tarmac on the way to check-in to lie flat on his back in the centre of the space.

The beauty of these two buildings stems from a geometric discipline in the centre of each plan, which becomes progressively corrupted towards the perimeter by real-world common sense. This is illustrated by the use of the served-and-servant idiom that results in lift and stair cores being articulated as detached component forms, projecting from each car park. Of course, there is a reason – the access and escape cores remove the departing motorist as far away as possible from exposure to the parking deck. In this way, the pair of buildings describe well the dichotomy between the ideal and the real. What distinguishes the airport's helical ramps from other examples is the concentric plan that places ascent and descent at its centre, a parti pris it shares with Ingenhoven Overdiek Architekten's Burda Parkhaus, in Offenburg. This plan lends the ascent greater moment when, while glancing up at the neo-Baroque ceiling, we glimpse a bowl of liquid sky contained by this concrete vessel. Beneath the oculus, motorists come and go in a great drum of space, open to the elements, that tracks the sun and is marked by the weather. At the heart of these two structures, the drums are remote silent places, activated only by the whirl of spiralling cars.

obliquity

4

innovation and programmatic experimentation

'Ramp', 'slope', 'incline', 'diagonal', 'acclivity', 'declivity', 'scarp', 'escarp' and 'rise': these terms all describe a condition other than flatness. We find obliquity in topography, and in rail and road, where it may describe a character and is useful when seeking to locate and to orient. Other words, such as 'tilt' and 'list', describe a state of collapse. Language is suggestive to our understanding of the oblique. The ramp – the result of the wheel, which distinguishes the motion of the car from that of the human body – sets the ramped multi-storey car park apart from other types of building.

obliquity

There are, essentially, three types of ramped car park: level decks with remote access ramps; split-level decks linked by 'stitching' ramps; and the continuous type, in which the ramp is integral to the parking deck. The permutations are numerous, particularly in the third category. In his 1965 book, Dietrich Klose provides a classification of nine ramped car parks, which are reproduced below.

Texts about ramped parking structures tend, like a manual, to dwell on the prosaic, upon gradient, speed and safety. What is interesting, however, is the clinometric reality, the visceral experience to be had from the ascent or descent, or the space that can be made from tilted, bowed and warped surfaces. These matter-of-fact descriptions overlook the remarkable sculptural effect of these movement systems, effects that until recently have been largely absent from other building types. Such effects were suggested as early as 1925 by Konstantin S. Melnikov, whose expressive proposals for Paris interwove a series of switchback ramps within a cube of parking decks. Driving along the ramps, he imagined, would be a pleasure for the motorist, a kind of sightseeing opportunity. Melnikov recognized the potential for enjoyment. He illustrated in the simple order of the lyrical plan the difference between stasis and helter-skelter movement, something that only the purest of diagrams can achieve. It is possible to imagine that Melnikov's motorist would experience 'flow' and become totally absorbed by the ride.

see case study pp.220–223 \\\\\\\\\\\\\\\\\\

Dietrich Klose, classification
of nine ramped car parks, 1965

Victor Gruen sought similar exhilaration for visitors to his car park on the roof of Milliron's department store (1948), in Los Angeles. Gruen rejected the more obvious scheme of building a two-storey department store with lifts in favour of what was considered cheaper at the time, a single-storey building with a reinforced roof that would take the weight of cars, and two ramps that would link the parking lot at grade with the parking lot on the roof. The design celebrates this journey with a pair of 6m-wide, 90m-long scissor-ramps, which, from the ground, look like isolated sections of freeway. At the base of the up-ramp, a large frame extends the elevation and marks the point of the ascent. But it was the two sixty-storey towers at Chicago's Marina City by Bertrand Goldberg that established a benchmark of insanity. The bottom third of each tower was constructed as one thin, continuous spiral deck, which was cantilevered from a circular array of columns. Consider the exhilaration to be had from driving nineteen storeys into the air and looking out over downtown Chicago; is the descent tedious, plain dangerous, or still interesting after nineteen circuits? Driving on more modest helical ramps suggests that such a descent would require the motorist's full concentration.

Geometry has a huge bearing on the driver's experience of the ascent and the descent. A linear ramp suggests a trajectory, is closely associated with roads and landscape, and creates the potential for a certain feeling of speed. By contrast, the helical ramp is more obviously the product of mathematics and engineering, and the result is quite literally artificial and unfamiliar. It is a more unique sensation to experience a spiralling effect, a road-vortex, deliriously revolving around some central point in space.

Localized ramps generate a kind of effect, but are of limited interest. Obliquity has the greatest impact where the ramp is integrated into the parking deck, and the building becomes one continuous inclined surface creating, as Virilio observed, disequilibrium in the human body. A building such as UN Studio's underground car park in Arnhem (1996–2007), with its folded linear decks, is a disorienting environment. With Parkhaus Saas-Fee, architects Steinmann & Schmid expose the individual to incline and counter-incline against a backdrop of mountains. Where soffit and deck end and the outside begins, the subtle incline effects a gentle rotation of the surrounding landscape, a sensation that is replicated by VMX Architects with Fietsenstalling, a bike park constructed over a canal in Amsterdam, with its destabilizing scissor-section. The contrast between deck and waterline confuses our reading of the horizon.

Unlike Arnhem Centraal, where the car park lies beneath a bus station, and Marina City, which is capped by apartments, other continuous surface structures (R. Jelinek-Karl's Rupert Street car park in Bristol, for example) add another dimension – the truncated form – to the incompleteness observed in the building matter. The motorist's ascent stops abruptly, without an architectural adjustment. One gets a similar sensation in reverse when descending the car park beneath Bloomsbury Square,

Victor Gruen, rooftop car park,
Milliron's department store, Los Angeles 1948

//////////////////////////////// see p.215

//////////////////////////////// see p.214

///////////////// see case study pp.240–243

R. Jelinek-Karl, Rupert Street, Bristol 1960
(see p.210)

Car park, Bloomsbury Square, London

see p.209 \\\\\\\\\\\\\\\\\\\\\\\\\\\\\\\\\\\\

see p.211 \\\\\\\\\\\\\\\\\\\\\\\\\\\\\\\\\\\\\\\

in London. But in the latter structure, without any external reference there is no way to measure one's descent or to predict the end. Instead, as a group of us cyclists discovered, it simply stops. The double-helix ends at a wall seven storeys below ground, without any change to the gradient or to the diameter of the helical descending deck. Again, it is a condition that one is acutely aware of when looking at VMX Architects' Fietsenstalling. The Owen Luder Partnership resolved this dilemma both formally and programmatically with a nightclub at the summit of Gateshead's Trinity Square, as did Roy Chamberlain Associates with an office pavilion at Young Street, in London. Both solutions are diminutive, unexpected and brilliant.

Probably the first hybrid was Louis Kahn's unbuilt 'dock' building (1956–57), which formed part of his city-centre proposal for Philadelphia and envisaged a drum of parking decks wrapped in offices and apartments. Given that the parking decks were part of a larger urban design strategy, there is no drawn record of how Kahn imagined that cars would move around inside the building. But just two years later, English architect Michael Webb, a member of Archigram, proposed a functional hybrid with his design for Sin Centre (1959–62), in London's Leicester Square. Interestingly, Webb makes reference to Kahn's 'docks'. The close integration of car park and 'entertainments palace' is no accident, and Webb described the building as a 'drive-in galleria' extending the street into the heart of the building.[62] He maintained that the circulatory systems, both vehicular and pedestrian, became important in facilitating the easy flow of large crowds of people through the different spaces. The two systems are 'specially designed units', and their juxtaposition 'generates the overall form of the building'. Venues, including a bowling alley, cinema, theatre, dance area, coffee bars and pubs, were planned in the spaces between the reel-to-reel parking helixes and pedestrian travolators, the 'rectangular' geometry of which, when compared to the geometry of the circular car ramps, made explicit Webb's intention that the building be derived from the order of the 'access systems'.

OMA's unbuilt 'Working Babel' (1989) project for a ferry terminal, in Zeebrugge, is another hybrid structure that stacks conference rooms, casino and swimming pool above offices and a hotel, a café, bar and restaurant, truck-drivers' facilities, separate car and truck parking, and, at the base, on-off vehicular access and bridges to the ferries.[63] Stacked up, the section mitigates the problems of sprawling and divisive infrastructures. The terminal bears an intriguing resemblance to the Downtown Athletic Club, in New York's Wall Street, which Rem Koolhaas discussed in his 1978 book, *Delirious New York*.[64] But instead of thirty-eight floors of club facilities linked by a backbone of lifts, the design for the ferry terminal, a 'cross between a ball and a cone', wraps a multitude of activities inside a single, nineteen-storey form, the dynamic plan and section of which are undeniably informed by the wheels of the trucks and cars that it serves.[65]

Much as Goldberg superimposed a centripetal apartment floor plan on top of a circular helical parking deck at Marina City, OMA also stacked circular segmental and concentric accommodation on top of their helical parking decks.

The architects finally realized their first vertical infrastructure/hybrid car park in Euralille. Early sketches of Euralille (1988–91) and the convention centre in Agadir (1990) suggest the degree to which OMA was preoccupied with the car, and illustrate cartoon roads dotted with cars that meander over synthetic landscapes and forests of columns seen through screens of glass. In one particular Euralille sketch, train, metro, car and pedestrian infrastructures appear suspended in aspic, the most notable of which are the roads that wind down into their underworld. If Zeebrugge alluded to the Tower of Babel, then Euralille took its cue from the *Carceri* drawings of Piranesi. In the end, the French authorities rejected the roads, and today the metro coexists with pedestrian bridges, lifts and escalators under the ever-watchful 'eye' of the car-park windows carved into the north and south faces of L'Espace Piranésien.

/////////////////// see case study pp.228–231

OMA were later commissioned to develop a masterplan for the Dutch town of Almere (1993), which earmarked a 9ha square of land next to the lake for the new town centre. Now nearing completion, the ground has been excavated 1.5m, just 0.5m above water level. Over the top, a deck has been constructed that folds to form a beach on the lake. The pitch of the folded deck varies; in part flat, elsewhere it inclines at between 2.7 per cent and 3.6 per cent. Beneath the deck are roads, loading docks and 3,300 parking spaces. A hypostyle of concrete columns rises to a height of 7.5m, dwarfing the mat of cars within. OMA defend the car parking that generated the socle landform into and onto which the town-centre complex is grafted because of its capacity to attract motorists and protect commerce from out-of-town retail and leisure facilities. Another OMA hybrid is Souterrain, in The Hague, that incorporates a tramline, two tram stations and underground car park built beneath the city centre. This 1.2km-long, cut-and-cover tunnel capitalizes on the creative spatial interference that the designers could derive from integrating these uses.

/////////////////// see case study pp.244–247

Other hybrids, including Morphosis's project for the Yuzen Vintage Car Museum (1991), in Los Angeles, and Burkhalter Sumi Architekten's new building for Hotel Zurichberg (1995), in Zurich, superimpose activities on top of subterranean parking. For the Yuzen museum, Morphosis conceived of a 'racetrack' embedded within a rectangular plan. Parking spaces line the perimeter of the racetrack, which inclines and revolves at the southern end of the site, linking one deck to the next. At the north end, tangential beams appear to spin out an illusory vortex adjacent to the lifts. This spatial/structural diagram is transposed to the exhibition floors above, and is expressed in a semicircular element that emerges above the building's curved roof form. By contrast, Burkhalter Sumi devised a diagrammatic plan for the Hotel Zurichberg

 //////////////////////////////// see p.212

Burkhalter Sumi Architekten, Hotel Zurichberg, Zurich 1995 (see p.213)

extension, an elliptical spiral of two storeys of bedrooms on top of three floors of parking. Outside there is no sight of the parking decks, just a spiral in which the steps in the horizontal timber cladding mark the gradual ascent of the windows. Inside, the doors on the ramp chart a similar ascent at the perimeter of a balcony, which revolves around a central void. This distant descendent of the Guggenheim Museum is tethered to the original house by an umbilical subterranean link, and to the forecourt by two parking ramps that surface some distance away from the elliptical form.

For the best part of a century, multi-storey car parks have been constructed using one or other of the prescribed blueprints; whether split-level or helix, the whole building would always conform to that one model. Then, in 1994, NL Architects, who were interested in the idea of repetition, used a series of textbook car parks to produce three new diagrammatic structures. Each diagram wove together the various ramp-types to make one vertical, a second horizontal, and the third a compact square in plan, and each employed a matrix of continuous-surface, helical-ramp, split-level and 'wheelwright', or 'hillock', systems. These playful drawings elaborated on the idea of the dehomogenized car park, and offered variety that, within the structure, resulted in localized identity. The architects maintained that their intentions were practical (it is easier to find one's car in a picturesque environment, for example), but what they did

NL Architects, three diagrammatic hybrid structures

was far more important and ingenious. In collaging the different ramp-types, the firm demythologized any functional assessment of one type over another. The fusion of these apparently mundane systems revealed their more subjective dimension. Along with the more detailed design Parkhouse/Carstadt, in Amsterdam, the drawings constitute an explicit critique of the typological norm, of the autonomous structure, mistakenly understood to be a utilitarian product justified by practicality. Although the experiments postdated the functional hybrids of OMA, they did not depend on interference to generate heterogeneous and picturesque environments. First Melnikov, today NL Architects – both have demonstrated the depth of intentionality that architects bring to the car park.

But when is a car park not a car park? Perhaps when it is a road or a field. Parkhouse/Carstadt is a 1km road tied into a tight knot, inclined, stacked and wedged into its inner-city site. The architects describe how 'the journey between the narrow streets becomes a pleasant ride over "hills" of programme, affording spectacular views across the historic city'.[66] Aranda/Lasch's 10-Mile Spiral was designed to decongest Las Vegas and to prevent traffic jams that would result in stationary (parked) vehicles. So, although cars would speed around this intestine mountain at 55mph, the Spiral is more structure than infrastructure, more building than road. The first is a car park masquerading as a road, the second a road masquerading as a car park. What makes the multi-storey car park recognizable – is it the function or the form? Then the field: first there was Khoury's hyperbolic paraboloid project, which predated Klose's 1965 book, and then OMA's 1993 Jussieu project. More recently, although not multi-storey, both Zaha Hadid's parking lot for Hoenheim North, in Strasbourg, and R&Sie(n)'s 'Asphalt Spot', in Tokamachi, have sought rhetorical expression in fields and waves of black tarmac and white painted lines. The setting of 'Asphalt Spot' in rural Japan against a backdrop of paddy fields and distant mountains goes further than any other in revealing the mimetic character of the car-park surface and the natural landscape in making something obviously synthetic and, at the same time, uniquely situated.

If the car park's surface can merge with the ground, our own project, 'Park and Jog', sought a scenario in which the parking structure could infuse city-space. The outcome is an ethical and aesthetic revision of edge-of-city commuting for motorists, who instead stop at a car-park terminus, 'Car(P)Ark', where they swap one mode of transport for another (bike, canoe, horse, etc.) before heading into town via a 1.2km 'Umbilical Park' and arriving at the 'Suit Park'. This utopian project signals a return to the optimistic contribution that Kahn and others believed, nearly half a century ago, the car park could make to the city. Instead of causing urban blight, these structures have the power to influence the character of our towns and cities and inform the mixed-use buildings that they support. The work of many architects, particularly the

Aranda/Lasch, 10-Mile Spiral, Las Vegas 2004
(see pp.216–217)

///////////////// see case study pp.82–85
///////////////////////////// see p.218

Buschow Henley, 'Park + Jog', Salford 1998
(see case study pp.236–239)

Dutch, points to a reversion to urban environments that seeks further integration for the car. Structures that were, for the most part, objects in our cities are now becoming more literal extensions of the infrastructure and the surrounding landscape. Whilst this idea rejects type, it has the more insidious effect of infiltrating other types. Still, the most radical proposition for integration must be MVRDV's unbuilt Leidschenveen town centre. These experiments are sensational, and would be behaviour-changing. The interleaving of oblique car decks with shops, a school, a church, etc., necessitates that one affects the other.

But to dwell on the exceptional is to miss the point of the normative condition; sometimes it is to stand on deck in the pitch and the yaw, to experience the destabilizing effect of these surfaces either behind the wheel or later on foot. Until very recently these have been the only Towers of Babel that architects could make. Now the form of the car park has become the preferred mode for exhilarating and shocking architecture. The sensation these designers crave can be found in any provincial town, where it is possible to remove oneself by means of a continuous (vehicular) ascent to a point in the open air high above the city. Back in the street, we observe the listing form and tilting planes before losing sight of them, and return to more familiar parts of the city.

double-helix ramp serves level decks, exterior

double-helix ramp serves level decks, interior

continuous-type ramp integral to parking deck

'stitching' ramps link split-level decks, exterior

'stitching' ramps link split-level decks, interior

infrastructure and architecture

SP 17
SECTIONAL PERSPECTIVE PROJECTION

Michael Webb
Sin Centre, London 1959–62

Preceding OMA's Jussieu Library and NL Architects' Parkhouse/Carstadt by over thirty years, Sin Centre sought to create what Webb described as a 'drive-in galleria', an extension of the street that utilizes the dynamic of helical car movement and linear pedestrian travolators to generate an architecture. The car park and mix of leisure uses were enveloped in a glazed roof, supported by tensile steel cables.

R. Jelinek-Karl
Rupert Street, Bristol 1960

Hill road or car park – the oval plan spirals up
around a central well to a point seven storeys
above the street, where the continuous surface
comes to an abrupt end. The 17m-wide deck
is supported on a series of transverse pre-cast
concrete cantilevered beams, each supported
by a pair of columns. In addition to structural
efficiency, the decision to cantilever accentuates
the fluidity of the decks seen in the faceted planes
of the perimeter barrier.

**Office for Metropolitan Architecture
'Working Babel', Zeebrugge 1989**

'Working Babel' blends building, roads, ramps
and bridges and epitomizes OMA's interest in
vertical infrastructures. This 'Babel' houses
offices, hotel, casino, car park, truck stop, bus
and taxi terminus, and illustrates how the geometry of a car park, here helical, affects conventional
uses. On the seventh storey, the car park gives
way to the truck-drivers' hall.

Morphosis
Yuzen Vintage Car Museum, Los Angeles
1991

This unexecuted project uses the motif of the helical ramp (distorted in one axis), embedded in a rectangular site to unite both the parking of contemporary vehicles (visitor parking) with the galleries exhibiting vintage cars above. The ramps are joined by the second motif of vertical car movement (a lift), which spears the project top to bottom in a single, dialectical journey.[67]

Burkhalter Sumi Architekten
Hotel Zurichberg, Zurich 1995

Like the tip of an iceberg, the new two-storey
hotel annexe, situated discreetly in a glade,
conceals a three-storey car park below ground.
Inside, the oval geometry of the parking decks
is transmitted into the inclined hallway and
stepping rooms, which revolve around a central
well daylit by a lantern above. Note the ascending
window positions and stepping joints in the
timber cladding.

Steinmann & Schmid Architekten
Parkhaus, Saas-Fee 1994–96

Parkhaus Saas-Fee, like Kahn's 'ports' and
Miozzi's Autorimessa, is a car terminus, with
the top two floors planned for offloading. As a
result, the ski resort is car-free, served by electric
carts. Built into the hillside, the twelve parking
decks fold up and down, linking one to the next.
Uniquely, the first glimpse the motorist gets
of Saas-Fee is not of the town but of entrance
barriers and the glazed drum, enclosing a helical
ramp that also links the parking decks. This is
a monumental piece of infrastructure that has a
profound effect on quality of life and the physical
environment. It is a utilitarian structure; the
concrete is rough, its folding form mimicking the
landscape, modifying one's outlook from a deck.

UN **Studio**
Arnhem Centraal, Arnhem 1997–2007

Arnhem Centraal's 1,200-space car park is situated beneath the bus station. It is a continuous-surface type, divided into three carriageways by V-shafts. These house the pedestrian circulation and provide a modicum of daylight to the brightly coloured spaces below ground. The inclined interiors are unusual, reminiscent of a road tunnel or the parking decks on a ferry.

Aranda/Lasch
10-Mile Spiral, Las Vegas 2004

On the main highway south of Las Vegas, a
rhetorical spiral seeks to tackle traffic congestion,
to delay arrival, to keep the motorist moving and
busy. As the architects say, it's a matter of perception. At the heart of this suburban gyratory is
a tower of roads, revealing the ambiguity of all
multi-storey parking structures in that they are
a continuance of both 'road' and, by necessity,
'building'. The form is the result of an algorithm
that generates a 'dirty' spiral.

```
Dim no: no = 70
Dim arrPoint, n
ReDim arrLine (no)
Dim account: account = 0
initial radius
Dim radius: radius = 10
create helix
For n = 0 To no Step 1
arrPoint = Array (radius)*Sin(n),
(radius)*Cos(n), n/2)
arrLine(n) = arrPoint
Dim random: random = Rnd()
If random < .5 Then
Radius = radius + .1 + (Rnd()*1.5)
Else
Radius = radius + .1 − (Rnd()*1.5)
End If
Next
```

'Dirty' Spiral

An algorithm (see opposite) is employed to derive a helix, whose radius 'varies randomly as it climbs and then falls back down to the valley floor'.

Extrude

A structural curb is extruded to 4.6m to stiffen the ramp.

Intersection – Load Transfer

Intersection points between these strips are transfer points through which the structure's loads are channelled to the ground.

Beams

The structure is optimized to allow views out to the valley: material is retained in the axial line of stress and removed where the curb is not doing any structural work.

Top row: $500 Car Slots – Matching vehicles win.

Second row: $5000 Car Roulette – Stop on your number and win.

Second row: $10,000 Tower – Every millionth car wins.

Bottom row: Free Car Wash – What happens in Vegas, stays in Vegas.

R&Sie(n)
'Asphalt Spot', Tokamachi 2003

'Asphalt Spot' was commissioned by the Art Front Gallery. Artificial topography is introduced into a rural setting, over which asphalt has been poured and white lines painted to create twenty parking bays. An exhibition room is created by a cluster of props that shore up the surfaces overhead. The visitor may walk or drive around the site to experience what R&Sie(n) refer to as 'disequilibrium'.

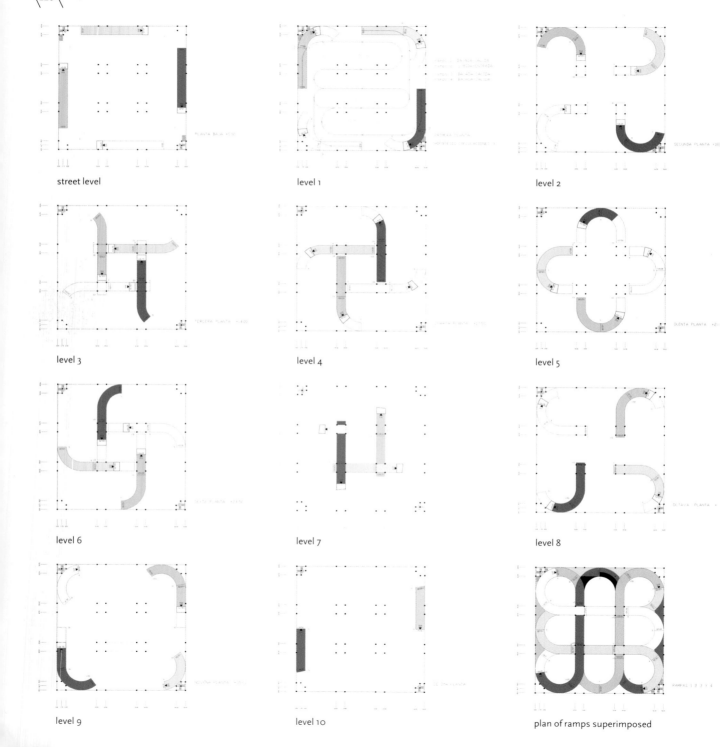

street level

level 1

level 2

level 3

level 4

level 5

level 6

level 7

level 8

level 9

level 10

plan of ramps superimposed

Konstantin S. Melnikov
Car Park for 1,000 Vehicles, Paris 1925

It was as a result of Melnikov's success in designing the winning Soviet pavilion for the 1925 Exposition Internationale des Arts Decoratifs et Industriels Modernes, in Paris,[68] that he was asked by local government officials to design a car park for 1,000 cars. He developed two designs, variously known as the 'first' and 'second variants', a 'minimal' and a 'maximal' version, and the 'first' and 'second versions'.[69] The first design expressed the oblique in its skeletal appearance (the maximal version), and the second, the orthogonal (the minimal version). Indeed, there is some confusion as to which is which. S. Frederick Starr, who met Melnikov, describes the skeletal option as the 'second variant', whereas Juan N. Baldeweg and Andrés Jaque, who describe the orthogonal option as the 'second version', quote passages written by Melnikov himself which suggest that theirs is the more accurate interpretation.

In a report dated 28 July 1925, Melnikov described how each realized design would be a 'palace with numerous floors for cars'.[70] He also outlined a set of principles for the car ramps: they will not cross; there will be a 90° curve between them; all the curves will have the same radius; there will be as few turns as possible; the whole surface will be used as a car park; the whole road will be used for ascending; the height of each floor will correspond to the height of the cars. He described the two options as 'project on an open allotment' and 'dimensional project (the form corresponds to the ascent)', which demanded linear sites such as boulevards and bridges.

Melnikov explained how he had 'proposed the construction of the car park over the bridges on the Seine for the Parisians who, as we know, love street life so much. An ingenious design occurred to me, consisting of two counterpoised protruding structures that maintained their balance by supporting each other. The building would contain 1,000 spaces, the cars would ascend and descend using a fixed number of ramps and they could occupy any of the free spaces without making more than one turn...'.[71] The two known drawings of this first variant describe a fourteen-storey structure, supported by four closely spaced piers in the centre of the river. The scissor-section exposed in elevation by the design is suspended two storeys above the bridge at the apex, and six storeys above at each bank. Here the structure is propped up by a caryatid at each end. The elevation is a composition of steeply inclined but truncated oblique lines. Access ramps on each side follow the same oblique line to the bridge deck.

He went on to describe the second project: '...[it] was set on a plot of land with a surface area of 50m by 50m. It included four spiral ramps that did not cross at any point. One of the spirals gave on to the centre of the façade of the building so that the cars would pass quickly by, in view and to the delight of the Parisian multitudes'.[72] The plan is divided by sixteen column clusters into a nine-square grid; a cluster of five in each corner, four clusters of four around the central square, and eight column pairs mid-elevation. The ground floor is 7m high, and the subsequent ten decks 3.5m

Konstantin S. Melnikov, elevation, section and plan, first variant

ramp 1

ramp 2

ramps 1 + 2 superimposed

ramp 3

ramp 4

ramps 3 + 4 superimposed

high. Threaded through this matrix are the four spiral ramps that Melnikov referred to, each following the shape of a 'w', a combination of straight ramps and 180° half-helical ramps. One ramp begins its ascent on each of the four elevations. The four ramps, superimposed in a rotating pattern, describe petal-shaped arcs of movement that criss-cross back and forth across the centre of the plan throughout a ten-storey ascent. At one point, in the middle of the elevation, the cladding is omitted to reveal a car on one of the sweeping helical ramps, a condition that would presumably have been replicated on each face. Finally, Melnikov's one plan at first-floor level shows 111 parked cars, but gives no indication of how the other 889 cars would be distributed.

Where the ramps describe a rotational symmetry, the static plan morphology exhibits mirror symmetry in both axes. The plan is divided into a tartan grid – ABABABA – where A (the structural cluster and ramp width) is approximately 3.5 m and B (the open space between the ramps and structure) is approximately 12 m. The elevation is divided into thirteen equal horizontal bays; when translated into the elevation, B equals three times A. There is a discrepancy, however, as the 50 m elevation divides equally into 3.85 m bays. Vertically this elevation divides equally into twelve bays of 3.5 m. The drawings describe a building, which is deliberately pure, both square and symmetrical, but strangely not quite a cube. What some have described as the minimal variant appears to suggest the ideal form for a multi-storey parking structure.

Melnikov imagined his design would be a pleasure, a kind of sightseeing opportunity opening up views over the capital. He recognized the potential for enjoyment. He also illustrated in the simple order of the lyrical plan the difference between stasis and helter-skelter movement, something that only the purist of diagrams can achieve as the turning of the wheel, the changing of gears, speeding up and slowing down all detract from the driver's dance. One only has to look at the plans to believe it is possible to experience flow, to become totally absorbed by the ride.

Baldeweg and Jaque's analytical drawings extrapolate the full design from Melnikov's two original plans, section and elevation. Their research highlights various inconsistencies between the structure, the ramps and the staircases. Seen from the side, the model bears a striking resemblance to the one that OMA produced earlier for the 1993 Jussieu Library, which employs the Domino frame to support a continuous internal landscape. Although Melnikov's plan is symmetrical and OMA's is not, and Melnikov's section comprises significantly more static decks, the combined effect is very similar.

Juan N. Baldeweg and Andrés Jaque, elevation, section and plan

Bertrand Goldberg
Marina City, Chicago 1962

As illustrated in the well-known painting by Pieter Bruegel the Elder, the Tower of Babel conveys the imagery of a monumental construction. This tower, part of the Old Testament account of the early human rejection of the rule of God, is imagined by Bruegel as a truncated cone, built using great arched, paired storeys reminiscent of the Coliseum in Rome. Each storey is united to the ground by a continuous helical ramp, which provides the means for transporting building materials from the port at the base into the heavens above. In Chicago, architect and engineer Bertrand Goldberg designed a building to resemble this biblical structure. Marina City, as it became known, dispensed with the bricks and mortar, arches and buttresses, but retained the continuous helical ramp and port setting. Goldberg's 32m-diameter towers cork-screw out of their riverside setting to a height of some nineteen storeys, providing a continuous parking structure. Above are a further forty storeys of apartments.

Goldberg was interested in harnessing prefabrication and mass production in the planning of communities, both of which, he believed, came before the more abstract and decadent issue of aesthetics. He prepared his design in contrast to Frank Lloyd Wright's vision of the utopian agrarian settlement, Broadacre City, which united the American traditions of farming and the suburb in one continuously settled Prairie mat. In many respects, Marina City reversed the American ideal of space, making the idea of proximity central to building a community. It brings together housing, offices, shops, a television theatre and cinema, a marina and a multi-storey parking structure in five buildings, and was, and perhaps still is, a clear sign of high-density living in North America. This was Goldberg's attempt to rehabilitate, repopulate and revitalize the then ailing downtown of Chicago. Yet this community still enjoys the idea of space. The elevated apartments enable residents to look out across the city, Lake Michigan and the surrounding countryside. Goldberg's intense use of the land results in an apparently absurd but romantic notion that people, in driving up into the heavens, manage the impossible.

The 'corncob' towers are in-situ concrete with a tubular core at the centre and a ring of sixteen columns at the perimeter. The apartments are arranged around the sixteen 'petals', while below the parking decks describe a simple circle, with spaces for thirty-two cars for each rotation and a total of 450 in each tower. Cars park radially around the perimeter, apparently enjoying the same views as their owners many floors above. Most remarkable is the 1km journey that the motorist makes from street level to the nineteenth-level parking deck, driving perilously close to a precipitous edge, steering wheel in a fixed lock. The building itself brings a whole new dimension to commuting and must be the cause of some traffic queues as motorists wait for one another to park on this single two-way track.

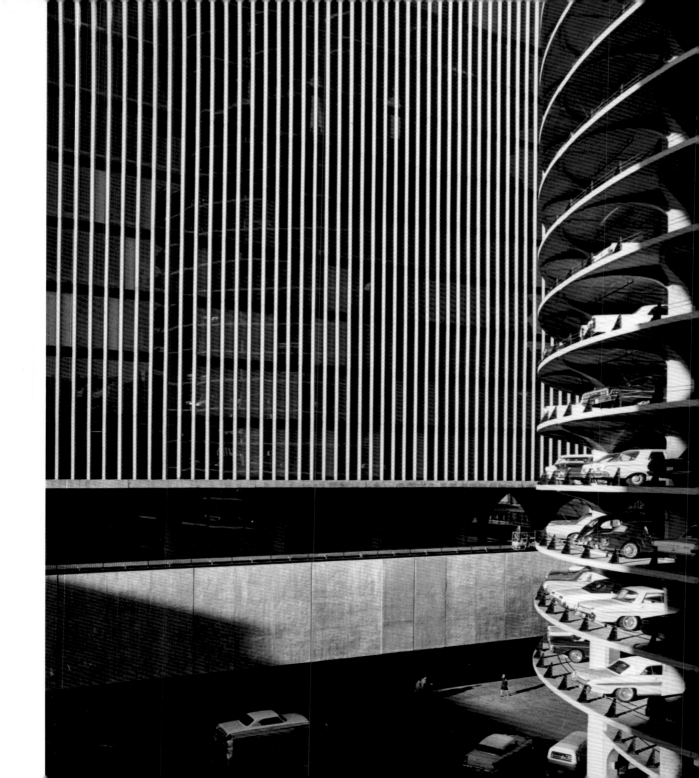

Goldberg believed in the city 'because people need to communicate personally with each other...a primitive instinct which architecture must understand, even if governments don't always understand'.[73] Parking at Marina City is integral to this vision; no parking structure is so tall or slender, or assumes so complete an embodiment of the spiral. As such, the scale, geometry and homogeneity of the structure are unprecedented. This must be the most heroic parking structure ever built.

Parking deck plan

Office for Metropolitan Architecture with Antoine Béal and Ludovic Blanckaert
L'Espace Piranésien, Euralille 1988–91

Euralille, masterplanned by OMA and Arup, is a swathe of development to the east of the historic centre of the French town of Lille, brought about by the construction of the Channel Tunnel. The masterplan strikes an oblique line between the old, above-ground railway station, and the new, below-ground Eurostar station. This oblique traces the roofline of Jean Nouvel's shopping centre, car park, offices, flats and hotel to the west, and the shelving floor of a new public park, which exposes the Eurostar tracks to the east. Towers above the station, designed by Claude Vasconi and Christian de Portzamparc, form part of the equation that allowed for the park.

The Eurostar station was planned on a north–south axis, to the east of which would run the boulevard Périphérique. In between, a long island of underground car parking was planned. Floris Alkemade, director of OMA and director in charge of Euralille, describes how, with road, rail, metro and pedestrian walkways converging on a single point in the city, the challenge was to make sense of a Gordian knot of infrastructure. This they did by carving a substantial cubic cavern deep into the ground, between the Eurostar station and the boulevard Périphérique, in the centre of the parking island. Originally, L'Espace Piranésien was envisaged by OMA as a dramatic mix of helical parking ramps, escalators, lifts and subway tracks. An aeroplane overhead in an early sketch was a rhetorical expression of the infrastructural impact that OMA hoped for the project.

L'Espace Piranésien is in effect an underground metro station open to the elements, its floor level having been established by the tracks. Unfortunately, the fire regulations imposed by the city forbade cars driving within a metro station. And, in addition, the proximity of nearby high-rise and public buildings brought further risk of fire. Although OMA's masterplan defined the site's oblique section and the distribution of station, towers, car park, park and Nouvel's building, their detailed design was the responsibility of a team of French architects and engineers. In reality, L'Espace Piranésien is less dramatic, but remains a substantial volume populated by decks, lifts and escalators that link the Eurostar station concourse with the streets above, and the car park and metro below. The underground parking structures, designed by Antoine Béal and Ludovic Blanckaert, project north beneath Le Corbusier Street and south more than 150 m. The parking decks are intimately located in the rock, vast horizontal expanses orientated back towards L'Espace Piranésien, where the north and south walls dividing it from the parking decks are punched with large, 'TV screen' windows. These originally opened up views from each deck out over the site; today, cloth screens obscure the view but allow the glow of diffused daylight into these dark spaces.

The south car park remains as it was when it was finished: exposed concrete surfaces punctuated only by grey rectangular 'road markings' overlaid with four circles, each carrying a digit, that denote the number of each space. Between the parked cars and carriageway, a path was marked with a band of small, similarly grey rectangles. Inside, four floors below street level, the sound of classical music suppresses any fears otherwise brought on by the gloom. By contrast, the north car park has largely been refurbished. The refurbishment sought to obscure all concrete surfaces (walls, floor and soffit) with paint in an attempt to sanitize these dark spaces. The original markings have been replaced with high-gloss painted reflective surfaces. Intriguingly, this emphasizes the compression felt when standing in a 'seam' of parking, and heightens one's awareness of the space beyond the windows.

The bold intervention of L'Espace Piranésien, with its windows on axis with the parking decks, gave these otherwise invisible parking structures a presence in the city. And for those parking their cars, the windows provide a point of orientation with the streets and landmarks above.

opposite, above:
south car park before refurbishment
opposite, below:
north car park after refurbishment

NL **Architects**
Parkhouse/Carstadt, Amsterdam 1994–95

The most obvious and striking feature about N L Architects' design for Parkhouse/ Carstadt is its contortionist shape, which raises questions about beauty, repetition versus complexity, typology and the relationship between architecture and infrastructure, even language. One has the impression that N L Architects are very interested in car parks. Although unbuilt, Parkhouse/Carstadt was planned for a specific site in the historic fourteenth-century core of Amsterdam, an area that attracts 40,000 shoppers per day, 14 million visitors a year. Space is limited. The project sought to take pressure off the available ground-floor retail space by making the storeys above accessible. The question is: can a car park be a catalyst for activity? Birds Portchmouth Russum's regeneration project, the inflatable Croydromia (1993) sought a similar solution in reusing the roof decks of 1960s car parks for leisure facilities, which could then capitalize on available convenient parking.

Prior to their development of Parkhouse/Carstadt, N L Architects produced three diagrammatic model car parks, which they portrayed in a number of playful drawings (see p.206). It was their intention that these car parks could offer the motorist variety and create internally localized identity. The firm emphasized the practical aspects of character when it came to finding one's car. Their studies were radical, however, and of vital importance to our understanding of intentionality in the design of a parking structure.

Having unpicked the problem of repetition and identity, they turned to the question of autonomy with their collage 'Graft Hybrids', described by Kamiel Klaase of N L Architects as a retroactive attempt to 'integrate the car' into a Hugh Ferriss-inspired American skyscraper. Here we see the stepped section of the block carved away to create ramped parking decks. In a further diagram, a parking configuration hovers above a square building into which it is embedded. The team notes how a 'more direct relation between parking space and programme becomes possible' (see M V R D V's Villa V P R O). 'If the cars that a building attracts are parked within the structure itself', they state, 'this could be called: Integrated Parking'. The architects note further that it has other advantages, including reducing the pressure on the public to park cars and the ability to bring parking and programme (offices, shops or cultural facilities) closer together. In the case of an office, why not 'Park at your Desk'?

'Graft Hybrids'

Parkhouse/Carstadt's plan is constrained by an unequal polygonal site, and its height by planning codes to 30 m. The firm's strategy was to incline the 19m by 2.5 m deck module at a 6 per cent pitch to ascend to 30 m above street level, which is possible in a length of 500 m; this is then mirrored for the descent. Altogether, the building is a 1km extension of Amsterdam's Nieuwezijds Voorburgwal. The road is then bent to form a horseshoe shape. Road trajectories ricochet off the site boundary to form a knot of parking decks on different levels, which interweave and carve voids out of the solid beneath the parking deck. The project creates 19,000 m² of parking, about 800 parking left: building elements   above: construction detail

spaces, and in the volume below, 35,000 m² of floor space for a department store, shops, offices, apartments, restaurants, conference centre and hotel. For much of the ascent/descent, the roadway creates shopfronts for and direct access to these facilities. The concept of integration was not unique; the now-demolished Tricorn Centre in Portsmouth, for example, located offices, shops and parking in a single complex, although perhaps without achieving quite the degree of integration or utilization of the drama of the oblique. The integration of the oblique is more apparent in Michael Webb's Sin Centre (1959–62), planned for London's Leicester Square, and MVRDV's Leidschenveen town-centre project (1997).

The Parkhouse/Carstadt project can be broken down into six elements: the road deck (the extension of the Nieuwezijds Voorburgwal); the trusses ('girders') that support the bridge sections of the road where they cross below; the linking pedestrian escalators; the elevations ('skin'); the pile foundations; and, finally, the horizontal floors of accommodation suspended within the contorted body beneath the roadway. The architects make one more observation about the material: asphalt. In addition to the integration of type, in making the link between 'roof' and 'road', there is also that of construction technology and nomenclature. They turned to the 1963 Oxford English dictionary, which describes asphalt as a material used in both roofs and road surfaces. The scheme, claim the architects, 'turns your journey into a pleasant ride over an inclined surface affording spectacular views across the historic city. Infrastructure and building become one; roof = road'. In their early diagrams of collaged ramp-types and drawings and models of Parkhouse/Carstadt, it is possible to see why the ramp or the continuous surface is of interest. In contrast to the tectonic and the static parking structures, these are experiments in the picturesque.

The building is a 1 km extension of Amsterdam's Nieuwezijds Voorburgwal.

Buschow Henley Architects
'Park + Jog', Salford 1998

'Park + Jog' was the product of an ideas competition to link two parts of the Salford University campus, which were divided by a six-lane road. The scheme links a suburban car park/transport interchange and city centre 'Suit Park' using a linear 'Umbilical Park'. Park + Jog, intended as a critique of the now conventional park-and-ride schemes used globally to reduce city-centre traffic, proposes a radical commuter model and the construction of a mixed-use 'Car (P)Ark', a four-storey, 1ha concrete structure.

Salford's Crescent Area highlights a common phenomenon in the twilight areas of the British city. Housing, once integrated with commerce and shopping, is now isolated by great stretches of road infrastructure that fan out, blighting this middle ground. These areas lack the 'density' of the centre and the craven space of the suburb. Each successive wave of sprawl adds to the expanse of this grey space. Park + Jog sweeps the road up into the multi-storey Car (P)Ark just west of University Square. Here, people can park their cars, change their clothes, pick up a bike or a canoe, or saddle a horse. Four lanes emerge from the car park as grass, sand, water and running track. Commuters then complete their journeys east into the Manchester city centre along the 1.2km Umbilical Park: walking, jogging, cycling, rollerblading, horse riding, swimming or rowing. The two remaining car lanes are connected up to a nearby gyratory.

Upon arriving in the city centre, the linear Umbilical Park is scooped up into the underbelly of the Suit Park, a structure grafted on to a railway viaduct where commuters can shower and change into their suits. Eight hours later, they're on their way home. Arriving back at the Suit Park, these health-conscious workers deposit their suits to be stored overnight, before returning via the Umbilical Park to the car park. After a shower, there's time for a drink in the rooftop café-bar of the Car (P)Ark before it's time to catch the train or return to the car.

An elliptical garden, with a double-helix car ramp, has been carved out of the Car (P)Ark, and around the perimeter of the garden are lifts and stairs linking the parking decks to the roof. An elliptical ramp links the Umbilical Park running track with the rooftop track of the Car (P)Ark. The roof itself is an active civic space, one of a series of new events that the Umbilical Park seeks to create. Rooftop structures include a pavilion with the café-bar, along with changing rooms, a crèche and a 'pet-crèche'. In addition to cars, the main decks accommodate horse stables and canoe and bike racks. The static geometry of the bland, 1ha parking decks contrasts with the dynamism and picturesque qualities of the elliptical garden and the lane-spaghetti that connects the decks to the road to the west and the park to the east.

Park + Jog unites a number of strands of city and suburban life, blending transport infrastructure, playing fields, health club and social centre. It takes the artificial condition that is commuting, and the equally artificial environment of the health club, and harnesses both to humanize this soulless tract of land, which is otherwise blighted by traffic. The linear park effectively stretches the insular health club out to inhabit a 'map of event-spaces'. Park + Jog sought to make a real change to people's way of life and to transform the Manchester/Salford conurbation. The model is shown extended to each of the radial routes – a ring of 1km Umbilical Parks, each with its own suburban car park/interchange and Suit Park that encircle the city. At intervals, these parks connect to the River Irwell and the Manchester Ship Canal. The waterways provide the 'circular' route, which links the parks to complete a comprehensive green commuter infrastructure. Park + Jog would radically alter the political situation for the suburb and the heartless commute it makes inevitable.

street level

level 1

level 2

level 3

roof level

vmx **Architects**
Fietsenstalling, Amsterdam 2001

New rules, no cars, and instead bicycles. Compare a bike to a car and one finds that it is shorter and considerably narrower. So, too, is vmx's congruent structure for 2,500 bikes, built over a canal opposite Lovers' Quay near Amsterdam's Centraal Station. Commissioned by local government in 1998, the project coincided with the construction of a new metro line, bus station and pedestrian underpass, and was intended to free up the entrance plaza in front of the station from the multitude of bicycles.

At 105m long and just 13.4 m wide, the building has the overriding characteristic of a line or measure. The plan is divided into two 6 m-wide decks that run parallel to the quay, linked at both ends and in the middle, and describe an asymmetric scissor-section. Adjacent decks follow the fall of the quay, a difference of 1.25 m and a gradient of 1/84. The outer decks fall 5.75 m counter to this – a gradient of 1/18, the pitch of which is nearly five times greater than that of the other decks. The oblique and counter-oblique section creates a one-storey difference at the midpoint, and a two-storey difference over its full length, hence the change from a two-storey structure at the east end, adjacent to the main bridge, to a four-storey one adjacent to the smaller bridge for cyclists. The diagram conforms to the continuous ramp model for a multi-storey car park with intermediate crossovers; the effect being that of a switchback alpine road, but with an Escher-like potential to lose oneself in a repeated ascent or descent.

Thirteen transverse concrete beams span stanchions located in the canal basin. The beam, on the line of the outer stanchion, provides the foundation for thirteen trussed steel columns, the width of which give rise to the 1.4 m dimension between the decks. With the exception of the lowest concrete deck adjacent to the quay, which is supported directly by the transverse beams, the remaining five steel decks are cantilevered from

these central supports. Factory prefabricated, each deck is divided into twelve 8.2 m-long, 6 m-wide, 0.5 m-deep monocoque cassettes that span the supporting steel beams and two similar 3.3 m cantilevered cassettes, one at each end. These were assembled so that the upper face of the monocoque rests on the cantilevered beams.

The greater load of decks and bikes on the waterside would naturally lead to the tree-like structure falling into the canal. A series of thirteen circular steel sections, however, tie the quayside decks and thus the whole cantilevered structure back to the concrete deck at the base, which is in turn restrained by the secondary (in this case, tensile) stanchions founded in the canal. This structural solution causes minimal obstruction to barges that are, as a result, able to manoeuvre beneath the waterside parking decks.

Each 6 m-wide deck is divided into a 2 m central carriageway, with a 2 m, 0.75 m-wide parking bay each side. The deck tapers, the top face falling away to the edge. In the centre, the head-height is typically just 2.5 m, the deck-to-deck height 3 m. Only the dimension between the quayside concrete deck and the first steel monocoque above differs, the central head-height here being about 3 m and the deck-to-deck height about 3.5 m. Red asphalt is used to cover the deck surface, the same material used throughout Amsterdam for its cycle paths. The bike park is connected directly to the main bridge at the east end, and to the quay at the middle and west end.

Fietsenstalling's extreme length is matched by its structural ingenuity, which serves to accentuate its stratified nature and to suggest that it be read as a critique of the 1960s car parks it seeks to emulate and, in a sense, hyper-realize.[74] From Lovers' Quay, the building is distilled down to just three oblique graphic lines – a sandwich of deck, railing and bicycle parts that can be measured against the level of the water beneath. It also fulfils a modern daydream for the urban cyclist who might wish to enjoy the thrill of the descent in this 'model village car park'.

Office for Metropolitan Architecture
Souterrain, The Hague 2004

The intestinal space Souterrain is a 1,250m-long tunnel running beneath The Hague's main shopping street, into which a tramline, two tram stations and a 375-space car park have been submerged. Here, infrastructure is architecture. Souterrain was commissioned by the city authority to pre-empt congestion and to enable a dramatic increase in density in the city centre. The commission was ideal for OMA, for whom the paradox in infrastructure is its unfortunate capacity to separate that which it is meant to connect, and their answer was to meld technique and intuition. The shape of the tunnel was initially defined by track curvature and inclines, and then by car-ramp inclines and car-turning radii. OMA also sought to link the station tunnels directly to the adjacent shopping malls above ground.

Souterrain is invisible at street level.

The architects' key decision was to sink the tramlines to a depth of 12m at most, deep enough beneath the surface to create cavernous station volumes, between which the double-decker car park would be inserted. The alternative would have been to drop the parking decks below the tramline and stations, which would have prevented the interference of use from having such a dramatic effect. The decks span caisson walls that retain the earth. Above the stations, the tails of the parking decks, just 200 mm thick, are suspended in the void by steel circular hangers. The decks are interwoven with car ramps, footbridges, stepped pedestrian ramps, stairs and lifts. Both the 1,250 m-long cavity and the entrails are modified in a continuously changing section, which, as the architects intended, helps to orient the visitor. Daylight does not play a part, but one does occasionally become aware of the sky.

During construction the tunnel sprang a leak, which was solved only by continuing the build under pressure, using the same technique employed for building a bridge caisson under water. Like deep-sea divers, construction workers used decompression chambers at the end of each shift. Not surprisingly, the expense and delay led to a search for cost savings, which in turn led to editing out the aluminium cladding for the retaining walls and the wood-clad winged casings for the tubular, concrete propping beams over the stations. Whilst these savings reveal the construction techniques to be those of infrastructure rather than building, the outcome is direct – the dynamic of movement framed in brutal construction. At one point the decision to expose the concrete structures led to local authority design officers cancelling the project, only to be overruled by the mayor. In contrast to the spare concrete retaining walls and soffits, the one surface that passengers touch, the station platform floor, has been finished in timber. The only disappointment is the timber screening that fire-separates the

parking decks from the station concourses. The timber itself seems incongruous, and the subdivisions detract from the gymnastic geometry and fine sections of the concrete decks.

The relatively narrow tunnel results in an echelon parking arrangement, which imbues the car park with a further dynamic. The resulting linearity suggests a road, made all the more literal by the inclusion of two roundabouts and various ramps and slip roads that link the decks to one another and to the street entrances above. A huge bamboo thicket fills one roundabout island, illuminated by strong fluorescent light that, from a distance, appears to be daylight and suggests an opening to the street-life above. Although OMA sought connections with the outside, it is disappointing that the planting is not open to the atmosphere.

As built, Souterrain is largely autonomous. It conveys the brutal reality of digging a hole, the transparent interference of use transcribed literally as superimposed layers that loom over or emerge from beneath one another, and spreads like butter the haptic qualities of timber throughout. Today the pedestrianized, shop-lined street above is almost deserted, and shows little or no signs of the drama that unfolds beneath. In part, this is the fault of the authorities and neighbouring businesses that would not allow the architects to extend their topographies at the Grote Markt station further into the public realm, creating a new square overhead and a demonstrative elevation for their subterranean architecture. The local restaurateurs' fear was that a 3° slope would be an unsuitable incline on which to drink a cup of coffee. Given OMA's research into inhabiting the oblique, it is ironic that the Dutch would decline a public space that, however dramatic, could not compete with that of an Italian hill town.

The multi-storey car park is a stealthy architecture that has been tracing the Zeitgeist for more than a century, projecting ideas of what is technically possible and what is emotionally interesting. The great examples all mark aesthetic progression. For an architect, the car park, in which function plays such a small part in the form, is an important commission.

conclusion

As Adolf Loos observed in 1910, 'only a very small part of architecture belongs to art: the tomb and the monument. Everything else that fulfils a function is to be excluded ...'.[75] Yes, there are dimensional norms, which, though not absolute, confer on these buildings some recognizable characteristics. Space, however, is unfigured, geometry and proportion at liberty, and environmental performance is irrelevant.

Simon Henley, 'Corset' car park, 1989
(student project)

Intention can be made explicit, ideas are laid bare – the phenomena that are both the primary source of the work and the product of others can be understood directly. It is possible to gauge an architect's interest in abstraction and representation, drama and craft, homogeneity and heterogeneity, complex and pure geometric forms, and notions of matter, order and repetition; otherwise function conceals and requires compromise. These skeletal structures, half built, conceal nothing.

We have the Dutch, particularly OMA, to thank for their insight into the oblique. The revolution occurred in 1993 with the Jussieu project, where the ramp went through a portal of perception. Before then the hyperbolic surface existed notably in roof structures and parking decks, but these were discrete poetic, and apparently pragmatic, applications of the geometry. Since that date, hyperbolic geometries have come to form part of the syntax of architectural expression. Consciously or unconsciously, architects employ the hyperbolic form to synthesize a sense of place and topography in situations where there are no longer any traces of the land, a condition that prevails in the city in an era of global culture. The antithetical nature of the multi-storey car park should, I believe, be recognized as a strong source for this type of expression.

Today, my interest in the car park is as an architect, intrigued by possibility. As a child I remember climbing between the split-level decks of various car parks in Bristol and Bath. When studying architecture in Liverpool, a friend and I cycled at dawn to the roof of the St Johns shopping centre car park, and since moving to London, I have led a number of cycle tours of car parks, where the joy to be had from these synthetic hills above and below ground could be shared. Wherever I travel, I search out these alien presences in the city, motoring up and down the ramps to experience the limits that the building imposes on the car. The contrast with the open road is like passing into a well-lit tunnel, in which movement is easy to measure and the reflective surfaces become a double enclosure of sound and space.

If I were to make a sweeping generalization about the contemporary parking structure, it is that the Dutch school seeks to shock, the Germans to delight, with the rest of the world falling into one or the other camp. These buildings belong to a bygone age when the city and its mundane places could legitimately be fantastic and shocking. In this Utopia, the state was optimistic and did not conceive of the vulnerable individual. Then something happened – perhaps it was Kubrick's *A Clockwork Orange* – the private psychological experience became a social nuisance. Buildings cannot afford to be both a temptation and a liability. Today it is interesting to observe that the architects of the new generation of car parks seem to seek a positive emotional response, whether sublime or exhilarating. And while it may now be natural to consider the great parking structures as architecture, it is just as important to recognize the anonymous ones. They may be less demonstrative and more mundane, but are no less beautiful.

p.248, top:
Simon Henley, *Untitled*, chalk on board, 2006
p.248, bottom:
Simon Henley, *Untitled*, chalk on canvas, 2006
opposite:
Simon Henley, *More Gaudian*
cloisters put over to parking 1, 1989

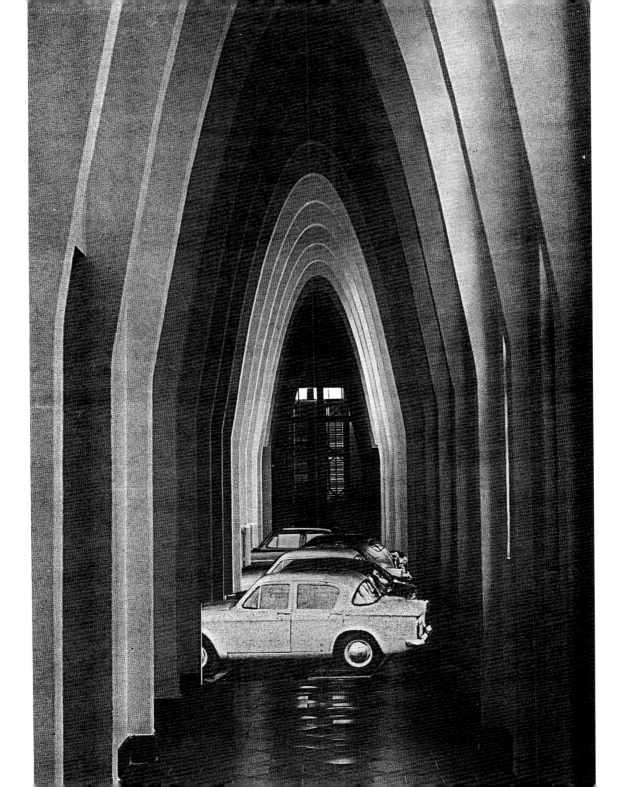

Introduction

1. Novelist J.G. Ballard (*Crash*, 1973); artists/ photographers Ed Ruscha, Rita McBride, Carsten Meier, Rut Blees Luxemburg; film directors Peter Yates (*Bullit*, 1968), Michael Hodges (*Get Carter*, 1971), Michael Winner (*Scorpio*, 1973), Walter Hill (*The Driver*, 1978).

2. J.B. Jackson, 'The Domestication of the Garage', in *The Necessity for Ruins and Other Topics* (Amherst, MA, 1980), 104.

3. Chicago Automobile Club, located in Plymouth Place, Chicago, is illustrated in *Architectural Record* 22:3 (September 1907): 214.

4. Jackson, 104.

5. H. Robertson, 'Motor Garages in Paris: Striking Treatments of a Modern Problem', *The Architect & Building News* 120:3117 (14 September 1928): 342.

6. V. Gruen, 'Retailing and the Automobile: A Romance Based Upon a Case of Mistaken Identity', *Architectural Record* 127:3 (March 1960): 195. Gruen cites United States Census Bureau records for data.

7. Ibid., 197.

8. W. Boesiger, *Richard Neutra: Buildings and Projects* (Zurich, 1951), 136. The project is illustrated with two model photographs and a very brief statement. There is no other record of this design.

9. See D. Klose, *Multi-Storey Car Parks and Garages* (London, 1965), 41, and *Parking*, ed. G. Baker and B. Funaro (New York, 1958), 149. Klose gives the date as 1948, whereas Baker and Funaro give a date of 1949.

10. Baker and Funaro, 149.

11. R. Banham, *Megastructure* (London, 1976), 168.

12. See A. Rossi, *The Architecture of the City* (1966; repr. Cambridge, MA, 1982) and C. Rowe and F. Koetter, *Collage City* (Cambridge, MA, 1978).

13. 19 m² reflects European dimensions.

14. R. Hattersley, *Fifty Years On: A Prejudiced History*

of Britain Since the War (London, 1997), 228.

15. 'Press Park: Car Park into Offices', *Architectural Review* 183:1094 (April 1988): 74. Transparent partitions were designed to compensate for the deep plan and low ceiling heights behind the façades. Plans, sections and colour photographs are reproduced in the article.

16. M. Graves, 'Roman Interventions', in 'AD Profile 20: Roma Interrotta', special issue, *Architectural Design* 49:3/4 (1979): 4.

Aesthetic Influence

17. See FARMAX: *Excursions on Density*, ed. W. Maas, J. van Rijs and R. Koek (Rotterdam, 1998), 394–409, and 'MVRDV 1991–97', special issue, *El Croquis* 86 (1997): 164–67.

18. K. Frampton, *Modern Architecture: A Critical History* (London, 1980), 85.

19. Ibid., 189–90.

20. P. Virilio, 'Architecture Principe', in AA *Documents 3: The Function of the Oblique : The Function of the Oblique : The Architecture of Claude Parent and Paul Virilio 1963–1969*, ed. Pamela Johnston (London, 1996), 12–13.

21. Floris Alkemade in discussion with the author.

22. K. Frampton, *Studies in Tectonic Culture: The Poetics of Construction in Nineteenth and Twentieth Century Architecture* (Cambridge, MA, 1995), 2.

23. Archizoom Associates, 'No-Stop City; Residential Parkings; Climatic Universal System', *Domus* 496:791 (March 1997): 49–55.

24. In Europe, the parking bay is 2.4 m wide by 4.8 m deep; in the US, it is 2.8 m by 5.8 m. European carriageways are 6.1 m with parking bays each side, a deck is 15.7 m wide. Echelon parking generates the only significant variation to the deck dimension by reducing the deck width and necessitating a one-way system.

25. Here each lift served twenty-nine stalls, the sixteen lifts served 464 cars in total. The Zidpark

system was designed to serve between twenty-four and sixty cars per lift on six to fifteen levels, and allowed for two cars to be parked either side of the lift on each level.

26. Architect and writer Sam Webb in discussion with the author.

27. Rotapark was invented by Griggs & Sons in the UK, funded by Lex Garages. Each revolving parking deck or 'shelf' could accommodate twenty-eight US or thirty-two European cars. Its optimum height was ten storeys, with a capacity of 320 cars.

28. 'Vertical Car Park "Rotapark"', *The Builder* (November 9, 1956): 796.

Matter

29 . S. Rabinowitz and C. Rattemeyer, *Rita McBride*, catalogue, exhibition, Annemarie Verna Galerie/Mai 36 Galerie, Zurich, 27 March–22 May, 1999 (New York, 1999). McBride has produced a number of sculptures reproducing car-park forms, including sand-cast bronzes *Parking Garage with Curve* (1992) and *Parking Structure with Curve* (1997).

30. See M. Gage, *Guide to Exposed Concrete Finishes* (London, 1970).

31. D. Leatherbarrow and M. Mostafavi, *On Weathering: The Life of Buildings in Time* (Cambridge, MA, 1993), 31–32.

32. See B. Woods, 'Turning Circle: Cullen Payne in Dublin', *Architecture Today* 159 (June 2005): 24–30.

Temple Street , New Haven

33. 'Four Current Projects by Paul Rudolph: A Parking Garage for 1500 Cars', *Architectural Record* 129:3 (March 1961): 152.

34. See A. Rossi, 103–7.

35. B.P. Spring and D. Canty, 'Concrete: A Special Report', *Architectural Forum* 117 (September 1962): 89.

36. Compare this to Le Corbusier's late work using *béton brut*. Leatherbarrow and Mostafavi note that

'Le Corbusier's buildings in rough concrete represent another tradition, one in which marks are seen to be inevitable…[the] weathering marks were seen as part of the finish of the building – even though this finished developed over time.' Leatherbarrow and Mostafavi, 110.

Tricorn Centre / Trinity Square

37. Owen Luder in discussion with the author.

38. Ibid.; R. Gordon, 'Modern Architecture for the Masses: The Owen Luder Partnership 1960–67', in 'The Sixties', special issue, *Journal of the Twentieth Century Society* 6 (2002): 71–80.

Veterans Memorial Coliseum

39. Project notes from the architects.

Braun Headquarters

40. M. Wilford and T. Muirhead, *James Stirling Michael Wilford and Associates: Buildings & Projects 1975–1992* (London, 1994), 169.

Car Park and Terminus, Hoenheim-Nord

41. 'Zaha Hadid: 1996/2001', special issue, *El Croquis* 103 (2001): 140.

Elevation

42. A charcoal sketch of the project was included in the exhibition 'Mies in Berlin', Museum of Modern Art, New York, 21 June–11 September 2001.

43. Klose, 102–5.

44. *Frank Gehry Buildings and Projects*, ed. P. Arnell and T. Bickford (New York, 1985), 184.

45. R. Venturi, D. Scott Brown and S. Izenour, *Learning From Las Vegas* (Cambridge, MA, 1972), 161. The authors are here referring to the 'Flamingo' sign at the Flamingo Hotel, Las Vegas.

46. *The Architecture of Frank Gehry*, catalogue, exhibition, Walker Art Center, Minneapolis, 21 September–16 November, 1986 (New York, 1986), 84.

47. Venturi, *et al.*, 139.

48. Ibid., 87.

Debenhams, London

49. Unpublished notes of The Concrete Society's visit to Debenhams car park, Welbeck Street, London (1970).

50. Frampton, *Studies in Tectonic Culture*, 2.

60 East Lake Street

51. See Baker and Funaro, 66–67. Parking Facility Nos 2, 3, 9 and 10 are illustrated.

52. Project notes from the architects.

53. Ibid.

Takasaki Parking Building

54. K. Kuma, 'Glass/Shadow', in 'Kengo Kuma: Digital Gardening', special issue, *SD* 11:398 (November 1997): 70.

55. B. Bognar, *Kengo Kuma Selected Works* (New York, 2004), 24, 33.

56. G. Lynn, 'Pointillism', in 'Kengo Kuma: Digital Gardening': 46.

57. K. Kuma, 'Relativity of Materials', *The Japan Architect* 38 (2000): 86.

Light

58. R. Furneaux Jordan, *A Concise History of Western Architecture* (London, 1969), 202.

Avenue de Chartres, Chichester

59. The architects in discussion with the author.

Parkhaus am Bollwerksturm

60. Project notes from the architects.

Hamburg Airport

61. See A. Pérez-Gómez, 'Symbolic Geometry in French Architecture in the Late Eighteenth Century', in *Architecture and the Crisis of Modern Science* (Cambridge, MA, 1983), 129–61.

Obliquity

62. *Archigram*, ed. P. Cook (1972; repr. New York, 1999), 12.

63. Drawings showing the different levels and uses for 'Working Babel' are illustrated in 'OMA/Rem Koolhaas, 1987–1998', special issue, *El Croquis* 53+79 (1998): 80–81.

64. R. Koolhaas, *Delirious New York: A Retroactive Manifesto for Manhattan* (1978; repr. New York, 1994), 152–159.

65. 'OMA/Rem Koolhaas: 1987–1998': 80–81.

66. *FARMAX: Excursions on Density*, 384.

Yuzen Vintage Car Museum

67. *Morphosis: Buildings and Projects, 1989–1992*, vol. 2 (New York, 1994), 240–55.

Car Park for 1,000 Vehicles

68. The project architect for the Soviet pavilion was Berthold Lubetkin, architect of the Penguin Pool at London Zoo (1933), which celebrated the playfulness of these animals with a pair of dynamic, interlocking concrete ramps.

69. S.F. Starr, *Melnikov: Solo Architect in a Mass Society* (Princeton, NJ, 1978), 103–105; *Living Bridges: The Inhabited Bridge, Past, Present and Future*, ed. P. Murray and M.A. Stevens, catalogue, exhibition, Royal Academy of Arts, London, 26 September–18 December 1996 (London, 1996), 97; J.N. Baldeweg and A. Jaque, *Melnikov: Car Park for 1000 Vehicles, 2nd Version, Paris, 1925* (Alcorón, Madrid, 2004), 44.

70. Baldeweg and Jaque, 45.

71. Ibid., 46.

72. Ibid, 46.

Marina City, Chicago

73. M. Ragon, *Goldberg: Dans La Ville, On the City* (Paris, 1985), 18.

Fietsenstalling, Amsterdam

74. Project notes from the architects.

Conclusion

75. A. Loos, 'Architecture' (1910), in *The Architecture of Adolf Loos*, trans. Wilfried Wang (London, 1985), 108.

Archigram, ed. P. Cook (1972; repr. New York, 1999).

The Architecture of Frank Gehry, catalogue, exhibition, Walker Art Center, Minneapolis, 21 September – 16 November, 1986 (New York, 1986).

Architectural Record 22:3 (September 1907): 214.

Archizoom Associates, 'No-Stop City; Residential Parkings; Climatic Universal System', *Domus* 496 (March 1997): 49–55.

R. Banham, *Megastructure* (London, 1976).

J.N. Baldeweg and A. Jaque, *Melnikov: Car Park for 1000 Vehicles, 2nd Version, Paris, 1925* (Alcorón, Madrid, 2004).

W. Boesiger, *Richard Neutra: Buildings and Projects* (Zurich, 1951).

B. Bognar, *Kengo Kuma Selected Works* (New York, 2004).

FARMAX: Excursions on Density, ed. W. Maas, J. van Rijs and R. Koek (Rotterdam, 1998).

'Four Current Projects by Paul Rudolph: A Parking Garage for 1500 Cars', *Architectural Record* 129:3 (March 1961): 152–154.

K. Frampton, *Modern Architecture: A Critical History* (London, 1980).

––––––, *Studies in Tectonic Culture: The Poetics of Construction in Nineteenth and Twentieth Century Architecture* (Cambridge, MA, 1995).

Frank Gehry: Buildings and Projects, ed. P. Arnell and T. Bickford (New York, 1985).

R. Furneaux Jordan, *A Concise History of Western Architecture* (London, 1969).

M. Gage, *Guide to Exposed Concrete Finishes* (London, 1970).

R. Gordon, 'Modern Architecture for the Masses: The Owen Luder Partnership 1960–67', in 'The Sixties', special issue, *Journal of the Twentieth Century Society* (2002): 71–80.

M. Graves, 'Roman Interventions', in 'AD Profile 20: Roma Interrotta', special issue, *Architectural Design* 49:3/4 (1979): 4–5.

V. Gruen, 'Retailing and the Automobile: A Romance Based Upon a Case of Mistaken Identity', *Architectural Record* 127:3 (March 1960): 192–210.

R. Hattersley, *Fifty Years On: A Prejudiced History of Britain Since the War* (London, 1997).

J.B. Jackson, 'The Domestication of the Garage', in *The Necessity for Ruins and Other Topics* (Amherst, MA, 1980).

D. Klose, *Multi-Storey Car Parks and Garages* (London, 1965).

R. Koolhaas, *Delirious New York: A Retroactive Manifesto for Manhattan* (1978; repr. New York, 1994).

K. Kuma, 'Glass/Shadow', in 'Kengo Kuma: Digital Gardening', special issue, *SD* 11:398 (November 1997): 70.

––––––, 'Relativity of Materials', *The Japan Architect* 38 (2000): 86.

D. Leatherbarrow and M. Mostafavi, *On Weathering: The Life of Buildings in Time* (Cambridge, MA, 1993).

Living Bridges: The Inhabited Bridge, Past, Present and Future, ed. P. Murray and M.A. Stevens, catalogue, exhibition, Royal Academy of Arts, London, 26 September–18 December 1996 (London, 1996).

A. Loos, 'Architecture' (1910), in *The Architecture of Adolf Loos*, trans. Wilfried Wang (London, 1985).

G. Lynn, 'Pointillism', in 'Kengo Kuma: Digital Gardening', special issue, *SD* 11:398 (November 1997): 46.

Morphosis: Buildings and Projects, 1989–1992, vol. 2 (New York, 1994).

'MVRDV: 1991–1997', special issue, *El Croquis* 86 (1997).

'OMA/Rem Koolhaas: 1987–1998', special issue, *El Croquis* 53+79 (1998).

Parking, ed. G. Baker and B. Funaro (New York, 1958).

A. Pérez-Gómez, *Architecture and the Crisis of Modern Science* (Cambridge, MA, 1983).

'Press Park: Car Park into Offices', *Architectural Review* 183:1094 (April 1988): 72–74.

S. Rabinowitz and C. Rattemeyer, *Rita McBride*, catalogue, exhibition, Annemarie Verna Galerie/ Mai 36 Galerie, Zurich, 27 March–22 May 1999 (New York, 1999).

M. Ragon, *Goldberg: Dans La Ville, On the City* (Paris, 1985).

H. Robertson, 'Motor Garages in Paris: Striking Treatments of a Modern Problem', *The Architect & Building News* 120:3117 (14 September 1928): 341–344.

A. Rossi, *The Architecture of the City* (1966; repr. Cambridge, MA, 1982).

'Vertical Car Park "Rotapark"', *The Builder* (November 9, 1956): 796–797.

C. Rowe and F. Koetter, *Collage City* (Cambridge, MA, 1978).

B.P. Spring and D. Canty, 'Concrete: A Special Report', *Architectural Forum* 117 (September 1962): 78–96.

S.F. Starr, *Melnikov: Solo Architect in a Mass Society* (Princeton, NJ, 1978).

R. Venturi, D. Scott Brown and S. Izenour, *Learning From Las Vegas* (Cambridge, MA, 1972).

P. Virilio, 'Architecture Principe', in AA *Documents 3: The Function of the Oblique: The Architecture of Claude Parent and Paul Virilio 1963–1969*, ed. Pamela Johnston (London, 1996).

M. Wilford and T. Muirhead, *James Stirling Michael Wilford and Associates: Buildings & Projects 1975–1992* (London, 1994).

B. Woods, 'Turning Circle: Cullen Payne in Dublin', *Architecture Today* 159 (June 2005): 24–30.

'Zaha Hadid: 1996–2001', special issue, *El Croquis* 103 (2001).

With thanks to Lucas Dietrich, Elain McAlpine and Cat Green at Thames & Hudson; to all contributing architects for providing drawings and texts and many photos free of copyright, especially Andrés Jaque for allowing the reproduction of his analytical/explanatory diagrams of Melnikov's Car Park for 1,000 Vehicles (pp.220, 222–223), Mike Webb for reworking his illustrations (p.209), Owen Luder for supplying various manuscripts including archive drawings of the Tricorn Centre, and Wilford Schupp Architekten for supplying the Braun Headquarters site plan (p.81); to Annabel Taylor for her help in researching the illustrations of Parc des Célestins, Megan Yates for her structural engineering advice, and Sue Foster for access to the Building Design archive; to my partners Ralph Buschow, Gavin Hale Brown and Ken Rorrison for supporting this endeavour; to Bruno Silvestre for his Portuguese translation and Rhona Lord for her help with Japanese correspondence; to Alex Flockhart (pp.115–117), Franziska Lindinger (pp.225, 227), Craig Linnell (p.104), Donncha O'Shea (pp.57, 59, 225), Guido Vericat (pp.119, 123), Conal McKelvey (p.67) and Susannah Waldron (pp.63–65) for preparing original case-study drawings; to Ros Diamond for her advice and editorial direction, Sue Barr (www.heathcotebarr.org) for her collaboration on the photography and Mark Diaper for his observations and the design of the book; and to my wife Claire for her thoughts and patience.

Aranda/Lasch 216–217; Luís Ferreira Alves 159; Autostadt GmbH 108; Sue Barr 33–40, 56, 57 (top), 59, 60 (top), 61 (top and bottom left), 62–68, 89–96, 130, 131, 145–152, 193–200; Courtesy of B. Braun Melsungen AG 14, 78 (top left), 79, 80 (top and bottom left); Bertrand Goldberg Archive, Ryerson & Burnham Archives, The Art Institute of Chicago 224; Birds Portchmouth Russum 167, 169; Rut Blees Luxemburg 6; Building Design Partnership 102 (middle); Burkhalter Sumi Architekten 205, 213; Orlando Cabanban, Bertrand Goldberg Archive, Ryerson & Burnham Archives, The Art Institute of Chicago 1, 226, 227 (left); David Chipperfield Architects 28; H.G. Esch, Hennef 2–3, 162; Mitsumasa Fujitsuka 138–141; Gehry Partners LLP 99 (bottom); Gigon/Guyer Architekten 54; Hedrich Blessing Collection, Chicago History Museum 118; Oliver Heissner 186–188; Simon Henley 21, 46, 47, 49, 57 (bottom), 58, 60 (bottom), 61 (bottom right), 78 (top right and bottom), 79, 80 (bottom right), 81, 99 (top and middle), 100 (top), 101, 102 (top and bottom), 103, 109, 115, 117, 154–157, 158 (middle and bottom), 171 (bottom), 172 (top and bottom right), 179, 181, 203 (bottom), 208, 210, 214, 230, 231 (top), 244–247, 250; Steven Holl Architects 163; IaN+ 112; Courtesy of Albert Kahn Associates, Inc 160–161; © 1977 Louis I. Kahn Collection, University of Pennsylvania and Pennsylvania Historical and Museum Commission 10; Nicholas Kane/Arcaid 166, 168; Karant & Associates, courtesy of

Tigerman Fugman McCurry 132, 134–137; Heiner Leiska 51, 105, 182–185; Courtesy of Lyon Parc Auto 15, 170, 171 (top), 172 (bottom left), 173; Bruce Martin 106; Ignacio Martinez Suárez 164; Morphosis 212; Jeroen Musch 242; NL Architects 232, 234; Office for Metropolitan Architecture 27 (top), 211, 229, 231 (bottom); Pablo Orcajo 52; R&Sie(n) 218; Courtesy of RIBA Library Photographs Collection 4–5, 8, 9 (bottom), 11, 13, 18, 25, 26, 42, 98, 100 (bottom), 114, 116, 120–122, 203 (top), 227 (right); Christian Richters 29, 174, 176, 178, 180, 215; Courtesy of Kevin Roche John Dinkeloo and Associates LLC 44, 70, 74–76; Ken Rorrison 158 (top); Hans-Christian Schink, Punctum Fotografie 110, 111; Jamie Shorten 48; Skidmore, Owings & Merrill 50; Annabel Taylor 104; VMX Architects 240–241, 243; Paul Warchol 45, 107; Dominique Marc Wehrli, Architekturbild 53; Hans Werlemans 27 (bottom left and right); Zaha Hadid Architects 82–85.